Neal Benezra

Olga M. Viso

Michael Brenson

Paul Schimmel

Juan Muñoz

Hirshhorn Museum and
Sculpture Garden,
Smithsonian Institution,
Washington, D.C.

The Art Institute of Chicago

Pages 1–12:
*The Burning of Madrid as Seen from
the Terrace of My House*, 1999

Cover and back cover:
Five Seated Figures, 1996 (cat. no. 54)

This catalogue was published in conjunction with the exhibition
"Juan Muñoz," organized by the Hirshhorn Museum and Sculpture Garden,
Smithsonian Institution, Washington, D.C., in association with
The Art Institute of Chicago.

EXHIBITION CURATOR: Neal Benezra, The Art Institute of Chicago
COORDINATING CURATOR: Olga M. Viso, Hirshhorn Museum and Sculpture Garden

Exhibition Dates
Hirshhorn Museum and Sculpture Garden: 18 October 2001–13 January 2002
Museum of Contemporary Art, Los Angeles: 21 April–28 July 2002
The Art Institute of Chicago: 14 September–8 December 2002
Contemporary Arts Museum, Houston: 24 January–30 March 2003

First edition
Printed in Belgium

05 04 03 02 01   9 8 7 6 5 4 3 2 1

Published by
The Art Institute of Chicago
111 South Michigan Avenue
Chicago, Illinois 60603
and
Hirshhorn Museum and Sculpture Garden
Smithsonian Institution
Independence Avenue at Seventh Street SW
Washington, D.C. 20560

Hardcover edition published in 2001 in
association with
The University of Chicago Press
1427 East 60th Street
Chicago, Illinois 60637

Produced by the Publications Department of
The Art Institute of Chicago,
Susan F. Rossen, Executive Director

Sarah E. Guernsey, Production
Catherine A. Steinmann, Editor
Designed and typeset by
    Anthony McCall Associates, New York
Separations by Professional Graphics, Inc.,
    Rockford, Illinois
Printed and bound by Snoeck-Ducaju & Zoon,
    Ghent, Belgium

Contents

Foreword

IT IS ONLY FITTING that the Hirshhorn Museum and Sculpture Garden should be the first museum in the United States to present a major retrospective of the work of the internationally acclaimed Spanish artist Juan Muñoz.

In 1995 the artist's five-part "conversation piece"—the last of a series that he had begun earlier in the decade—entered the Hirshhorn's collection and was installed in a prominent position on the museum's plaza. Two years later recent work by Muñoz was the subject of a one-gallery "Directions" exhibition at the Hirshhorn. The close conjunction of these two occurrences and the excitement and interest that was generated led to the realization that the public might be better served by taking a longer and deeper look at the artist's work.

The idea for this exhibition originated with Neal Benezra, former Assistant Director for Art and Public Programs, in the late 1990s, during his tenure at the Hirshhorn. As Deputy Director and Frances and Thomas Dittmer Curator of Modern and Contemporary Art at The Art Institute of Chicago, Benezra continued his work on the project and served as the exhibition's guest curator. Working closely with him was Olga M. Viso, the Hirshhorn's Curator of Contemporary Art, who coordinated the exhibition and its U.S. tour. It was indeed a pleasure for the Hirshhorn and its staff to organize this exhibition in association with the Art Institute and a longtime friend and colleague. We are grateful to James N. Wood, Director and President of the Art Institute, for cooperating with our institution on the exhibition and for assuming responsibility for producing this fine catalogue.

We are pleased that the exhibition is traveling to the Art Institute as well as to the Museum of Contemporary Art, Los Angeles, and the Contemporary Arts Museum, Houston. We appreciate the early support of our colleagues in Los Angeles, Jeremy Strick, Director, and Paul Schimmel, Chief Curator; and, in Houston, Marti Mayo, Director, and

Lynn Herbert, Chief Curator. Our gratitude further extends to the many individuals and public institutions around the world who agreed to part with their works for the show's lengthy tour. Their names can be found listed on page 21 of this publication.

Major corporate support for the exhibition was provided by Terra Networks; we are indebted to Joaquim Agut, Chairman, and Antonio Botas, Director of Marketing and Corporate Relations, for their strong enthusiasm for Muñoz's work and the exhibition's U.S. tour. Terra Networks worked closely with the artist and our two institutions to develop an educational Web site for the exhibition. We are also grateful to Pepe Cobo for facilitating our relationship with Terra Networks.

Hirshhorn friends Aaron and Barbara Levine supplied major assistance for the project early in its planning stages. We are indebted to them for their ongoing dedication to our museum and its exhibitions and programs. A significant in-kind contribution was made by Armstrong World Industries, which provided custom linoleum flooring materials and worked closely with the artist, Hirshhorn Museum staff, and local installation crews at each exhibition venue. Waterjet Works of Dallas, Texas, handled the precision cutting of the linoleum materials that was required to produce the floor designs by Juan Muñoz. We are grateful to Douglas Schmauder, Executive Contract Market Representative, and Lien Chu, Senior Contract Market Representative of Armstrong, as well as Philip Einsohn, Principal of Waterjet Works, for their interest in collaborating with us on this project. Elayne Mordes of Baltimore kindly introduced Armstrong to contacts at the Hirshhorn Museum; we acknowledge her efforts on our behalf.

This handsome publication, produced for the exhibition by the Art Institute, was generously underwritten in part by the Sociedad Estatal de Acción Cultural Exterior (SECAX) of Spain. Juan Carlos Elorza, President of SECAX, and José Guirao Cabrera, Secretary of State for International

Cooperation of the Ministry of Foreign Affairs in Madrid, were extremely helpful in facilitating this sponsorship. Borja Coca also made an important contribution toward the realization of the book, and we are grateful for his generous spirit.

Numerous dedicated staff members at each museum contributed to the project in substantial ways; their names appear in the acknowledgments that follow. In Washington, public programs for the exhibition were supported in part by the Latino Initiatives Fund, administered by the Smithsonian Center for Latino Initiatives. In Chicago, the exhibition was supported by the Woman's Board of The Art Institute of Chicago and Judith Neisser.

Our greatest debt is, of course, to Juan Muñoz himself, who took an active role in all aspects of the planning of this project. Without his vision and focused determination, this exhibition would not have been possible.

JAMES T. DEMETRION
Director
Hirshhorn Museum and Sculpture Garden
Smithsonian Institution
Washington, D.C.

Acknowledgments

18

JUAN MUÑOZ HAS A long and distinguished record of exhibitions in Europe. The exhibition that this catalogue accompanies, however, is his first to tour in the United States. Although I have known the artist and his work for many years, my first substantial introduction came in 1990, when my friend and colleague Susanne Ghez organized the artist's first museum show in this country for The Renaissance Society at The University of Chicago. Since that time, Muñoz and I have stayed in close contact, and over the past decade I have visited him often in the course of my travels in Europe. Given the artist's many connections with Chicago and Washington, D.C., it is altogether appropriate that the Hirshhorn Museum and The Art Institute of Chicago should share in the organization of this important exhibition.

My debts are many and my gratitude is great to all those who helped me in the development of the present show. The project was initiated while I served as Assistant Director for Art and Public Programs at the Hirshhorn Museum and Sculpture Garden, and I am enormously grateful to Director James T. Demetrion for his belief in the artist and the support he offered the project. When I assumed my current position at The Art Institute of Chicago, Director and President James N. Wood graciously encouraged me to continue my work, enabling the present collaboration between our two institutions to take place. Two individuals deserve very special mention for their work on the project. Olga M. Viso, Curator of Contemporary Art at the Hirshhorn, who coordinated the exhibition, willingly shouldered the burden of organizing the loans after my departure and authored a fine essay in this catalogue. Stephanie D'Alessandro, Assistant Curator in the Department of Modern and Contemporary Art at the Art Institute, worked closely with me in organizing this catalogue, and she is responsible for its Documentation section, which constitutes the most complete record of the artist's career to date.

Numerous staff members at both museums contributed to the project in substantial ways. At the Hirshhorn Museum, Beverly Lang Pierce, Assistant Director for Administration; Brian Kavanagh and Barbara Freund in Registration; Edward Schiesser, Robert Allen, and Albert Masino in the Exhibits and Design department; Anna Brooke and the Library staff; Laurence Hoffman and the Conservation staff; Lee Stalsworth, Chief Photographer; and Fletcher Johnston and the Building Management staff all contributed mightily to the success of this show. In the Department of Public Programs, Linda Powell and the Education staff; Sidney Lawrence, Head of Public Affairs; my former assistant Frances Woltz; and Karen Perry, Curatorial Assistant, were all instrumental in developing the exhibition. In the early stages of planning the exhibition, I benefitted from support from research intern Tania Owcharenko Duvergne. In addition, Olga Viso was ably assisted by former interns Amy Gotzler and Kristen Hileman.

At the Art Institute, I am most grateful to Dorothy Schroeder, Assistant Director for Exhibitions and Budgets; Susan F. Rossen, Executive Director of Publications; and Kate Pasquith, Executive Secretary, for their patient support. I am also grateful to Jack Brown, Executive Director of the Ryerson and Burnham Libraries, and, for their outstanding research assistance, library staff members Peter Blank, Lauren Lessing, Marcie Neth, and Susan Perry. In addition, I extend my gratitude to Robert W. Eskridge and his staff in Museum Education, Edward W. Horner and his staff in Development, Mary Solt and the staff of Museum Registration, Eileen Harakal and the staff of Public Affairs, Lyn Delliquadri and her staff in Graphic Design and Communication Services, and Frank P. Zuccari and the Conservation staff. I would also like to thank my staff in the Department of Modern and Contemporary Art, especially Nicholas Barron, Department Specialist, John Tweedie, Department Technician, and former research intern Mette Scheppers, for their excellent work.

This beautiful catalogue was produced by the Art

Institute's Publications Department. Catherine Steinmann skillfully edited the catalogue, with the able assistance of Diana Fabian and Jessica Kennedy. Sarah Guernsey expertly shepherded it through the design and production process, and Karen Altschul and Christopher Cook acquired many of its comparative photographs. The catalogue was designed with great skill and sensitivity by Anthony McCall, Doug Clouse, and David Zaza of Anthony McCall Associates, New York. Pat Goley of Professional Graphics, Inc., Rockford, Illinois, produced fine color separations for the plates and illustrations. I would like to thank writer and art critic Michael Brenson for the outstanding essay he contributed, and Paul Schimmel, Chief Curator at the Museum of Contemporary Art, Los Angeles, for his insightful interview with the artist. I am also grateful to The University of Chicago Press, especially Susan Bielstein, Anthony Burton, Pamela Heath, and Carol Kasper, for its strong commitment to this project.

It has often been a challenge to locate the artist's works, and I am indebted to the numerous gallerists who have worked with the artist through the years for their assistance. Marian Goodman, Elaine Budin, Lane Coburn, Jeannie Freilich-Sondik, and Richard Sigmund, Marian Goodman Gallery; Nicholas Logsdail, Lisson Gallery; Jean Bernier and Marina Eliades, Galerie Bernier/Eliades; and their respective staffs all deserve my thanks. We were also aided in a very considerable way in this regard by Laura Carpenter, Joost Declercq, Dorothée Fischer, Anthony Grant, Jane Hamlyn, Xavier Hufkens, Ghislaine Hussenot, Rafael Jablonka, James Kelly, Marga Paz, and Thomas Segal.

A great many individuals generously supported my work with Juan Muñoz during the last few years, and I am most grateful to the following individuals for their kindness, support, and hospitality, and for sharing information with me: Cleopatra Alexander, John and Beverly Berger, Blake Byrne, José Guirao Cabrera, Hervé Chandès, Paolo Colombo, Maria de Corral, Kristien Daem, Catherine Forni, Jocelyn and Andre Gordts, Katherine Hatch, Ingrid Kurz, Aaron and Barbara Levine, James Lingwood, Attilio Maranzano, Denise Mattia, Fons van Meijgaarden, Marvin and Elayne Mordes, Amber Noland, Vlasta Odell, Janet Passehl, Denise Ragona, Alicia Rodriguez, Sheila Russell, Isabel Sagües, Julião Sarmento, Patricia Shea, Morad Tavallali and Pascale Dubois, Vicente Todolí, and Donald and Shirley Young.

I also wish to offer special thanks to two Spaniards, Pepe Cobo and Borja Coca, for their unwavering and quite extraordinary support for this project. Beyond their contributions as lenders to this exhibition, both have a great passion for the work of Juan Muñoz, and both provided exceptional support at critical moments on our journey. Similarly, I am grateful to the artist's assistants, past and present—Natalia Camacho, Ana Fernández-Cid, Luz Amanda García Jiménez, Carolina Grau, Julian Lopez, and Ruben Polanco—for their many contributions.

Finally, I wish to thank Juan Muñoz, whose generosity and commitment to this project are unparalleled in my experience in working with artists. Juan spared no effort and accepted no obstacle in ensuring that our vision for the show might be realized. Ours was an extraordinary collaboration in every way. In the process our families became close friends, and so it is most appropriate that I close by thanking our respective spouses, Cristina Iglesias and Maria Makela, for their own very special contributions.

NEAL BENEZRA
Deputy Director and
Frances and Thomas Dittmer Curator
of Modern and Contemporary Art
The Art Institute of Chicago

Corporate support for the
exhibition was provided by
Terra Networks with major assistance
from Aaron and Barbara Levine.

The exhibition catalogue was
made possible in part by the
Sociedad Estatal de Acción Cultural
Exterior of Spain and Borja Coca.

Armstrong World Industries and
Waterjet Works provided in-kind
assistance with the special flooring
installations.

In Washington, public programs for
the exhibition were sponsored in
part by the Latino Initiatives Fund,
administered by the Smithsonian
Center for Latino Initiatives.

In Chicago, the exhibition was
supported by the Woman's Board
of The Art Institute of Chicago
and Judith Neisser.

Lenders to the Exhibition

The Art Institute of Chicago

Francis de Beir

Bouwfonds Kunststichting, Hoevelaken

Fondation Cartier pour l'art contemporain, Paris

Mr. and Mrs. Stuart M. Christhilf III

Pepe Cobo, Seville

Carlos and Rosa de la Cruz Collection

Lena and Bernard Dubois

Mimi Dusselier, Belgium

Konrad Fischer Galerie, Dusseldorf

Marsha Fogel

Mr. and Mrs. Philip Gersh

Carol and Arthur Goldberg

Marian Goodman Gallery, New York

Camille O. Hoffmann

Colecciones I.C.O., Madrid

Sres. de Iglesias Collection

Eddy de Jaek

Linda and Jerry Janger, Los Angeles

LAC-Switzerland

Raymond Learsy

Jacqueline and Marc Leland, Washington, D.C.

Aaron and Barbara Levine

The LeWitt Collection, Chester, Conn.

R. Matthys

Collection Migros Museum, Zurich

Marvin and Elayne Mordes, Baltimore

Juan Muñoz

Judith Neisser

Marilyn Oshman, Houston

Anita and Burton Reiner

Deedie Rose, Dallas

Rubell Family Collection, Miami

Collection Sanders, Amsterdam

Dean Valentine and Amy Adelson, Los Angeles

Jan Vercruysse, Belgium

Ginny Williams Family Foundation, The Collection of
    Ginny Williams

Private collections (4)

Sculpture and Paradox   *Neal Benezra*

IN 1990 JUAN MUÑOZ published "On a Square," a brief text in which he described a lecture delivered by the Mexican poet Octavio Paz (see pp. 67–68). In the lecture, Paz recounted the history of a large stone sculpture of the Aztec goddess Coatlique that had once been mounted atop the Great Temple of Tenochtitlan. According to Paz, at some point the sculpture had been removed from the temple and buried in the center of Mexico City, where it was discovered in 1790 by workmen making street repairs. Coatlique was unearthed and placed on public view at the Royal University of Mexico along with a collection of plaster copies of Greek and Roman sculptures that had recently been donated to the university by Charles III of Spain.

So great was the sculpture's power that native Mexicans visited the university to worship Coatlique. The sculpture came to be considered an affront to Greco-Roman ideals of beauty and a subtle threat to colonial rule, and the university determined that it should be returned to its original site, beneath the streets of Mexico City. Before this was done, however, the scholar Antonio de Leon y Gama was able to study the work. His notes were published in 1804 and were subsequently read by the German scholar Alexander von Humboldt. During a visit to Mexico, Humboldt was able to persuade authorities to exhume the sculpture, although following his examination it was buried yet again. Coatlique was not uncovered permanently until Mexico won its independence from Spain in 1821, when the sculpture was returned to the university and placed nearly hidden from view in the corner of a courtyard and later in a hallway behind a screen. Today, however, Coatlique resides in the Museo Nacional de Antropología, an unquestioned masterpiece of Aztec sculpture.

Muñoz recounted Paz's lecture in some detail, evoking the darkened and crowded lecture hall and the distant voice of the speaker. Yet the event was a complete fabrication. Muñoz had discovered the history of Coatlique in an actual text by Paz, "The Art of Mexico: Material and Meaning," in the author's *Essays on Mexican Art*, published in 1987.[1] While Paz there recounted the story of Coatlique as the point of departure for a discussion of the increased secularization of art in the modern age and the evolving perception of ancient Mexican art in European eyes, Muñoz borrowed the Paz text for his own rather different purposes. Although Muñoz certainly shared Paz's fascination with the "vicissitudes of the Coatlicue—turning from goddess into demon, from demon into monster, and from monster into masterpiece," his own interest in the story lay elsewhere. As a sculptor, Muñoz was intrigued by Coatlique because the sculpture had retained its power despite spending so much of its history out of sight, either buried underground or inaccessible in storage. Muñoz retold the history of Coatlique in order to contrast it with the countless public sculptures depicting obscure generals or politicians that dominate so many city squares and yet are scarcely noticed despite their extraordinary visibility and prominence. It is precisely the equivocal existence that Coatlique had led that fascinated Muñoz, the idea that a work of art may possess extraordinary power and inspire an impassioned response even while—and perhaps because—it cannot

FIG. 1   *Two Figures for Middelheim*, 1993 (page 22)
FIG. 2   *Untitled*, 1979–80

2

24

be seen. For Muñoz, it is this "enigma of the arousal of feelings," the persistent mystery of the relationship between the artist, the object, and the viewer, that is the essence of art.

Muñoz's text is important in introducing his own work for several reasons. "On a Square" and the other texts he has published throughout his career in various exhibition catalogues, journals, and newspapers show him to be an artist of letters as well as a sculptor, as adept with ideas and the written word as he is with his hands. While his published work includes texts on individual artists and writers, some historical and some contemporary, he has also authored pieces that hover, in a tantalizing way, between prose and fiction, chronicling events that may or may not have occurred—the reader can never be sure. Muñoz's transformation of the Paz text into an event in which the artist becomes an onlooker is an example of his conceptual and theatrical gamesmanship, a tool that he employs to extraordinary advantage in his sculpture as well. In the Paz text, Muñoz found support for an alternative understanding of the potential emotional and psychological power of a work of art. While Muñoz is committed to resolving the form and the content of a particular object, a parallel interest centers on its conceptual and emotional underpinning. This has allowed him to steer his own course between an exclusive dependence on either formal concerns or subject matter, the two extremes that too often delimit contemporary practice. Muñoz rejects these limitations, simultaneously opening his work to a panoramic range of references and borrowing freely from the history of art as well as from architecture,

literature, music, and the theater. Ultimately he does so not to clarify or resolve his position, but rather to complicate and enrich a body of work dominated by silence and absence and their psychological implications.

Juan Muñoz became an artist nearly by chance.[2] He was born in Madrid in 1953, the second of seven children whose father was a building contractor. Muñoz admits to having been an indifferent student with a willful personality, and he recalls one incident in particular that had a powerful impact on him. Although generally bored with his grade-school work, Muñoz took special interest in a science project that involved the human ear. He recalls studying the form and workings of the ear very carefully, making several diagrams to complete the assignment. Despite the care he took with the project, and his realization that this was the first time he was engaged with his schoolwork, he received a poor grade. In a fit of rage, he cursed at his teacher in class and, at the age of twelve, was expelled from school. Although Muñoz would not become seriously interested in art for another ten years, some of his earliest works involve both drawings and cast renderings of ears, and sound has played a fundamental role in his work throughout his career.

In 1965, Muñoz's parents enrolled him, along with his older brother, Vicente, at the Colegio Alameda de Osuna. There Muñoz received a classical education and came under the powerful and lasting influence of his Latin instructor, Santiago Amón. Born in Vizcaya in 1927, Amón was among a generation of Spanish intellectuals who came of age under the dictatorship of General Francisco Franco. The staunch conservatism of the Spanish government offered little freedom and few prospects to left-wing intellectuals such as Amón, who taught high school to earn a living while working as a poet, cultural critic, and writer on art. Amón was perhaps best known as the art critic for the Spanish daily newspaper *El País*, and he was a founder of *Nueva Forma*, an influential journal published from 1966 to 1975 that advocated the cultural values of modernist art, literature, and design in the waning years of the Franco regime. He also authored a monograph on Pablo Picasso as well as numerous articles on contemporary artists.[3] Although his life was cut short by a 1988 helicopter crash, Amón had already had a profound impact on the highly intelligent and passionate but somewhat unruly young Muñoz. He inspired his student not so much to become an artist, but rather to develop his mind by reading broadly and extensively. Muñoz would later pay tribute to Amón in various ways in both his writing and his sculpture.

Spain was to remain oppressive until the death of Franco in 1976. After graduating from high school in 1970, Muñoz, eager to leave his home and the Spanish capital, embarked on a twelve-year period of travel in Europe and the United States. Seeking to counter the cultural and geographical isolation of Franco's Spain, Muñoz traveled in order to meet people and gain access to other cultures. He shared a room with his brother while supporting himself as a dishwasher in London, worked as a house painter and dabbled in left-wing politics in Stockholm, and returned occasionally to Madrid to earn money working in his father's construction company. Although he still had no intention of becoming an artist, Muñoz briefly considered studying filmmaking, at one point even making a short, 16-mm film in which he documented public sculpture in Madrid.

The period he spent living in London was particularly important. It was there that Muñoz "became passionate about art and the act of looking." Muñoz studied art history independently and today believes that he was better suited by nature to be an art historian or perhaps an architect than an artist. The impetus to consider making art came only at the urging of his brother, who possessed a natural aptitude for painting and who had taken private art lessons as a child. Although Vicente had stopped painting by the age of 16, he purchased art materials for his brother and encouraged him to begin working. This occurred while the two were living in London in the mid 1970s, when Muñoz spent almost all of his free time on weekends at the Tate Gallery and the National Gallery, developing a detailed and quite particular knowledge of their collections.

In 1976, Muñoz received a scholarship from the British Council and attended Central School of Art and Design (now known as Central Saint Martins College of Art and Design) in London, where he studied lithography. Today Muñoz emphasizes that he pursued a formalized course of study less because he loved printmaking than because the modest stipend provided the financial support necessary for him to live in London. Muñoz visited home in 1978 and returned to London the following year, this time attending Croydon School of Art (now known as Croydon College), where he studied advanced printmaking. To supplement his income, Muñoz worked as a fine-art printer and began to experiment with sculpture for the first time.

London was a hotbed of progressive sculptural activity at the time, with young artists such as Tony Cragg, Richard Deacon, Barry Flanagan, Richard Long, and Bill Woodrow all working against the distinguished tradition of cast and carved monumental sculpture that had been dominated for decades by Henry Moore and the more recent formal abstraction of Anthony Caro. Muñoz met Deacon and Woodrow and began to study sculpture in earnest. Although he made a few traditionally modeled and carved figures in plaster and stone, he almost immediately gravitated toward more experimental, informal modes of working. These early pieces often incorporated mechanical devices, sound, and motion. One such piece included reel-to-reel tape players and wall-mounted objects that acted as take-up reels, making sound literally visible (fig. 2). For another piece he devised a motorized, fabric-covered, kite-like

FIG. 3 *Croydon Drawing*, 1980
FIG. 4 Juan Muñoz, Malaga, 1980

3

26

object that moved up and down the façade of a building. Although these initial efforts today might seem unnecessarily complex and somewhat overwrought, they do show Muñoz to have been conversant with current trends in conceptual and process art, in particular the work of Bruce Nauman and other artists who, in the late 1960s and 1970s, deformalized and even eliminated the art object. On the other hand, Muñoz was also capable of more subtle gestures: on one occasion he drew a small figure in white chalk on the façade of a building in Croydon and then, on a rainy day, photographed pedestrians as they ignored the image (fig. 3).[4]

This equivocal form of making art preoccupied the artist as he continued his travels. After he returned to Madrid again in 1980 to work briefly for his father, he gained access to an abandoned bullfighting ring in Malaga, where he constructed a makeshift woven minaret and had himself photographed erecting and then tipping it over (fig. 4). This was the first of many instances in which Muñoz focused on the minaret, the slender towers attached to mosques that are often surrounded by one or more balconies from which the call to prayer is made. Muñoz's travels continued the following year when he moved to New York, where he received a Fulbright Fellowship. In New York, Muñoz attended Pratt Graphic Center, once again studying printmaking in a nominal way, and obtained a position as an artist-in-residence at P.S.1. Contemporary Art Center.

Although he made only a single work on paper during the year he spent in New York, Muñoz continued to experiment with process-based sculpture. Whereas in London he had been engaged in making objects that

moved, Muñoz now began to investigate the casting process, composing sculptures that consisted of the form of the mold alone rather than of the object that it formed. He also continued to focus on the photo-documentation of his own activities: in one instance he improvised a wooden springboard and then photographed himself jumping from it (see figs. 5a–c), and in another he made a series of photographs of himself swinging a long wooden handle (see figs. 6a–c).

As he had done in London, Muñoz read extensively while in New York, studying art history, criticism, and theory. He also began to keep journals in which he wrote about art for the first time. He recalls being strongly influenced by Philip Guston and Barnett Newman, and among his papers are extensive quotations from the writings of the latter as well as of sculptors such as Robert Morris and Robert Smithson, and from Michael Fried's seminal text "Art and Objecthood." Muñoz's notations focus principally on the contemporary redefinition of the relationship between the work of art, the space it inhabits, and the role of the artist in structuring the experience of viewing.[5] Running through these texts is the essence of the revolution that was brought about by many leading artists in the 1960s and 1970s and that would influence Muñoz so decisively. In redefining art as the experience of objects and actions of the artist and the viewer alike, these Minimalist and post-Minimalist sculptors effected a new and greater emphasis on the viewer and the perception of space, as well as a cerebral rather than a formal approach. Although this sculptural revolution was first undertaken in the United States, these same

4

ideas permeated contemporary English sculpture as well, and Muñoz had encountered the same concepts in London in the mid and late 1970s, in the early work of Deacon, Woodrow, and others, that he was experiencing in New York in 1981–82. Muñoz's own process-oriented work—characterized by objects that move through space, photo-documentation of activities both inside the studio and out, and experiments with sound—reveals his familiarity with the most progressive currents in contemporary sculpture. Given the conservative nature of the Spanish art world during these years, Muñoz's extensive travels in Western Europe and residence in London and New York would prove to be of inestimable importance as he increasingly committed himself to a career as an artist.

While Muñoz continued to experiment with the making of art, as his stay in New York was coming to an end, he began to contemplate how he might support himself when he returned to Spain. Although Franco had died in 1975 and a democratic government had been established, Muñoz was painfully aware that no progressive contemporary art movement existed in Spain and that he would have no professional prospects there. Muñoz remained as interested in art history, theory, and criticism as in the making of art, and he began to consider a career as a curator or critic in Madrid, mindful of the examples of artists such as Donald Judd, who worked as a critic early in his career.

Before he left New York to return to Madrid in 1982, Muñoz was able to meet and interview the artist Richard Serra. Muñoz admired Serra greatly, and he prepared extensively for the meeting, carefully developing his thoughts and questions. Through the interview, Muñoz attempted to understand what it meant to be a public sculptor working outside of Europe. The text is filled with questions that invite comparisons between the public cultures of Europe, with its more extensive history and an urban environment based on the pedestrian, and of the United States, with its modern industrial environment dominated by the automobile. Underlying the conversation is Muñoz's emerging doubt concerning modernist sculpture, as well as his interest in establishing the central role of the viewer in the form and content of public sculpture.[6]

Coincidentally, it was through Serra that Muñoz gained an opportunity to work as a curator when he returned to Madrid in 1982. Serra was friendly with the influential Spanish curator Carmen Giménez, who at that time was working in the Ministry of Culture in Madrid, and he encouraged Muñoz to meet her on his return. Muñoz did so, and with her support he quickly conceived an exhibition on the subject of

FIGS. 5a–c Juan Muñoz, P.S.1 Contemporary
Art Center, Long Island City,
New York, 1982
FIGS. 6a–c Juan Muñoz, New York, 1982

5a

5b

5c

the relationship between sculpture and architecture.
While Giménez offered advice and guidance, Muñoz
developed the exhibition, formulating the list of participants, selecting the works, and locating a venue for
the exhibition in Madrid, the Palacio de las Alhajas.

As impressive as Muñoz's organizational skills
was the roster of artists and architects that he enlisted
for the show. Muñoz invited the architects Emilio
Ambasz, Peter Eisenman, Frank Gehry, Leon Krier, and
Robert Venturi, and the sculptors Eduardo Chillida,
Mario Merz, Joel Shapiro, and Charles Simonds, as well
as Serra, to participate. This was an extraordinary roster
of talent, and the exhibition, "Correspondencias: 5
arquitectos, 5 escultores," which opened in October
1982, offered many of these individuals their first opportunity to exhibit in the new, post-Franco Spain. For the
catalogue, Muñoz published brief texts by several of the
participants and by a number of critics and historians,
among them Germano Celant and Paz. He also invited
his former teacher, Santiago Amón, to contribute a text.
Muñoz's own first essay, "Notes on Three" (see pp.
56–57), was published in the catalogue. The title was of
paramount importance, as in the essay he discussed
the historical relationship between architecture, sculpture, and the viewer. For example, he juxtaposed
Eisenman's intellectually ambitious, spatially open
designs for houses with Shapiro's diminutive and
utterly solid, self-contained, early bronze house-sculp-
tures. The essay also reveals Muñoz's ability to merge
fact and fiction toward meaningful ends. For example,
he imagined the Chilean painter Roberto Matta walking
the streets of Paris together with his young son:

It is equally possible or fictitious to imagine
that during one of those walks the boy would
take a special interest in the complexity of
the flying buttresses and arches at the church
of Sacré-Coeur. Allow us to imagine, in the
permissible exagerration of fiction, the
moment when he, now inside, observed, with
special devotion, the rose window, which, in
the manner of an epicenter, simultaneously

unites and divides the church's interior light. Years later, Gordon Matta-Clark, former architecture student, conceived sculpture as the act of cutting a series of circles into the guts of several abandoned buildings. . . .

This telling fragment contains invented but imaginable fiction while remaining true to the essential history of art. This inventiveness—and the pleasure taken in bending the truth while respecting the outline of history—would become a striking characteristic of Muñoz's subsequent writing.

Although the exhibition was quite a success, and later it traveled to Bilbao, where it was presented at the Museo de Bellas Artes, Muñoz again found himself without a job, money, or prospects. In fact, so dire was his economic situation that at the end of the exhibition he actually hired himself out to Mario Merz to deinstall the sculpture the Italian artist had made for the exhibition. Despite his financial predicament, Muñoz embarked immediately on a second project, a show titled "La imagen del animal: Arte prehistórico, arte contemporáneo." This exhibition was perhaps even more ambitious than the first: taking prehistoric images from the Altamira caves as a starting point, Muñoz borrowed works from several Spanish archaeological museums and paired them with works featuring images of animals by leading contemporary artists such as Merz, Miquel Barcelo, Joseph Beuys, Cragg, Per Kirkeby, Jannis Kounellis, Malcolm Morley, Jaume Plensa, Julião Sarmento, and Woodrow. Muñoz also included a work of his own in the exhibition, *Portrait* (1983), an imprint of a pair of feet cast from a garden sculpture that he had purchased. He also exhibited a work by a young Spanish artist, Cristina Iglesias, whom Muñoz had met in London and with whom he was now living in Torrelodones, a Madrid suburb. "La imagen del animal" opened at the Casa del Monte in December 1983 in Madrid and was subsequently shown at the Fundació "la Caixa" in Barcelona. The catalogue included several texts, written by Spanish archaeologists as well as contemporary artists such as Beuys and Merz. Muñoz also contributed a text, "The First/The Last," in which he concentrated on the nonillusory representation of space

6a

6b

6c

FIG. 7 Installation view of "Juan Muñoz: Últimos trabajos," Galería Fernando Vijande, Madrid, 1984, with *General Miaja Looking for the Guadiana River* installed on four columns

FIG. 8 Bunker overlooking Juan Muñoz's house in Torrelodones, Spain

30

7

in cave art as well as in the work of his contemporaries.

Although Muñoz had set aside $15,000 from the exhibition budget for his own salary, he still had no prospects for future employment. After considerable soul-searching and extensive conversations with Iglesias, he decided to abandon curatorial work and used his salary to buy welding equipment and to pursue sculpture in a serious way. Since 1979 Muñoz had exhibited in occasional group shows in London, Fribourg, and Berlin, and he now spent the summer and fall of 1984 preparing a body of work for his first solo exhibition, at Galería Fernando Vijande in Madrid. Although short-lived, from its founding in 1981, the Vijande gallery was one of the leading progressive commercial galleries in Spain, exhibiting such international artists as

Kounellis and Andy Warhol as well as Spaniards such as Plensa, Chema Cobo, Antonio Muntadas, Jose Maria Sicilia, and Susana Solano. In 1983, Muñoz had participated in a group show at the gallery, "Seis españoles en Madrid." His first solo show, "Juan Muñoz: Últimos trabajos," opened in November 1984. Muñoz had prepared a large body of welded-iron work with which he filled Vijande's cavernous space (see fig. 7). He again exhibited *Portrait*, along with a number of other works that featured cast imprints of the body or diminutive heads and bodies. Disembodied ears appeared in a few works, recalling both Muñoz's unfortunate grade-school experience and his recent attempts to incorporate sound into his sculpture. Even at this early stage, Muñoz was assigning allusive titles drawn from a variety

8

of art forms to his work; the title of an Ezra Pound book, *If This Be Treason* (1948), actually formed the basis of one sculpture.[7]

The most important works Muñoz made for the exhibition—sculptures that would provide him with a rich body of subject matter for several years to come—were those that involved small architectural elements such as balconies, minarets, spiral staircases, and watchtowers. One such work, which bears the beautiful title *If Only She Knew* (1984; cat. no. 1), is a type of minaret raised on tall, spindly legs that contains several small, carved-wood male figures as well as a single female figure carved from stone, all seemingly trapped beneath a peaked roof. For the most part, however, the works of this type only imply a figurative presence. One of the first of these nonfigurative works was a very small, welded-metal, wall-mounted object in the form of a spiral staircase. Although this piece was originally titled simply *Staircase*, Muñoz soon retitled it *Spiral Staircase* (1984; cat. no. 2).[8] The sculpture had great power for the artist; he recalled feeling that it was the first sculpture that was really his own, and he took it from his studio and mounted it in the living room of his house so that he might live with it. Although it is one of the smallest sculptures the artist has ever made, it is among the most evocative pieces of his career. In an interview published in the catalogue with the Belgian curator Jan Debbaut, Muñoz might well have been discussing the piece when he said, "I believe that a sculpture retains its interest when it remains strange to me. . . . At times I think I always try to construct a sculpture that will betray my memories, that will remain foreign."[9]

Muñoz also included in the exhibition a series of four metal balcony sculptures that he mounted on columns in the Vijande gallery. The four-part work that resulted—*General Miaja Looking for the Guadiana River* (1984; see fig. 7)—dominated the show. The references in the title are numerous and intriguingly complex. General Miaja (José Miaja Menant; 1878–1958) was an important figure in the Spanish Civil War, best known as the Republican commander who led the defense of Madrid after the government abandoned the city in advance of Franco's armies in November 1936.[10] Miaja is a deeply ironic figure; although he began the war as a staunch anti-Communist, he found himself in command of a badly disorganized but impassioned band of Communist and anarchist freedom fighters and Madrid civilians. Miaja was celebrated as a hero by the forces of the left, and he eventually joined the Communist party. It is perhaps noteworthy that Franco's armies approached Madrid from the west and northwest, since Torrelodones, where Muñoz continues to live, lies to the northwest of Madrid. Remarkably, on a rocky bluff immediately visible from his house is an observation bunker (fig. 8) that, although of unknown origin, served as an imaginative point of departure for the work. The other reference in the title is to the Guadiana River that flows across south-central Spain, through Portugal, and into the Gulf of Cadiz. It interests Muñoz because in many places the porous limestone through which it flows produces a low water table, causing the river to actually disappear below ground only to reappear again miles away. Beyond the allusive title, the work itself recalls the balconies that appear in the paintings of Francisco de

Goya and Édouard Manet (see fig. 9), and, conceptually, the "watchtower" paintings that Sigmar Polke was making in Germany in the early 1980s. For his part, Muñoz has often associated the work with *The Tartar Steppe*, a novel by the Italian writer Dino Buzzati that Muñoz read at the time in which a soldier spends years assigned to a distant outpost to guard against an enemy who never materializes.[11]

The Vijande gallery exhibition was reviewed by Francisco Calvo Serraller, an art critic for *El País*. In his article, "La tercera mirada del misterio," Calvo Serraller referred to Muñoz's work as a curator, noting that the same engagement with the viewer that characterized the two exhibitions he had organized was also a seminal component of his sculpture. He emphasized that Muñoz's formative years as an artist had been spent in London and New York rather than in Madrid and that the sources of his art were with the Arte Povera artists Merz and Kounellis, as well as Beuys, Nauman, and Serra, rather than with Spanish modernism. In a revealing statement, Calvo Serraller noted that Muñoz

> does not bother to conceal his loyalties, the points of transition and stimulation, but they indicate to us in any event the cosmopolitan resonance . . . in which they unfold. Even though our artists do not usually move with ease through this territory of mental subtlety that J. Muñoz has chosen and, therefore, the Spanish observer is not particularly receptive to it at the moment, the exhibition of pieces in the Vijande Gallery proceeds

9

> with much dignity, a mixture of coherence and mystery.[12]

If Spain remained something of an artistic outpost in the early 1980s, the situation was changing rapidly, and the timing of Muñoz's first exhibition could scarcely have been better. Commercial galleries in Spain were beginning to exhibit international contemporary art, and Spanish curators such as Giménez, Maria de Corral, Gloria Moure, and Vicente Todolí were organizing important exhibitions in Madrid, Barcelona, and Valencia. The international art fair ARCO was now held annually in Madrid, and a new Spanish national museum of modern art—the Museo Nacional Centro de Arte Reina Sofía, which would open in 1988—was in the planning stages. Critics, curators, and collectors from the rest of Europe and North America were coming to the "new Spain," and Muñoz and other young artists clearly benefited from this sudden attention.[13] Indeed, Muñoz's career took off following the Vijande show, and he received more offers to exhibit than he could readily accept. The Portuguese painter Julião Sarmento, a friend of Muñoz, introduced him to the Lisbon dealer Luis Serpa, and through Serpa Muñoz exhibited work at the Cómicos Gallery in March 1985. Rudy Fuchs, then director of the Stedelijk van Abbemuseum in Eindhoven, the Netherlands, saw the show, as did Jan Hoet, director of the Museum van Hedendaagse Kunst in Ghent, Belgium. Each invited Muñoz to participate in an exhibition: Fuchs in a show of young, principally European artists that included Iglesias and Sarmento, among others, in May and June of 1985, and Hoet in the celebrated exhibition "Chambre d'amis," which took place during the summer of 1986. Also in 1986, Maria de Corral included Muñoz and three other young Spaniards in the Aperto section of the Venice Biennale.

For Aperto in Venice, Muñoz made a body of work centered on a sculpture titled *North of the Storm* (1986; fig. 10). This was a welded-metal sculpture in the form of a table with a variety of small objects mounted on top. These included a wagon with wheels and an actual switchblade knife as well as several miniature architectural forms, a staircase and a tower among them. In addition Muñoz made a group of free-standing and hanging sculptures featuring intricate and somewhat awkward objects that moved and turned. Accompanying the sculptures in the *North of the Storm* project was a 45-rpm record that Muñoz had made with his brother-in-law, the composer and musician Alberto Iglesias. This was the first of several collaborations between the two artists, and it was Muñoz's first actual sound piece.

Almost immediately, however, Muñoz concluded that these pieces were an artistic "dead end" and that the Venice installation was a "complete disaster." He also decided that the large number and small scale of many of the works in the Vijande show had detracted from its overall impact and that in the future he should limit the number of works included in a given exhibition. Most importantly, he decided to focus on architectural forms, granting them approximately human scale so that they might assume a more complex psychological dimension.

The change in Muñoz's work was immediate and profound. He quickly began to make larger sculptures that contained a much greater range of complex

10

references. For "Chambre d'amis," for instance, an exhibition that was located in private residences around Ghent, Muñoz made *Balcony on the Ceiling of a Basement* (1986; see Viso, fig. 8), a large and wonderfully eccentric sculpture mounted on the ceiling of a basement room. For a show at Galerie Joost Declercq in Ghent in the fall of 1986, Muñoz transformed and took full possession of the gallery space by including works that either were mounted very high on the wall or reconstituted the floor. This exhibition, which was his most ambitious to date, included just two works. The first was *Hotel Declercq I–IV* (1986; cat. nos. 14–17), a series of welded metal balconies, each accompanied by a handmade hotel sign extending from the wall. An additional pair of balconies (*Double Balcony*; cat. no. 13), one mounted above the other and resembling successive floors of the same building, was also included. Galerie Joost Declercq was a vast and quite raw industrial space, and, by mounting a series of balconies high up on its walls, Muñoz situated the viewer in the role of a pedestrian on the street below. The other work, *The Wasteland* (1986; cat. no. 19), included a complex patterned floor and a small papier-mâché ventriloquist's dummy seated on a low shelf. This was the first of several instances in which the artist created patterned floors as an element in his sculptural environments, simultaneously recalling antique Roman architecture and the work of Carl Andre. For Muñoz the floor suggested the stage and the complex psychological relationship between the viewer and the actor, in this case a small figure whose feet did not quite touch the floor. As Muñoz would later note, "The floor developed out of a desire to build something that was real, something people could walk across. . . . It was also a necessary device for locating the figure. . . . The floor becomes a gigantic prop for such a piece."[14] If, on the one hand, the floor engages the viewer and invites him to move forward and examine the dummy, it simultaneously creates distance. Muñoz described it as a "Baroque device, a stage set for the image."[15] Although Muñoz had made small figures for works such as *If Only She Knew*, the ventriloquist's dummy in this new work assumed far greater importance:

> To begin with, it remained in the studio for quite awhile; later I would carry it into the living room. . . . Although I don't usually handle my sculptures too carefully, I would always carry that ventriloquist's dummy in an upward position and with the utmost care. That's when I decided to show it.[16]

11

In discussing this small figure, Muñoz has mentioned the impact that Edgar Degas' *L'Homme et le pantin* (known today as *Henri Michel-Lévy*; 1878; fig. 11), a painting of a man and puppet that he had seen often in the Gulbenkian Collection in Lisbon, had upon him. For Muñoz, the ventriloquist's dummy provided an opportunity to make a figure without engaging in naturalism. As he would note in 1991,

> I made a perfect copy of one such ventriloquist's doll, because a ventriloquist is always a storyteller. But a ventriloquist's doll without the ventriloquist also becomes a story teller. He sits there, waiting for you in order to talk. He still doesn't speak, but his identity endows him with some capacity to tell a story.[17]

Clearly, Muñoz was engaging in an equivocal sort of figuration; in working to move beyond the implicit presence but ultimate absence of the figure in his balcony sculptures, he included figures in his work that possessed narrative possibilities and psychological implications but that hovered, nonetheless, between actual figures and animated objects.

The title *The Wasteland* refers to T. S. Eliot's landmark poem, first published in 1922. In this poetic Tower of Babel, which consists of five separate parts with numerous voices and explanatory notes, Eliot balanced images of chaos and stability. Written from 1915 to 1922, the poem contains many references to classical literature and speaks to the despair and isolation that developed during World War I and its aftermath. Among Muñoz's notes are many quotations from Eliot. Muñoz clearly admired the writer's willingness to enrich the meaning of a work through the interweaving of a series of disparate fragments and his embrace of historical tradition for the purposes of expanding modernism. Eliot's model has served Muñoz remarkably well throughout his career.

It was with the Declercq show that Muñoz began to realize his promise as an artist. After having spent several years thinking and writing about Minimalism, post-Minimalism, architecture, and the complex tripartite relationship of object, space, and viewer, Muñoz created an environment that was not merely filled with objects but also imbued with complex psychological implications. Although the figure was absent from the *Hotel Declercq* pieces, viewers were nonetheless encouraged to imagine themselves either occupying the balcony or strolling on a city street while looking upward, in Muñoz's words, "at the intersection between watching the walking that goes on underneath and walking while watching what goes on up above."[18] In *The Wasteland*, the oddly troubling, highly theatrical separation that the patterned floor created between the ventriloquist's dummy and the viewers also engaged them in a powerful way. Whereas Judd, Serra, and others had expanded sculpture by taking the object off the pedestal, they nonetheless exercised near total control over the architectural spaces surrounding their works. Muñoz had no wish to restrict the viewer's experience to such an extent. He opened up the sculptor's space to the visitor's subjective interaction and, most importantly, introduced the figure into his work.

Muñoz found himself in the company of artists

12

such as Robert Gober and Charles Ray in the United States, Thomas Schütte in Germany, and Jeff Wall in Canada, among many others, who were beginning to reinvent both the figure and the possibility of narrative in contemporary art. Interestingly, the type of figuration with which these young artists were engaged owed nothing to the short-lived, overwrought neo-Expressionism that was in such vogue at that time. Rather, to varying degrees, these artists were all engaged with the figure while retaining the formal discipline of Minimalism, the involvement with a wide range of materials of Arte Povera, and the intellectual restraint of Conceptual Art. Wall created figurative work with strong psychological connotations; in fact, in 1990 he would take up the theme of the ventriloquist (see fig. 12), which Muñoz had already begun to explore in works such as *The Wasteland*. Artists such as Gober, Ray, and Schütte now effectively reversed the accepted trope

35

FIG. 13   Robert Gober, *Untitled*, 1990

As with these artists, however, the figure would maintain an equivocal existence in Muñoz's work in the late 1980s, appearing, disappearing, and reappearing in a variety of forms. For instance, in 1986 Muñoz made *One Month Before* (cat. no. 18), a sculpture composed of a freestanding bookcase with a pair of legs resting on one of its shelves. It is a startling image that recalls the abrupt fragmentation of the body that appeared in Gober's work at this time, though it does not include the clothing and artificial hair that lends such a surreal and troubling aspect to the latter artist's work (see fig. 13).

Simultaneously, however, Muñoz began to produce a series of works in which the figure was present only implicitly, in particular, a series of sculptures representing banisters—objects with an obviously functional purpose in guiding hand and body that Muñoz transformed in a number of surprising ways. Muñoz began to show these works at Marga Paz Gallery in Madrid in 1988. Included were works such as *The Other Banister* (1988; cat. no. 23), a straightforward replication of the actual object, and *De Sol a Sol* (1990; cat. no. 33), which takes a more whimsical form, snaking lyrically along a wall. In other cases, however, Muñoz was far more extreme, relishing the opportunity to take an ordinary object that invites reassurance and make of it an object of danger. For instance, *First Banister* (1987; see Brenson, fig. 5) is similar to *The Other Banister* except that an open switchblade knife is mounted on it in a nearly invisible position where the trusting hand might be severely cut. Others in the series are simply dysfunctional: *Banister* (1991; cat. no. 35) sweeps upward with a flourish at one end, while *Nîmes Banister* (1994) brushes paradoxically against the wall in the middle, making it impossible for the hand to pass. For Muñoz, the banister was a simple, functional form, yet one that offered endless possibilities for elaboration and reinterpretation. For a period of several years it would offer the artist an objective image, one that he could endow with a wide variety of psychological possibilities without the intrusion of a figure.

These works focused on interior architectural forms paralleled another body of Muñoz's work, a series of "raincoat drawings," executed in white chalk on a commercial black fabric that is used in Spain to make

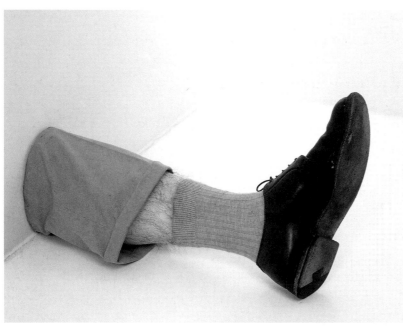

13

of the modernist artist as one who gravitates from figuration toward abstraction. Instead, these three artists began their careers as principally nonfigurative artists and subsequently moved toward the figure. Throughout the mid 1980s, Gober concentrated on sculptures in the form of sinks, cribs, chairs, and beds; Ray made still-lifes and a variety of abstract sculptures; and Schütte focused on architectural models. Yet theirs was never an art of pure abstraction, and the figure was strongly implicit throughout their early work. When each turned to the figure it was with the greatest restraint: Gober began to make sculptures of radically cropped body parts such as legs, buttocks, and torsos; Ray photographed himself and made sculptures featuring mannequins; and Schütte included small figures in his architectural models.

raincoats. The first work in the series, *Ventriloquist Looking at a Double Interior* (1988; second version, 2001; cat. no. 26), is the most complex. Like *The Wasteland*, the work contains a ventriloquist's dummy, but this time the figure sits on a low wall and looks blankly at a pair of interior scenes drawn in white chalk on black fabric. This is the only instance in which Muñoz related a figure to these works. The view is oddly disjunctive because the interior scenes depict the same space viewed from different directions—thus the same chair is seen from the front on the left and from the back on the right. Muñoz would go on to make approximately forty such drawings of beds, chairs, rugs, and other ordinary objects set in darkened and quietly haunting domestic settings. Muñoz has described the apparent normality of these images: "A normal room is very interesting. I find the normal very suggestive. You can build stories from a very normal situation. Any normal situation is ready for something to happen."[19] Although he has emphasized that these scenes are imaginary, Muñoz has also commented,

> When I was a kid living at home, I used
> to come back to the house every day.
> Occasionally—I don't know why—my mother
> changed the furniture around between the
> rooms. So you came in and opened the door
> of your room and found that your room was
> no longer your room—it was your brother's.
> And a different room somewhere up the
> hall was now your room, with all your stuff
> in it, your posters on the wall. Then you
> grew used to it—until the rooms were
> changed again. So I grew up with this experi-
> ence of dislocation. You feel uncomfortable,
> yet it's extremely normal. I suppose that
> this relationship between the normal and
> the discomforting is part of the territory
> of the work.[20]

At the same time Muñoz was creating the banister sculptures and raincoat drawings, he was continuing to explore the figure. This had begun with the ventriloquist's dummy in *The Wasteland* and the fragmented figure in *One Month Before*, and in the late 1980s, his

figurative work took other, equally surprising forms. In 1988 Muñoz was invited by the Munich art dealer Rudiger Schöttle to participate in a project that focused on the relationship of contemporary art to gardens and the theater. Eventually realized at the P.S.1 Contemporary Art Center in New York in early 1989 under the title "Theatergarden Bestiarium," the show included artists such as James Coleman, Dan Graham, Rodney Graham, and Wall, among others. References to the theater had already been implicit in Muñoz's work, and he now made *The Prompter* (1988; cat. no. 24), which, like the *The Wasteland*, includes a patterned floor, but is more obviously a stage because it is raised off the ground. One of several sculptures that involves dwarves, the piece is viewed from the perspective of the audience, with the small prompter's box and the legs of a dwarf visible along with a drum that sits discarded at the rear.

The work has a complex derivation. Following a conversation with Schöttle in Munich concerning the project, Muñoz visited the Nymphenburg Gardens, which had served as the summer residence of the Bavarian monarchy since the late seventeenth century. During his visit, Muñoz was intrigued to learn that one of the principal designers of the extensive eighteenth-century architectural complex was François de Cuvilliés I (1695–1768), a French-trained, Bavarian architect.[21] At the age of eleven, de Cuvilliés had entered the service of Maximilian II Emanuel (1662–1726) as court dwarf. Educated first at the Bavarian court, de Cuvilliés later studied architecture in Paris, and in 1728 he was appointed court architect in Munich. Muñoz had long been troubled by the discomfort he felt when he encountered dwarves, and this, in part, attracted him to them as a subject for his art. Muñoz also knew that dwarves had often occupied central roles in the political and social life of the court during the Baroque period, and he was familiar with the prominent role they played in the work of the great Spanish painter Diego Velázquez. In fact, Muñoz included a reproduction of a Velázquez painting of a court dwarf that he knew well from the Prado, *Don Diego de Acedo* (1644), with a text he authored, titled "The Prompter" (see p. 66), for the exhibition catalogue accompanying "Theatergarden Bestiarium."

Interestingly, although *The Prompter* was shown

37

14

for the first time in New York, Muñoz also applied the French title *Le Souffleur* to the work, and he used the two titles almost interchangeably from the outset. The French title was inspired by an Honoré Daumier lithograph, published in the French journal *Le Charivari* in 1870, that shows Adolphe Thiers (1797–1877), the first president of the Third French Republic, inside a prompter's box following a script (fig. 14). In researching the history of the prompter's box, Muñoz had encountered histories of the theater that included reproductions of the lithograph. Muñoz has described the prompter's box as "a house of memory, the mind you never see but is always there. . . . like a stage set with no representation, no play, only one man trying to remember, trying not to forget."[22] Muñoz had long been attracted to the complex relationship of memory and forgetting, and in his "Theatergarden Bestiarium" catalogue text he paraphrased Jorge Luis Borges on the subject, noting that the Argentine considered "forgetting as a form superior to memory."[23]

The implicit reference to narrative storytelling and the stage that appeared in the earlier work was now becoming more literal. While Muñoz's theater possessed an audience, a prompter, and a prop, however, it lacked a plot or actors. There are traces of both Samuel Beckett and Luigi Pirandello in this work's reference to the theater as a drama of discomfiting situations involving empty stages, absent actors, failed communication, and the active engagement of the audience. In the language of contemporary art, Muñoz was seeking a middle ground between the resolute formal control of simple objects in space as issued by Minimalist sculptors and

the human psychology reflected in more traditional figurative art.

Muñoz's approach, in which he filled his work with a multitude of references to art history, literature, and theater, among others, proved somewhat controversial. Muñoz acknowledged this in a 1987 interview:

Someone, a few months ago, mentioned to me that he could see, in my work, a dangerous, excessive bent towards literature. Although it worried me for a while, I retorted, in my defense, that yes indeed, I was a storyteller. And though this answer first seemed like taking a great leap, I am now gradually becoming used to the notion.[24]

This is a revealing statement, both for the direction that Muñoz's work was taking and for what it shows about the often oppressive character of discourse about contemporary art. Muñoz's work, in which he employed self-consciously theatrical sculptural devices in pursuit of narrative content, was outside the scope of progressive thinking about contemporary art at that time. The reaction against neo-Expressionism was so prevalent in the late 1980s that any artist working with narrative content and theatrical means was dismissed as "romantic." In a 1991 interview, Muñoz would lash out against his critics and those who sought to restrict contemporary practice:

> It is true that there is a change in sensibility but it's more to do with being bored with denial. We have become aware of the millions of stories that we did not allow ourselves to tell over the last ten years because of our suspicion of the conditions of expression. Now we can express without being expressionistic.[25]

The Prompter signaled the beginning of a period in which Muñoz expanded his use of the figure in a number of directions. For example, he made other sculptural installations involving dwarves and quasi-theatrical props, such as *Dwarf with Three Columns* (1988; cat. no. 22), in which the figure stands motionless among three terracotta columns. The following year, Muñoz departed even more dramatically from contemporary practice. He had worked previously with literary and dramatic themes, and he now made the first in a series of bronze sculptures devoted to dance and to ballerinas that allude to Edgar Degas' images of dancers in pastel and bronze, works that are among the highest achievements of modern French art. Muñoz knew and had enormous respect for Degas' work, and he approached the subject of ballerinas with only the greatest trepidation.[26] Just as he had mined literary and theatrical traditions with respect and admiration, Muñoz now engaged with the work of Degas in a similar way. Beyond this, Muñoz was concerned for the fate of these new works in the court of contemporary art-world opinion. To make the figure of a ballerina, and in bronze, no less, was simply beyond the margins of acceptability in progressive art-world circles, and Muñoz knew he risked rejection among certain critics and curators. He assumed, perhaps correctly, that his position as a progressive artist was at stake because these works would be perceived by many as both too traditional and too accessible.

Nevertheless, Muñoz pushed ahead with the project, making a number of small bronze figures. All possessed round bottoms rather than legs, defying the possibility of movement that was implicit in their

15

interaction, gestures, and surroundings. Most often he composed them individually or in pairs on patterned floors atop traditional tabletop bases. These bases, often surfaced in parqueted wood or polished stone, served as small stages. Perhaps the most engaging and impressive piece in the series is *Ballerinas in Apartment* (1990; fig. 15), the only example that includes three figures. They are set in a miniature architectural environment, all with small bells attached to their hands. This and other works in the series have the character of a scale model for a stage set; indeed, when Muñoz exhibited the ballerina sculptures for the first time at the Marga Paz Gallery in Madrid in 1989, their theatrical power was unmistakable.

The ballerinas occupied Muñoz from 1989 through 1991. The body of work was the centerpiece of two

39

important museum exhibitions, one organized jointly by The Renaissance Society at The University of Chicago and the Centre d'Art Contemporain in Geneva, Switzerland, in 1990, the other by the Museum Haus Lange in Krefeld, Germany, in 1991. In publications accompanying both exhibitions, Muñoz contributed an extended essay titled *Segment* (see pp. 69–75), unquestionably his most important piece of writing to date. Although Muñoz had long since committed himself to sculpture, he had continued to write, developing an extensive resume of published essays on art during the 1980s. Following the two catalogue essays that he had written as a curator in 1982–83, Muñoz contributed a series of essays to *Figura*, a short-lived journal published in Seville and edited by the artists Pepe Espaliú and Guillermo Paneque. Perhaps the most engaging of these was "Borromini-Kounellis: On the Luminous Opacity of Signs" (1985; see pp. 60–61), which featured a lively and unexpected comparison of the work of the Baroque architect Francesco Borromini with that of Kounellis. In 1988 Muñoz published "The Time of the Pose" (see pp. 64–65), an equally original comparison, in this case of Parmigianino's *Lady with Three Children* (1537–39) with *Riots in St. James Square, February 17, 1936*, a photograph made in Barcelona during the Spanish Civil War by the Catalan artist Agusti Centelles.

Having spent several years in London, Muñoz knew contemporary English sculpture well, and he published other essays in *Figura* in 1985, which focus on artists such as Anthony Caro, Richard Deacon, Ian Hamilton Finlay, and Richard Long. Muñoz's commentary on English sculpture continued in 1986, when he served as a consultant for the exhibition "Entre el objecto y la imagen: Escultura britànica contemporáneo," which was presented at the Palacio de Velázquez in Madrid. For the catalogue Muñoz contributed "A Man up a Lamppost" (see pp. 62–63), a brief essay on Jacob Epstein's seminal sculpture *Rock Drill* (1915). Epstein, who had been enormously enthusiastic about the machine in the years prior to World War I, composed the sculpture in two parts, setting a white plaster mechanical figure of his own making astride an enormous mechanical rock drill that he had purchased. Epstein exhibited the work only once, in London in 1915; with the devastation of World War I, he came to reconsider his embrace of the machine, and he eventually abandoned the drill that was the lower half, casting the figure from the waist up in bronze and thereby making of it a somewhat more conventional modern sculpture. *Rock Drill* was one of the most powerful—if short lived—sculptures of its time, a devastating emblem of raw industrial power, and perhaps the most unlikely and original found-object sculpture ever made.[27]

In his essay, Muñoz recalled having often seen the final bronze sculpture at the Tate, finding it in a remote gallery, "past rooms full of allegorical images of ladies and horses . . . surrounded by paintings by Turner's disciples, or by friends of Vorticism or others of uncertain pedigree." Muñoz had seen an important Vorticism exhibition at the Hayward Gallery in London in 1974, where a reconstruction of Epstein's original sculpture was exhibited.[28] Muñoz was fascinated by the history of *Rock Drill*: a powerful, even shocking work was placed on public view; the artist then removed it from sight and later abandoned its most compelling element; he then cast the remainder in bronze; the finished work was consigned to a secondary position in the history of modern sculpture; and, finally, the original was reconstructed sixty years later, providing the prevailing memory of the celebrated original. While Muñoz recognized the precedent that *Rock Drill* provided for the found-object sculpture of Cragg, Woodrow, and others, he was also intrigued by the work because it had "escaped the basic requirements of [its] age, the impeccable consummation of [its] aesthetic destiny." These words are especially important in that they came at a time when Muñoz, too, was achieving independence from the creative expectations of his own time.

Although Muñoz's art criticism was growing increasingly insightful and personal, *Segment*, the essay he published in 1990, is of a far different order. The text is introduced by an anonymous preface in which the author described himself as a friend of an archaeologist named André Friedmann. During an expedition to the Peruvian highlands, Friedmann had located a village called Zurite and a small architectural structure there called "la posa." Friedmann had apparently studied Zurite and "la posa" extensively, but he had died in a helicopter crash before his notes could be published; the reader presumes that *Segment* represents a posthumous account of Friedmann's fieldwork. The preface concludes, "may these notes be the payment of a debt incurred in time and a sign of friendship, or rather a certain proximity, as for years we shared identical balconies on opposite sides of the same street."

The essay begins with a very detailed description of Zurite, which, we are told, is located at an altitude of 3,391 meters in the Vilcabamba mountains near a tributary of the Apurimac river in Peru. The village has 3,402 inhabitants, who grow quinoa, coca, and potatoes and herd alpacas and vicunas. The author illustrated "la posa" in a grainy, black-and-white photograph and described it as a simple structure constructed every year of sticks, scrap wood, and rope off the main plaza of the village. What interested Friedmann about "la posa" was that it was without discernible function; barely a shell, it neither protected man against the elements nor offered privacy. Asked to describe the feeling of being inside "la posa," the villagers invariably described it as simply a dark and quiet room. Most remarkably, according to the author, "la posa" was burned to the ground every year, and the accompanying photograph shows the structure after it has been set on fire.

Following the description is a long treatise on ephemeral architecture. Wide-ranging references are made to the history of architecture and to architects, historians, and theorists ranging from historical figures such as Vitruvius, Etienne-Louis Boullée, and Gottfried Semper to the contemporary writers Francesco Dal Co, Andre Leroi-Gourhan, Emmanuel Lévinas, and Vincent Scully, all of whom are quoted extensively. Summarizing Friedmann's research, the author described these structures as "continuously perishing houses. As time goes by, their only permanence lies in their description."

Segment is a skillfully written, thought-provoking essay. Although presented as anonymous, it was, of course, written by Muñoz. Blending pseudo-erudition with effective storytelling, Muñoz created a meticulously contrived, quasi-anthropological tale that, like so many of his texts, mixes fact and fiction. In fact, actual studies of the history of Andean architecture describe and illustrate religious processions in a village named Zurite that conclude with a fireworks display set off from a small hut called a "posa."[29] André Friedmann, the character whose anthropological fieldwork is the basis for the essay is, in fact, a surrogate for Santiago Amón, Muñoz's former teacher and friend. Amón had not been an archaeologist and had never worked in Peru, yet Muñoz invented this professional guise for him in order to pay him homage. Perhaps most extraordinary is Muñoz's introductory reference to sharing "identical balconies on opposite sides of the same street." This element of *Segment* is, in fact, true: while Muñoz had been Amón's student, he and his family had lived directly across the street from his teacher. In 1991, the year after *Segment* was published, the artist made *Opposite Balconies* (fig. 16), which consists of two balconies separated by a narrow space. This autobiographical reference sheds new and surprising light on all of Muñoz's balcony sculptures of the 1980s.

Beyond Muñoz's tribute, the content of his essay and the style of writing are also noteworthy. In elaborating a world filled with paradox, Muñoz seamlessly blended allusions to arcane factual material with fictitious material. The unavoidable comparison here is with the writing of Borges, many of whose stories are filled with images of spiral staircases, balconies, mirrors, and other evocative objects, and whose principal subject is the weaving of paradoxical situations and the collapse of rational certainties. Muñoz admits a debt to Borges here, in particular for a style of writing in which erudite references seduce the reader into a false state of confidence in the author's intentions.

At this time, Muñoz was beginning work on a series of "conversation pieces," sculptures that would occupy him for much of the 1990s and that, for many observers, have become his signature works. In many ways the phrase "conversation piece" is a misnomer: the term originated in the early eighteenth century to describe Dutch and English paintings in which identifiable figures are set in specific contexts and are engaged in conversation and other forms of social interaction.[30] By contrast, Muñoz's "conversation pieces" involve groups of anonymous figures set in generic spaces who relate to one another in a complex but ultimately obscure psychological manner.

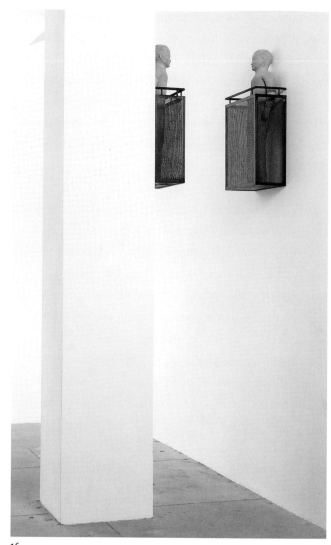

16

When Muñoz began the first of the "conversation piece" sculptures late in 1990, he resolved that they neither relate too closely to human scale nor bear personalized facial expressions or gestures.

I didn't want to be constantly inventing unnecessary variations on a theme. . . . I also felt that maybe I was walking into a territory where I would get lost in mannerist decisions, mannerist in the negative sense of endlessly reworking a gesture, or retouching a nose or an eye.[31]

Initially, the "conversation piece" figures were smaller than life size and bore round bottoms, no hands, and faces that were only generally articulated. Fabricated in resin in the studio and then cast in bronze, these sculptures were general figurative types, with no distinction in clothing or facial expression and only slight differences in the turn of a head or in the gesture of a hand.

Muñoz's "conversation pieces" evolved quite logically from both the patterned floor pieces such as *The Wasteland* and *The Prompter* and the ballerinas of 1989–91. Whereas in the early patterned floor pieces, Muñoz was concerned with creating empty but psychologically charged stages, with the ballerinas Muñoz had grown comfortable with himself as a figurative sculptor working in bronze. Yet he was not quite ready to project his sculptures at a larger scale in space. For Muñoz the idea of making larger figurative sculptures offered challenges different from those that he had faced

previously. As Muñoz studied modern figurative sculpture, he found himself attracted to works that

have a certain indifference to time. . . . Some of the best figurative sculptures seem to be aware of the impossibility of looking alive and aware of the boundaries they can occupy. The most successful ones are the ones that state those limits, the space between being just a sculpture and the man walking on the street. Not for a split second can you confuse one with the other.[32]

Muñoz has referred to Alberto Giacometti in this regard, believing that the power of his work resides in the distance from naturalism that he achieved while nonetheless working within a figurative genre. By first replacing the legs of the "conversation piece" sculptures with round bottoms and later employing legs without feet, Muñoz had invented his own means to suggest "the possibility of moving about and of hope, of conviction and lack of conviction, impossibility, uncertainty." Ultimately, Muñoz was convinced of the need to make sculpture that avoided any form of naturalism: "The more realistic they are meant to be, the less interior life they have."[33]

The first works in this new series were exhibited at New York's Marian Goodman Gallery in the spring of 1991. Subsequent works of this type were shown in a variety of important group exhibitions in the early 1990s, perhaps most impressively in *Conversation Piece I–V* (cat. nos. 36–40), which was exhibited at the Carnegie International in Pittsburgh in 1991. By 1993, Muñoz began to seek a greater degree of characterization without sacrificing the figurative type that he had established. He now made resin versions, creating a tan patina by employing studio assistants to paint the figures with resin and then literally throw sand at the wet surfaces. The stiff poses and generic hand and facial expressions of the initial bronzes gave way to figures that twist and turn and respond physically and psychologically to one another. Muñoz also gradually expanded the number of sculptures in his installations, choreographing these ensembles as though they were troupes of actors. If Giacometti's example had been helpful in conceiving a figurative type, Georges-Pierre Seurat's offered support when Muñoz began to compose them into ensembles. Describing the French painter's *Bathers at Asnières* (1884; fig. 17), a painting he knew well from the National Gallery in London, Muñoz stated:

> The space between all these people looking at a river, there is such a distance between them all. Each one is standing so still. And so mute. And each one seems to be occupying a space of silence. They are placed with perfect equilibrium between them. Looking at it I realised I wasn't interested in the mathematical formulation behind the work. I was interested in the incredible loneliness of the characters. On the other hand, no pain, no suffering is described, just the

43

17

condition of each of them. But it is also a relaxed Sunday scene. I thought: this is the image of the soul looking at the desert. I realise that I go back again and again to looking at certain images. In the Seurat there is a position of stillness and muteness combined with an incredible transparency. The indifference of the sunny afternoon is paralleled with a tremendous tension.[34]

This sense of profound psychological isolation within a social situation was conveyed in *Conversation Piece (Dublin)* (1994; see Brenson, fig. 1), in which he placed twenty-two figures in a large outdoor courtyard at the Irish Museum of Modern Art. Animated in their gestures and bearing, the figures are engaged in conversation and appear ready to move despite their round bottoms. The theatrical tenor of this installation

44

is unmistakable: Muñoz had moved from designing the empty stage to filling that stage with actors.

In contrast to the Dublin piece, with its high-pitched intensity, is a piece Muñoz made in the same year, *A Winter's Journey* (1994; see p. 151), whose title refers to the Franz Schubert song cycle of 1827. In this work, one of artist's most intimate, Muñoz combined a pair of figures, one carrying the other, and placed them on a large patterned floor.[35] With this sculpture Muñoz abandoned the round-bottomed bases, replacing them with legs that he would ultimately remove the feet from. Between 1995 and 2000, Muñoz employed this variation on the "conversation piece" type in several impressive installations. The centerpiece of a 1996 exhibition organized by the Museo Nacional Centro de Arte Reina Sofía and installed in the Palacio de Velázquez, Madrid, was a piece made up of thirty-one figures and titled *Square (Madrid)* (see figs. 18a–b). An element appeared in these figures that was new to Muñoz's work: Asian faces with expressions suggesting laughter. The artist generally refers to these figures as Chinese, and in their number and their typological sameness they recall the third-century-B.C. terracotta warriors excavated from a gravesite near Xi'an, China. Perhaps more importantly, Muñoz recognized that Western eyes are often unaccustomed to distinguishing specific Asian facial characteristics, and he exploited this inability to perceive difference in his ongoing effort to "depersonalize" his sculptures. Despite the sameness of their facial expressions, Muñoz's figures bore a variety of poses, with hands held at their waists, down at their sides, or behind their backs. Although several figures stood apart, the principal

group was arranged in a circle, their laughter perhaps suggesting that a joke had been told at the expense of one among them. Most importantly, Muñoz designed the installation so that the viewer could view the piece only from above, from the mezzanine overlooking the gallery.

At the same time as the Palacio de Velázquez exhibition, Muñoz developed perhaps one of his most ambitious projects to date, "A Place Called Abroad," for the Dia Center for the Arts in New York (see figs. 19a–b). Muñoz had long been fascinated by the relationship of the individual to architecture, and this installation produced a remarkable conjunction of those interests. In his "conversation pieces," he had realized a figurative type whose very lack of articulation enhanced its psychological depth. In this work Muñoz designed an architectural setting of equally powerful ambiguity, in which all the windows were shuttered and the doors were closed; there was neither sound nor signage, and neither time nor place. The artist transformed one floor of the institution's raw industrial space into a disorienting and forbidding, uniformly gray streetscape meant to suggest the experience of walking through a silent city at night. This architectural environment recalled the image conjured up by a fictional villager in Muñoz's essay *Segment*, who described "la posa" as a dark and silent place, as well as the sense of absence that pervades the artist's "raincoat drawings." Upon entering the installation, viewers walked some distance and turned a corner, suddenly encountering a figure seated before a wood panel and a pair of figures huddled together on a bench. Rising up behind them was a staircase leading to a floor above, which ended abruptly at a blank wall. Further along on the main street, viewers entered a small room occupied by five figures (see *Five Seated Figures*; cat. no. 54). Two were engaged in animated conversation, two others looked on, and, at the back of the room, a fifth figure turned away to look into a large mirror hung at an angle to allow viewers to see the grouping from a second point of view. Returning to the street, viewers finally reached *Shadow and Mouth*, a room with two figures (fig. 19b). One was seated at a small bench close to a wall. Illuminated theatrically by a side light, the figure was

18a

18b

19a

19b

seen in precise silhouette. Only upon careful observation of the shadow was it possible to recognize that the figure's mouth was slowly, silently moving. Seated at a table several feet away, a second figure looked on; he, too, was seen in double in a shadow cast on the wall behind.

Although "A Place Called Abroad" was site-specific, Muñoz was invited to reinvent it for SITE Santa Fe in New Mexico in 1998. The new installation, "Streetwise," was similar, but in it the artist eliminated a number of elements and added several others. Among the additions was a pair of rooms in which Muñoz placed figures before wall-sized photographic backdrops of apartment-building façades and cobblestoned streets. Whereas in the New York installation Muñoz had focused exclusively on the experience of pedestrians, for Santa Fe he produced new works such as *Loaded Car* (1998; cat. no. 56). Just as his figures were intentionally smaller than human scale in order to separate them from life, Muñoz now made a small-scale sculpture of a car from sheet metal, turning it on its side as though it had been wrecked and abandoned. Close inspection through its windows reveals a Piranesian maze of miniature streets and curving stairways. One of the most powerful works in either installation, *Towards the Corner* (1998; cat. no. 57), was made for Santa Fe. This work consists of a set of bleachers that the viewer initially approaches from behind. On these bleachers six figures sit and one stands, and all laugh uproariously; as the viewer moves toward the corner they are facing in order to better understand the sculpture, he or she unwittingly becomes the subject of their mirth, the butt of their joke.

Muñoz has pursued this type of role reversal— with sculpture transformed into viewer, and viewer into object—in a more recent work, *Many Times* (2000; cat. no. 58). When first installed at the Louisiana Museum for Moderne Kunst in Denmark, this piece consisted of no fewer than one hundred figures, all with Asian facial features, all dressed in identical gray coats. In this work, however, Muñoz grouped the entire cast on a narrow catwalk overlooking the gallery. While some of the figures seemed to take note of the viewers looking up from below, others seemed oblivious to anything other than their own animated interaction. From his earliest works,

Muñoz has often required his viewers to look steeply upward to see balcony sculptures, a vantage point he had reversed in the *Square (Madrid)* installation, where he allowed the piece to be seen only from a mezzanine above. By creating a catwalk that surrounded a gallery on three sides and populating it with figures, Muñoz reversed the relationship and placed the visitor on stage, to the evident amusement of his sculptures. The dark humor of this piece resembles nothing so much as Francisco de Goya's celebrated frescoes in the Chapel of San Antonio de la Florida (1798) in Madrid, in which the vaulted ceiling is ringed with shadowy figures.

Muñoz's career during the 1990s is marked by his evolution as a sculptor in the commonly accepted sense of the word. His invention and ongoing elaboration of the "conversation pieces" and their variations characterizes this growth. Over time he both expanded the number and refined the expressive range and psychological complexity of these sculptures, eventually reversing the traditional roles of viewer and sculpture. Because of the recognition Muñoz was receiving as a sculptor, during the 1990s he was offered numerous opportunities to install work permanently outdoors. He has often issued harsh critiques of the manner in which modern sculptors and their advocates have willfully placed sculptures in prominent outdoor sites without regard for the character or implications of a particular site;[36] nonetheless, during the course of the decade, Muñoz made two permanently sited outdoor pieces that are particularly successful. *Two Figures for Middelheim* (1993; fig. 1) consists of a pair of bronze figures that he hung from a pair of trees in an open-air sculpture museum in Antwerp,

Belgium. Installed high upon opposite sides of a tree-lined path, the figures bend plaintively from the waist and recall images of martyred saints in Christian art. For *Last Conversation Piece* (1994–95; see Brenson, fig. 8), at the Hirshhorn Museum and Sculpture Garden in Washington, D.C., Muñoz created a composition of three central figures who struggle almost violently with one another while two additional figures look on with apparent concern a short distance away.

The title of the Hirshhorn piece is significant. *Last Conversation Piece* would indeed prove to be the final work in the series, and it signaled both the artist's weariness with the theme and his desire not to be locked into a single sculptural genre.[37] The artist has, at times, expressed a desire to reduce the role of the figure in his work and, eventually, to eliminate it altogether. In fact, the history of Muñoz's work of the 1990s is quite complex and extends well beyond the "conversation pieces," which have come to dominate the public perception of the artist. Muñoz had never abandoned his longstanding interest in critical writing and text- and sound-based work, as well as other alternative, even more ephemeral, media. Indeed, just at the time Muñoz's work was assuming figurative form, the artist was also making work in a variety of other forms that proposed a redefinition of the art object and its elimination altogether.

This alternative history might begin in the fall of 1991, when Muñoz and Iglesias, with their young daughter Lucia, rented an apartment and studio space in the Trastevere quarter in Rome, where they lived and worked for a year. Although Muñoz returned to Madrid often to continue working on the "conversation piece" sculptures that would be shown at the "Documenta" exhibition in Kassel, Germany, in the summer of 1992, most of his time in Rome was spent writing and conceiving text and sound pieces. One of the first pieces he completed while in Rome was "The Prohibited Image" (see p. 77), a text he had begun as early as 1987 and that was published in 1992. The starting point for this essay was Muñoz's fascination with a preface written by the noted art historian E. H. Gombrich in 1978 for the book *Legend, Myth, and Magic in the Image of the Artist*, first published by Ernst Kris and Otto Kurz

in 1934.[38] In his text Gombrich noted that Kurz had devoted his later years to the study of iconoclasm, although his work remained unpublished at his death in 1975. Muñoz had been intrigued by Kurz since the early 1980s, at which time he had made *Minaret for Otto Kurz* (1985; cat. no. 12), a fanciful miniature minaret mounted on spindly legs atop a Turkish carpet. At that time Muñoz had visited the archives of the Warburg and Courtauld Institute in London, where Kurz had worked for many years as director of the library. There he uncovered Kurz's papers, and, after an extensive search, located six files containing small notecards. Muñoz photocopied these cards, which bore

> hundreds of unconnected notes under
> the heading 'Prohibited.' Like topographical
> records, these notes must have allowed
> Kurz to trace out a detailed map of the prohi-
> bition of images in the history of representa-
> tion. Possibly, like the other texts by this
> meticulous Viennese art historian, this book
> that never existed could have consisted of a
> continuous, precise, and exact footnote.

As with *Segment*, Muñoz's text is convincing in its attention to obscure details. The difference in this case, of course, is that Muñoz was himself passionately interested in learning about the tradition of iconoclasm because he was torn in his own work between representation and a deep desire to make work in a more ephemeral form.

While in Rome, Muñoz made several audiotape pieces. The artist had worked consistently with sound from the time he lived in London, in the 1970s, and while in Rome he developed ideas that would be realized over the course of the next several years. For instance, he collaborated once again with Alberto Iglesias on *Building for Music* (1992), a sound piece devoted to the architectural and acoustic design of a fictional opera house that was broadcast on the radio in Arnhem, the Netherlands, during the exhibition "Sonsbeek 93."

Muñoz was particularly interested in card tricks at this time, having read S. W. Erdnase's seminal text

20a

20b

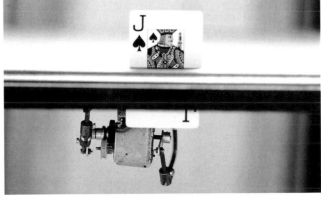

20c

The Expert at the Card Table. For the catalogue accompanying the 1991 Carnegie International exhibition, Muñoz wrote "A Drawing-Room Trick," an essay on card tricks that he adapted from Harry Houdini's "The Dancing Sailor," a text published in 1922 that Muñoz had found in the New York Public Library.[39] Later, Muñoz made *Table with Hold-Out* (1994; figs. 20a–c), a whimsical sculpture consisting of a table equipped with a mechanical device that made hidden playing cards appear.

While in Rome he also collaborated with the composer Gavin Bryars on a sound tape, *A Man in a Room, Gambling* (1992). For this piece Muñoz wrote and then narrated a series of ten texts describing card tricks, and Bryars composed the accompanying music and orchestrated a series of ambient sounds that were tape-recorded for the purpose. The work was broadcast by the BBC, in Great Britain as well as in Austria and Canada, and it was later issued as a compact disc.[40]

In these sound pieces, Muñoz pursued an art form that was episodic rather than objective, one that may be witnessed but also missed. His work with sound ultimately owes much to the groundbreaking work of John Cage, and, as Bryars himself noted concerning the broadcast of these pieces on radio,

> The use of such public broadcast facilities widens the impact of Juan Muñoz's work in fields that have hardly been investigated as legitimate media for visual expression. The impact of such broadcasts is, of course, minimal and constitutes little more than a gentle prod. But then this is the essential nature of work in an ambient framework.[41]

This anti-formal, text-based aspect of Muñoz's work found its way into the larger body of his work in additional ways. For instance, for the catalogue of an exhibition at the IVAM Centre del Carme in Valencia in 1992, Muñoz included a series of dialogues between two characters, each one limited to the length of one published page. While one was based on an excerpt from the Buzzati novel *The Tartar Steppe*, a favorite of the artist, most were transcriptions of mundane conversations tape-recorded in cafés or bars. There is a strongly absurdist tone to these fragmentary dialogues, one that is reminiscent of Beckett and Pirandello.[42]

One of the anonymous dialogues includes the following exchange:

> "What did you say?"
> "I didn't say anything."
> "You never say anything. No. But you keep coming back to it."

This fragment—so reminiscent of the dialogue of Beckett's plays—found its way into the first of several sculptures that Muñoz would make featuring miniature resin figures, *Stuttering Piece* (1993; cat. no. 48), in which two figures are seated on tiny resin boxes and this brief, tape-recorded dialogue is played monotonously into the surrounding space. The following year he made *Living in a Shoe Box (For Konrad Fischer)* (1994; cat. no. 49), in which a pair of miniature figures sits inside a shoe box that moves back and forth on a set of model train tracks mounted high on a wall. The existential absurdity of this sculpture again recalls Beckett, especially one of the playwright's most celebrated stage images from *Endgame* (1958), in which the characters Nell and Nagg spend the entire play in dustbins.

On occasion, Muñoz has pressed the idea of the absurd even further in his work. For an exhibition at the Stedelijk van Abbemuseum in Eindhoven in 1991, Muñoz made *Waiting for Jerry* (1991; fig. 21). In a darkened, empty room, a simple mouse hole was cut from the foot of a wall. Light was visible through the hole and the theme music to the animated children's series *Tom and Jerry* was audible. In this work, in which an unseen cat waits to pounce on a mouse that may or may not exist, we see a darker side of the artist's humor.

This same dark humor found its equivalent in another, very different project, undertaken eight years later. In 1999, the artist constructed a series of small cardboard architectural maquettes. Loosely related to his project for Dia, these maquettes were composed of streets and the façades of buildings complete with windows and balconies. After assembling these maquettes into a vast cityscape, Muñoz invited the Italian photographer Attilio Maranzano to photograph them as Muñoz set them on fire. Muñoz lives to the northwest of Madrid, and on clear days one can readily see the skyline of the city from his patio; this partially explains the title of the resulting photo essay, *The Burning of Madrid as Seen from the Terrace of My House* (1999; see pp. 1–12).[43]

On one level, a history of Juan Muñoz could be written that would chronicle his development as a sculptor. Beginning in the late 1970s, this is the story of an artist who schooled himself in the progressive movements of the time, Minimalism, Arte Povera, post-Minimalism, and Conceptualism, and began to produce work that was infused with the evidence of his own activity. Soon he came to make objects, and by the mid to late 1980s, his sculptural objects—balconies, banisters, and patterned floors—assumed greater authority, both formally and psychologically. In the late 1980s, Muñoz turned increasingly to the figure, and, with his invention of the "conversation piece" sculptures around 1990, emerged as a figurative sculptor, making highly theatrical installations of multi-figure compositions that are entirely original and compelling in their psychological content.

Throughout the modern period, artists have placed a high value on achieving a signature style, a combination of form and content identifiable as the artist's own. Yet Muñoz, like many of his contemporaries, is uncomfortable with this aspect of modernism, and he has neither an interest in, nor patience with, this form of achievement. Muñoz is the most restless of artists, and he distrusts the seductions of a comfortable late modernism in which an artist sows certain creative seeds and then spends the rest of his career methodically harvesting the same crop year after year.

So while Muñoz has achieved a position of great respect as one of the most inventive figurative sculptors of his time, he has done much to expand upon and, in a sense, to undermine the status that he has earned for himself. A fully three-dimensional history must include his work as a curator, critic, and essayist, and in his writings, the titles of his sculptures, and the references he makes to art history, literature, music, and the theater,

FIG. 21   *Waiting for Jerry*, 1991

21

he has consistently focused on topics that are riddled with paradox. Whether examining the Aztec masterpiece Coatlique, Jacob Epstein's *Rock Drill*, the quasifictional "la posa," the writings of T. S. Eliot and Jose Luis Borges, or iconoclasm, card tricks, and children's cartoons, Muñoz has concentrated on objects or forms of cultural experience that derive their power and meaning from absence, memory, and paradox. In his own work as an artist, Muñoz's continual struggle is to create experiences that awaken similar impulses in himself and his viewer. While Muñoz's work often assumes figurative form, the artist is equally committed to a creative life in which sculpture is but one choice among a great many, in which the nature of the experience is its meaning and not the form.

NOTES

The texts by Juan Muñoz that have been quoted from in this essay are reprinted elsewhere in this catalogue (see pp. 55–81); therefore I have not provided bibliographical citations below. For a complete list of the artist's writings, see pp. 194–95. For their suggestions and assistance in preparing this essay, I am greatly indebted to Olga M. Viso; Stephanie D'Alessandro, Assistant Curator, and Mette Schepers, former research intern, both in the Department of Modern and Contemporary Art at The Art Institute of Chicago; and Tania Owcharenko Duvergne, former research intern at the Hirshhorn Museum and Sculpture Garden.

1. The Paz essay, "The Art of Mexico: Material and Meaning," was published in the author's *Essays on Mexican Art* (New York, San Diego, and London: Harcourt Brace, 1987): 29–43. I am most grateful to my Art Institute colleague Richard Townsend for his suggestions regarding Coatlique. See also Justino Fernández, *Coatlicue: Estética del arte indígena antiguo* (Mexico City: Centro de Estudios Filosoficos, 1954).

2. Much of the previously unpublished biographical information—as well as the non-footnoted quotations—contained in this essay are the product of my many conversations with Juan Muñoz during the past several years. I am enormously grateful to the artist for his great generosity in sharing this information, as well as his archives, with me.

3. Santiago Amón, who tutored Muñoz privately in addition to teaching him Latin in school, was the author of numerous essays, books, and catalogues on contemporary Spanish art, modern architecture, and design. He also published widely on philosophers such as Henri Bergson and Martin Heidegger and the writers Marcel Proust and Franz Kafka, and he produced two volumes of poetry, *Tiempo de infancia* and *Alba que bala* (1968). His art and cultural criticism was published regularly in the Spanish newspaper *El País* and in the journals *ABC*, *Diario 16*, *Nueva Forma*, *Revista de occidente*, and *La vanguardia*. He was also the author of *Picasso* (1973) and *Marca-Relli* (1978). See Madrid, Centro Cultural de la Villa, *Nueva Forma: Arquitectura, arte y cultura 1966–1975*, exh. cat. (1996).

4. See James Lingwood, "Monologues and Dialogues," in Madrid, Museo Nacional Centro de Arte Reina Sofia, *Juan Muñoz: Monólogos y diálogos/Monologues and Dialogues*, exh. cat. by James Lingwood (1996): 16–17.

5. Included among the artist's papers are extended citations from: Barnett Newman, "Interview with David Sylvester," in *Barnett Newman: Selected Writings and Interviews* (New York: Alfred A. Knopf, 1990; broadcast by the BBC, 17 November 1965; first published in *The Listener*, 10 August 1972); Michael Fried, "Art and Objecthood," *Artforum* 5 (June 1967); Robert Morris, "Notes on Sculpture, Part 3," *Artforum* 5 (June 1967); and Robert Smithson, "Fragments of an Interview with P. A. Norvell," in Lucy R. Lippard, ed., *Six Years: The Dematerialization of the Art Object from 1966–1972* (London: Studio Vista, 1973).

6. The text of this unpublished interview is included among the artist's papers.

7. Although the title *If This Be Treason* has been employed by a great many authors and playwrights, Muñoz has confirmed that it was Pound's 1948 publication on E. E. Cummings and James Joyce that he had in mind when making the sculpture.

8. The phrase "spiral staircase" *("escalera de caracol")* appears in an extended citation included among the artist's papers from "Seis problemas para don Isidro Parodi," in J. L. Borges and A. Bioy Casares, *Cuentos de H. Bustos Domecqu* (Barcelona: Editorial Seix Barral, 1985): 7–118.

9. Quoted in Juan Muñoz, "Fragments from a Conversation," interview by Jan Debbaut, in Madrid, Galería Fernando Vijande, *Juan Muñoz: Últimos trabajos* (Madrid: F. Vijande, 1984): n. pag.

10. For Miaja, see Anthony Beevor, *The Spanish Civil War* (New York: Peter Bedrick Books, 1982): 129–40, and Burnett Bolloten, *The Spanish Revolution: The Left and the Struggle for Power during the Civil War* (Chapel Hill: The University of North Carolina Press, 1979): 259–301.

11. Dino Buzzati, *The Tartar Steppe* (Boston: David R. Godine Publishers, 1995).

12. Francisco Calvo Serraller, "La tercera mirada del misterio," *El País* (Madrid), 17 November 1984, Art section.

13. See Dan Cameron, "Spain is Different," *Arts Magazine* 61, no. 1 (September 1986): 14–17; Jutta Koether and Diedrich Diederischsen, "Jutta and Diedrich Go to Spain: Spanish Art and Culture Viewed from Madrid," *Artscribe*, no. 59 (September–October 1986): 56–61; and Liliana Albertazzi, "Espagne aujourd'hui," *Galeries Magazine*, no. 17 (February–March 1987): 50, 57, 116–17.

14. Quoted in an interview with Iwona Blazwick, James Lingwood, and Andrea Schlieker, in London, Institute of Contemporary Arts and Serpentine Gallery, *Possible Worlds: Sculpture from Europe*, exh. cat. by Iwona Blazwick, James Lingwood, and Andrea Schlieker (1990–91): 58.

15. Quoted in "A Conversation between Juan Muñoz and Jean-Marc Poinsot," in Bordeaux, Capc Musée d'Art Contemporain, *Juan Muñoz: Sculptures de 1985 à 1987*, exh. cat. by Jean-Marc Poinsot (1987): 44.

16. Ibid.

17. Quoted in Jan Braet, "Fluiten in het donker," *Knack*, no. 48 (December 1991): 111; translation by Eric McMillan. In the Bordeaux catalogue (*Juan Muñoz: Sculptures de 1985 à 1987*; note 15),

Muñoz included a reproduction of the Degas painting. The artist discussed the painting in some detail on page 44, where he mentioned making regular visits to see the painting when he was in Lisbon and his fascination with it.

18. Quoted in "A Conversation between Juan Muñoz and Jean-Marc Poinsot" (note 15): 43.

19. Quoted in Juan Muñoz, "A Conversation, New York, 22 January 1995," interview by James Lingwood, *Parkett*, no. 43 (January 1995): 44.

20. Ibid.: 45.

21. From "Cuvilliés, (Jean) François (Vincent Joseph) de, I," in *The Grove Dictionary of Art Online* (www.groveart.com, Nov. 2000).

22. Quoted in *Possible Worlds* (note 14): 59. Included among the artist's papers is an extended text that Muñoz had translated and that is devoted to the history of the prompter's box. The source is *Les Annales Dramatiques: Dictionnaire Général de Théâtre* (Paris, 1911), which includes a reproduction of the Daumier print.

23. Muñoz's statement is actually a reinterpretation of a statement Borges made in response to an interviewer's question: "But why is time ungraspable?"—to which the Argentine writer responded, "Undoubtedly, because time is made up of memory. We are each, to a great extent, made up of poor and frail memory. And that memory is made up largely of forgetfulness." Quoted in *Twenty-Four Conversations with Borges* (Housatonic, Mass.: Lascaux Publishers, 1984): 62.

24. Quoted in "A Conversation between Juan Muñoz and Jean-Marc Poinsot" (note 15): 43.

25. Quoted in *Possible Worlds* (note 14): 61.

26. Degas' work continues to intrigue and inspire the artist. For example, Muñoz's recent sculpture *A Hanging Figure* (1997; cat. no. 55) is based on the French artist's *Miss La La at the Cirque Fernando* (1879), a painting Muñoz knows well from the National Gallery, London.

27. For a complete history of Epstein's *Rock Drill*, see Richard Cork's essay in *Jacob Epstein: Sculpture and Drawings* (Leeds City Art Galleries, 1987): 160–71.

28. The 1974 exhibition in which the reconstruction was included was "Vorticism and Its Allies"; see London, Arts Council of Great Britain, *Vorticism and Its Allies*, exh. cat. (1974): cat. no. 244.

29. See Teresa Gisbert and Jose de Mesa, *Arquitectura Andina: 1530–1830* (La Paz: Coleccion Arsanz y Vela, 1985), in particular the chapter titled "Arquitectura Efímera Fiesta y Alegoría" (pp. 209–30), which is devoted to ephemeral festival architecture. Included in this chapter are two photographs illustrating a religious procession in Zurite passing by the same structure illustrated by Muñoz. In one the structure is set alight by fireworks.

30. See Mario Praz, *Conversation Pieces* (University Park and London: The Pennsylvania State University Press, 1971): 33–37.

31. Quoted in Juan Muñoz, "A Conversation, September 1996," interview by James Lingwood, in Madrid, Museo Nacional Centro de Arte Reina Sofia, *Juan Muñoz: Monólogos y diálogos/Monologues and Dialogues*, exh. cat. by James Lingwood (1996): 157.

32. Ibid.: 159.

33. The first quotation is included in *Possible Worlds* (note 14): 59; the second is from Muñoz, "A Conversation, September 1996" (note 31): 159.

34. Quoted in *Possible Worlds* (note 14): 61.

35. The content of this installation is reminiscent of a Borges story, "Averroes' Search" (1949), about a medieval Arab scholar living in Cordoba. In one passage, Averroes stands on his balcony and observes three children playing in a courtyard below; one rides on the shoulders of another, while a third plays in the dirt. Averroes recognizes that, in effect, the three are acting out the roles of muezzin, minaret, and Muslim worshipper. "Averroes' Search" is included in Borges' *Labyrinths: Selected Stories and Other Writings* (New York: New Directions, 1964), 148–55.

36. Among a number of statements that Muñoz has made concerning contemporary public sculpture is the following: "The great unfinished assignment for artists of the twentieth century is public sculpture. In this sense, sculptors have thoroughly failed. We have not known, with the possible exception of Serra and a few others, how to integrate our work into public spaces, how to find the symbolic value that the general had on his horse. Public sculpture has turned into an exercise in opportunism in which politicians and street artists participate." Quoted in an interview by Rafael Sierra, *El Mundo* (Madrid), 9 November 1996: 14; translation by Adriana Rosado & Bonewitz, Inc.

37. As evidence of this, when the piece was patinated in advance of its installation at the Hirshhorn, the artist insisted that it be done in a nontraditional blue-gray color, rather than the more customary dark brown, and that the figures not be waxed to a glossy finish. The Hirshhorn's sculpture garden is replete with examples of bronze sculptures—by Aristide Maillol, Henry Moore, and Auguste Rodin—that are patinated dark brown, and the artist wished to have his work be understood as separate from traditional public bronze sculpture.

38. See E. H. Gombrich, "Preface," *Legend, Myth, and Magic in the Image of the Artist* (New Haven and London: Yale University Press, 1979): ix–xiv.

39. In "A Drawing-Room Trick," Muñoz noted that the text was "adapted by the artist from a book found in the Lincoln Center Public Library, New York, call number MZC-75.623." That book is Harry Houdini, *Houdini's Paper Magic* (New York: E. P. Dutton, 1922); "The Dancing Sailor" appears on pp. 33–36.

40. Gavin Bryars, *A Man in a Room, Gambling* (Audio CD; Point Music 456 514-2, 1997).

41. Gavin Bryars, "A Man in a Room, Gambling," *Parkett*, no. 43 (March 1995): 55.

42. Muñoz is keenly interested in Pirandello's work. As a preface to the Valencia catalogue, Muñoz transcribed a segment of dialogue from the Italian's celebrated play *Six Characters in Search of an Author* (1921). In 1994, Muñoz's essay "The Face of Pirandello" was published; it is reprinted in this catalogue on pp. 78–79.

43. This project was first published in *Janus 3* (March 1999): 22–27. It is worth recalling that in *Segment*, the villagers burned "la posa" to the ground as well.

53

Juan Muñoz

Selected Texts

Notes on Three

First published as "Notas afines a tres," in Madrid, Ministerio de Obras Públicas y Urbanismo, Correspondencias: 5 arquitectos, 5 escultores, exh. cat. by Carmen Giménez and Juan Muñoz (1982).

Page 54: Juan Muñoz's studio, Madrid, 1999

IN THE BEGINNING was the menhir. Allow us the scientific fiction to assert that thermodynamics begins after the menhir materializes. To be precise, its second law, the one about entropy: the progressive erosion and disordering of matter and mind, or in its vernacular translation we call oblivion. The menhir, a unique volume erected in space, neither covers nor shelters. Nothing supports it; it supports nothing. A sculptural element above all others. Perceiving it is like perceiving a moment in time. Whatever practical purpose it may have had, if it ever had one, has been forgotten.

Face-to-face with spatial infinity, primitive man raises up a stone (for us, a sculpture). Next to it, he raises another (still a sculpture), and on top of the two he sets a third, in this way inaugurating formal disorder. Roof, arch, or burial site, the dolmen, because of oblivion and the passing of time, became a symbol of its own architectonic mystery.

It is possible to imagine the great Chilean painter Roberto Matta taking his son for a walk through the streets of Paris, where he lived for a time. It is equally possible or fictitious to imagine that during one of those walks the boy would take a special interest in the complexity of the flying buttresses and arches at the church of Sacré-Coeur. Allow us to imagine, in the permissible exaggeration of fiction, the moment when he, now inside, observed, with special devotion, the rose window, which, in the manner of an epicenter, simultaneously unites and divides the church's interior light. Years later, Gordon Matta-Clark, former architecture student, conceived sculpture as the act of cutting a series of circles into the guts of several abandoned buildings, right through the walls and floors. This action, which allowed light to pass from one side to another and also from the fifth floor to the basement through these ellipses and circles incised into the structure, might well be taken as a warning to those who imagined a possible dialogue between the practitioners of both professions.

Sculptors have repeatedly suggested setting aside the nominal reason why the Guggenheim Museum was built in order to present it in terms of its vacuity. Frank Lloyd Wright himself clearly hinted at this notion because of his obvious disdain for the objects that were to occupy it. This central work of modern architecture is actually a grand sculpture that renders non-viable any work that occupies it. In Wright's hands, a museum for modern art became a self-referential sign that pointed to its modernity and its art at the cost of suppressing its character as a museum.

The centrifugal movement of its interior seeks to absorb the art shown there and succeeds in imposing itself on it. At the Eduardo Chillida retrospective, his works, even those that share the building's spiral form, had to assert more than ever before their centripetal and interior space. Faced with the same challenge, Joseph Beuys directed that the light levels and the temperature of the building be lowered.

Any museum is designed to house paintings on its walls and, between its walls, sculptures. Of all extant museums, one alone seems to have been built with the respect its immobile inhabitants demanded. Even so, when Richard Serra erected his seventy-ton sculpture a few meters away from the Berlin Nationalgalerie designed by Mies van der Rohe, his attitude was clear. For his work to be constructed, the structure of the building had to be reinforced, which he allowed to be surmised as more a result of Mies's shortsightedness than a conditioning factor about the potential of the sculpture. Of course it is also true that Mies, a major influence on Minimalism, always favored anthropomorphic or decorative sculptures in the mode of Henry Moore in order to emphasize the abstract clarity of his structures.

When Piano and Rogers canceled the installation of a huge steel curve, another work by Serra, in the area adjacent to the Centre Georges Pompidou, arguing that people would not be able to pass through to the nearby subway entrance, the sculptor jokingly responded that perhaps what the architects really meant was that in order to enter the subway, people would have to walk around the sculpture.

On the other hand, when Serra refused to place two huge pieces in the Western Plaza (Washington, D.C.) because he believed that his language was being manipulated and presented as columns, the architect Robert Venturi declared that he could use the language of any artist or even that of the devil himself any way he chose.

Over the course of the history of modern art, whenever we find a possible rapprochement between architecture and sculpture, there spontaneously arises a great difficulty in uniting both visions of space. Let us say that what is understood as space is the multiplicity of up and down, inside and outside, full and empty, shadow and light, right and left, opacity and transparency, along with difficulty and surprise. (Perhaps the difficulty does not arise out of the space itself, the weight, volume, or even the surprise.) Ultimately, the conflict between both activities lies in the necessary social utility of architecture and the absolute uselessness of sculpture. Nevertheless, let us say once more that among all the arts, these two begin and end in their concern with space. Inhabited space, uninhabited, or to-be-inhabited space; even space as a metaphor.

But between space and the attitude with which architects and sculptors contemplate it, there stands a third element: the observer. To say that architecture belongs to daytime space and sculpture to nocturnal space would be once again to exclude the observer. It is better to restore his role to him and declare that any form in space is understood in relation to the dimensions of the human body. Every object around which and within which we move is perceived beginning with the size of our own organism and its limits. Interior and exterior limits, like arches, in the face of which the only thing we can do is circumvent or cross them.

I have chosen two museums as a meeting place to explain certain divergencies. Let the intentions of two creators in both disciplines illustrate the necessary collaboration of the viewer: on one hand, Peter Eisenman's House XI, where he created a glass room, visible but inaccessible, a metaphor about shared habitation, a plastic theorem placed in the radial epicenter of the house. On the other, a work by Joel Shapiro, the house in the center of the rectangle, tiny, well established in its setting but at the same time fearful of slipping off one of the corners. Everything a house symbolizes is there.

Vasari writes that one day Francesco Parmigianino decided to paint his own reflection in a convex mirror, so he ordered a carpenter to make him a wooden sphere the same size as the mirror. When it was finished, he cut it in half in order to paint on it. If, helped by Alice's pill, an imaginary traveler could enter Shapiro's house and find there Eisenman's closed room, he would certainly see through the glass Parmigianino's wooden sphere before it was cut.

It is true that even today glances are exchanged, but discerning the continuous divergence between architecture and sculpture presupposes understanding that both the active spectator and the traveler, like the two groups of creators, share a concept of space common to all three.

"We know not the meaning of dragons, just as we know not the meaning of the Universe, but there is something in their image that harmonizes with the imagination of mankind. . . ."

— Jorge Luis Borges

The First/The Last

First published as "Los primeros/Los últimos," in Madrid, Palacio de las Alhajas, Caja de Ahorros y Monte de Piedad, La imagen del animal: Arte prehistórico, arte contemporáneo, exh. cat. by Juan Muñoz (Madrid: Ministerio de Cultura with the collaboration of The British Council, 1983).

SIGFRIED GIEDION, the great historian to whom this show is a modest homage, used to say that all life in its continuous movement struggles between constancy and change.

Let the image of the animal (the subject of artistic expression in prehistory and now) serve as the constant in an equation where the human capacity for renewal and creativity is a variable that shows us its will to change.

We can study the stylistic changes in modern art without referring to animals, but primeval art can only be comprehended if we follow the successive changes in zoomorphic representation over the millennia.

I believe that the simultaneous presentation of a prehistoric artistic image and another almost devoid of history should provoke an atemporal appreciation of both creative works.

Knowing when the best cave paintings were produced neither adds to nor diminishes the sense of mystery that these works produce in the viewer. It might be said that those images do possess a meaning. Even so, we have no access to it, and even if we did, that meaning would never exhaust their mystery.

The first question that the contemplation of paleolithic art raises is the following: What is its intention? Again and again, the animal depicted rebels against our rationality and demands a third gaze which situates us at the focal point of mystery.

The observation of cave paintings suggests that what we call the subject of the work (the image of the animal) was for Paleolithic man a tower from which to observe reality. In prehistoric art, the animal is the summary of all aspirations. It is a conjuring device used to bring reality closer to desire. Magdalenian man lives inextricably bound to animals as a source of rites and food. Self-observation is realized by means of the "other" that walks, hunts, makes a home for itself, and procreates. Fertility and death are explained on the walls of Altamira and Ekain with greater intensity than in any other historical era. Because never since then has the representer needed the represented to such a great degree.

What does the experience of Paleolithic art forms mean for the twentieth-century artist or observer? Would it be possible to appreciate them to the same degree without the visual "deposit" Picasso and Merz have bequeathed us? Without people like Sigfried Giedion or Abbot Brevil, contemporaries of those artists, who extracted from the polychrome work of Altamira and the simple outlines of Pech-Merle the extraordinary aesthetic value they always had.

What importance would a cultured man of the sixteenth century have conceded to cave painting, when during his time all aesthetic consideration depended on the degree of likeness with what was represented?

Each change in the social structure implies a transformation in the way we perceive reality. This new perception stimulates changes in the artistic forms of society.

When, in Hellenic culture, man defines himself as the center of rationality, the other/the animal, in its various representations, is relegated to an auxiliary role. Only when its body is added to or removed from the human one, thus symbolizing a deity, can it ascend to the altar.

Over the course of the Middle Ages, man dreamed away his fears and desires through zoomorphic images which have only sporadically reappeared in the past century. For instance, the animal as totemic element in Brancusi and the module that explains Theo Van Doesburg's neoplasticism. That is, until this image is taken up by Picasso's lucidity with a profundity of meaning only comparable to that of the Magdalenian era.

The artist of the Quarternary and the contemporary artist share a single vision. For both, the act of tracing the silhouette of an animal is also the act of constructing a vision of the world in forms. This silhouette/painting relates to the real world, refers to it, and is part of it. What distinguishes the prehistoric creator from the one of today resides in the consciousness of the latter that this act also refers to itself and is art alone.

We must remember that this idea of art, which began in the Renaissance and attained its modern meaning in Mannerism, would have been totally incomprehensible to primitive man. Even so, our contemporary understanding of cave painting is linked to the notion of art as an aesthetic object.

Of all existing theories, in my opinion, it is Panofsky's that comes closest, with the greatest clarity, to a possible definition that would be useful to understand one of the propositions of this exhibit. Panofsky makes the possible importance art has for a given society depend on its capacity as a symbolic language. And its capacity to link the spiritual and intellectual beliefs of that society.

For prehistoric man, this symbolic function (incomprehensible to us at this time) possibly bears with it a degree of utility for which reason it was created.

A painting establishes a relationship with the viewer, society, its culture and beliefs by means of a determined environment. Cave painting functioned as an intermediary between all antecedent elements.

The modern artist, aware of the partial uselessness of art and immersed in the creation of the so-called art object, cannot participate in any of the coordinates that motivated drawing on stone.

The break established in the twentieth century with regard to the secular tradition of realism in art comes about through the representation of space. Cézanne renounces the illusory space characteristic of painting that precedes him and presents the plane of the canvas as the primary reality.

I believe that the principal source of artistic interest in this exhibition derives from the problematic of space.

Among scientists and philosophers, space is generally thought to be continuous and homogeneous.

The task of sculpture appears to be the healthy intention of proving the contrary.

Every fortunate visitor to one of the caverns holding cave art is surprised at the places chosen for the paintings. Frequently we pass under a huge vault with none. But just beyond, on a tilted wall or in a corner barely a meter high (where in order to paint it was necessary to lie face up), zoomorphic images appear. An animal drawn in vertical position appears next to another upside down, or at an angle, centimeters away from a third that may be half the size and face in the opposite direction from the first. The multiplicity of directions, in some cases images superimposed on others, does not create an impression of contradictory rhythms in the observer. The opposites complement one another in the unique context of the cave. The transparency of each animal represented allows the animals near one another to appear in a space alien to the norms of perpendicularity.

The observer might compare this spatial concept with that of the present in the most recent tendencies in art. For the prehistoric creator, the wall of the cave was an infinite space. For the contemporary artist, the rectangle signifies an infinite space. The spatial depth of the wrinkled wall exists for the cave painter without the vanishing point that provokes illusion. With no other reference than the wall, these images belong to a single, indissoluble unity. The modern artist is reluctant to accept the illusionism of perspective. In inventing a new image, the artist, instead of comparing it with what is real, adds it to the world of the possible. Cave painting has no depth. For contemporary painting—in general—the depth is a plane surface. Even when it is painted with a field of colors, it essentially lacks, in the same way, any depth.

These correspondences allow today's painters to feel formally closer to cave art than they do to their immediate past. In the new tendencies, the image of the animal seems to want to leave the canvas. The brushstroke is violent. Graphic expression and the flow of lines treat

the extremes of the canvas more like an undetermined approach than as an example of rigor. The images share with the Aurignacian silhouettes of deer this pendular equilibrium in continuous movement.

Some of the artists in this exhibition are here because of their unquestionable quality. This includes Mario Merz, the cornerstone. Others are here as examples of the "new modernity." Like Paleolithic man, they share the belief that the representation alludes to something beyond itself. For the primeval creator and the contemporary artist, the work (of art) is allegorical. What this allegory means is different in each case. Nevertheless, the best objects among those assembled here show that the true creator or believer is a medium between reality and sign.

It remains for the viewer to make the parallel analysis of past and present. And this includes the presence of the past in the present.

Borromini-Kounellis: On the Luminous Opacity of Signs

First published as "De la luminosa opacidad de los signos: Borromini-Kounellis," Figura, no. 6 (fall 1985): 94–95.

THE VALIANT POET Valente left a treatise, written in unintelligible characters, on the mathematics of color. Its title was "On the Obstinate Possibility of Light."

March 1663

It is Sunday in the church of Saint Agnese in the Piazza Navona. Immense in their intensity, the footfalls of an Italian peasant entering on a sunny morning. It is possible to imagine him crossing the portico, passing through the nave, under the barrel vaults, making his way to the altar. There, facing him: magnificence. Volutes, decoration everywhere. All ornamentation because that is what Baroque theatricality demands.

Nevertheless, something in this river of effects contradicts its original reason for being. Attention is not led toward spiritual absorption, veneration, or the sacred. Instead, it seems the spectacle was a metaphor for itself. Every vault and promontory is its own architectonic contradiction. The bronze, stucco, and glass follow one another like parts that do not manage to make a whole. The left rises over the upper section and before it reaches bottom, the right collides with the corner. Everything seems in perpetual motion.

Borromini's church owes its being in the world to existing in the very space its theatricality invents. In truth, the columns here neither hold anything in place nor support anything. In its highest reaches, it resolves itself in decoration, and in that way it recreates itself.

The gaze that passes from effect to effect without continuity finds no place to catch its breath. Borromini's church, like Schwitters' *Merzbau*, demonstrates that it could have continued to grow. Immobile in a constantly fluctuating world, the Baroque building is, for the eye, a place (like the earth itself, the only reason for being for the never-represented God) in *perpetuum mobile*.

A modern simile, if there were one, could well be like walking hurriedly along an airport conveyor belt.

In Baroque scenography, in order for the epiphany to appear illuminated, the spectator must be in darkness. This is why Borromini locates the church's focal point in the skylight. And, let us add: What sort of circle would a compass in motion trace? Would it not be a spiral staircase, tilted walls, concave forms, convex cornices, elevated elements? The flow of light falls on the overhangs, then transforms into a mask, doubly luminous in the recesses. Which leads us to assert that the epiphany, the concept represented here, is light itself.

Borromini must have known that there was no face beneath the mask. Baroque stagecraft, promoted by the Council of Trent, fascinating machinery that dazzled the faithful, was conceived by its creator in the image and likeness of mystery. Period.

The center of any Borromini church, the lantern, is always elliptical. It has two centers. The beam of light that descends from it resembles a slow, helicoidal, ascending movement. And vice versa. Two in one. The spiral staircase seems to rise at the same time it drops and twists its geometric zero.

There is no indoctrination in Borromini, no Holy Church. For which reason, beyond the luminous effect, there is not even a God. Everything is epiphany, representation of the whole by means of the whole itself, by means of the mystery of light in space, by means of the mystery of light, of space.

All those volutes, those broken lines, those columns that barely support anything, awaiting the clarity that comes from the cupola, recall the poem by the great José Lezama Lima: "like clouds galloping, but later the lightning bolt of grace does its work." What lightning bolt is that which, emanating from the ellipse, works on form and makes it plausible? Perhaps it is the same one that transforms the concave into the accomplice of the convex, that makes shadow coincide with volume.

We feel something similar standing before one of Jannis Kounellis's objects.

Let us just say it once and for all: the lucid Greek's sculpture, beyond its apparent epiphany of mystery, is in itself strangeness.

If the truly surprising (the operative

grace) is being and, therefore, being-in-space, let us add that the place transforms into the child and the enclave of the incomprehensible.

In the work of both creators, the emphasis is on making it possible for something to take place, and that something is the act that engenders light.

In 1971, Jannis Kounellis builds a truly complex image. The image of something that is moved toward without being arrived at. Sculpture or metaphor for a landscape of tributary streams without a river into which to empty, it is composed of several butane tanks with their rubber hoses and their blowtorch nozzles from which pour flames. The locus, the room, has been occupied by light. The light moves toward an escape point, but where is it? Exactly like the cornices in Sant'Andrea delle Frate, the lines take a direction, but which? Space has curled up on itself. Here there is no center, but nevertheless the drawing on the floor seems to correspond to another order. It is possible to guess that Kounellis, just as obsessively as Borromini, has chosen the geometric form of the ellipse. Two centers and none. Our attention moves from one to the other. The eye moves, but it is now de-centered.

Both residents of Rome, bearing the tools of their trade, stand before space, conscious of not being able to transgress it and, at the same time, astonished. Furthermore, they are amazed by the qualities Martin Heidegger has glossed. Because "before it, there is no reference point, and after it there is no signal to guide us to something else." It makes sense to continue Heidegger's comparison in order to explain that both the twist in Borromini and the deepening of the myth in Kounellis take place in spaces "where a god is going to appear or from which the gods have just fled or where the manifestation of the divine takes too long in coming." But what might those "tools of the trade" be with which these two work and manage to invest space with otherness? For the Italian architect, the building is a piece of stage machinery he uses to achieve the global effect of chiaroscuro that again and again indicates the strangeness of illuminated space. Should we not add to this capricious discourse on uncertain relationships, how symmetrical it is that Kounellis emphasizes the conflict in the everyday use of an object between the light it emits and the shadow that allows it to exist?

That bluish butane light, in no way alien to chiaroscuro: Does it not place the spectator in the shadow? A subtle paradox perpetrated by the cunning Greek, who seeks that which belongs only to the spectator's gaze upon the object itself. The immobile presented to the eye as something centrifugal. There are arguments that would justify the genealogical proximity with more authority. Arguments that are certainly more shallow, like the recurrent theatricality both employ, but instead suggest, properly, that language is capricious, that nothing or almost nothing can elude the arrival of night except its clarity.

Epilogue

Let us publicly allow a certain distance with the opportune pictorial concern of the great Greek creator, at the same time that we recall the obsessive tilted wall of Borromini's creation.

61

A Man up a Lamppost (Between British Sculpture and Sculpture Itself)

First published as "Un hombre subido a una farola (Entre la escultura britànica y la escultura a solas)" in Madrid, Palacio de Velázquez, Entre el objeto y la imagen: Escultura britànica contemporánea, exh. cat. (Madrid and London: Ministerio de Cultura, Dirección General de Bellas Artes y Archivos and The British Council, 1986).

JUST BARELY AN INFLECTION, and yet beautiful. Just that. A light, beautiful inflection. Because when all is said, the plot, all plots, are the same. Except that each age tells them with that light. . . .

Such is the suspicion about which Jorge Luis Borges writes. No doubt about it, a composer of tangos would suspect that the Tate Gallery's ambiguous reputation (dividing a work by Jacob Epstein and thereby making two sculptures out of one) bears a certain resemblance to the well-known miracle of the loaves and fishes.[1]

Let us look into this daring tale and unite the sundered pieces in order to glimpse (like light) the concerns of British sculpture.

For years, it was necessary to make one's way past rooms full of allegorical images of ladies and horses and down a flight of stairs to reach a corridor that was neither wide nor narrow nor particularly well-lit. Once there, surrounded by paintings by Turner's disciples, or by friends of Vorticism or others of uncertain pedigree, one would find the sculpture of a man's trunk. Half human, half image of the future. In that peculiar limbo, the piece seemed to have found its own true *locus*. Between "history" and "oblivion." (It is worthwhile to remember, as Borges is so fond of doing, that oblivion is a form, perhaps the highest form, of memory.) Just halfway between the galleries on the floor above and the storage space in the basement.

The Upper Half, or the Carburetor
Through the years, with the trunk cut off above the pelvis and the forearms sliced off in the classical manner, it came to resemble a traditional modern sculpture. Even so, those same forms—the shoulders, the back, the neck—seemed to have been made from spare parts of an automobile. The thorax itself recalled the carburetor of a motorcycle. The fascination with machines, a hallmark of early twentieth-century modernism, is found in this piece by Epstein, one of its most ardent advocates. All of it, and even man himself, could be made up from anything already in existence and thus could exchange identities.

What Epstein added to the first of his two sculptures was no mere reconsideration of materials. This work, intended to be cast in bronze, bears a radical metaphor: man conceives of man in his own image and likeness. Let us propose a simile that is rather domestic but useful. The little car that Picasso transformed into an ape (*Baboon and Young*, 1951) is, in Epstein's hands, dismantled and reconstructed as a face. Two almost diametrically opposed trajectories. For Picasso, everything is likeness. For Epstein, car and man are as one and interchangeable.

The Lower Half, or the Concrete
To consider the lower half is to look at a kind of technological insect. It raises man from the ground and without pretense puts him back there again. Ironically, or perhaps metaphorically, the drill rises in the air in order to reach greater depths.

Epstein's work existed as a mere trunk until 1974. In the learned Hayward exhibition held that year, it was reconstructed and restored to its original state.[2] First of all, let's admit it, it was a great aesthetic surprise. A machine with three legs, the support, is a kind of minaret from which to look into the distance (distances). Its form has an internal grammatical logic that is as exact as its technical requirements demanded. The English sculptor, like several of his compatriots years afterward, turned his admiration to the readymade object, constructed without sculptural intention. What separates Epstein from the most recent generation is his march from the object backward. From the ship to its wake, memory. Let us use Picasso's little car again to shine, like a lantern, some clarification on the matter. Picasso privileges form because form is his real interest, the original reason for being. The car is already a face. Epstein not only leaves the object and its form intact but, more than simply alluding to its function, makes this the very cause and motivation for his sculpture.

A Lamppost up a Man, or Castling
Halfway between man and the manmade. *Rock Drill*, driller drill. The translator.

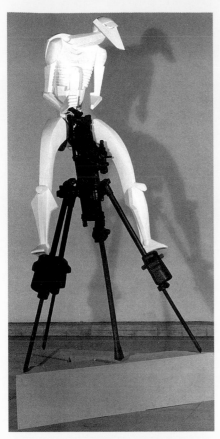

Reconstruction of Jacob Epstein's *Rock Drill*, (1913–15), 1973–74

Man fascinated by the bovine extends his man-made legs to raise himself up. The machine, like a mechanical horse, elevates the man to fulfill his function of going deeper: two objects from nature that nature did not unite. Through sculpture Epstein makes one out of two. Artist of a single sculpture (like Duchamp-Villon, Gabo, Smithson, or McCracken), Epstein here creates a threshold. When Hayward presented the complete sculpture, it had changed yet again. Now the human part was of white plaster instead of the original black bronze. One might wonder if it was Epstein's timidity or the reconstructor's lack of funds that diverted this symbiosis of forms through color. Perhaps the final meaning of this work is to make the upper half indistinguishable from the lower half. To be: between. In any case, what Epstein accomplishes is, in addition to a qualitative leap, an act of clarification. To take a bottle and to blow across its mouth is, in a sense, to extend the scope of its function. To place it upside down on a table is to link it with the function of balance. To take a glass of water and empty it is to return it to its true essence. To cover a shadow with glasses and bottles is to emphasize the body that casts it. Epstein, in reality, takes the bottle and empties its contents into a glass. Period. He has poured a drink. Exactly.

Let us go back to Picasso's little car. What Epstein does with it is to open the door and put a driver inside.

Among Other Sculptures
Among the multiplicity of sculptures exhibited in the halls of the Tate Gallery, only some seem to have escaped the basic requirements of their age, the impeccable consummation of their aesthetic destiny: González, David Smith, its continiuty into Caro's *Early One Morning*. Two contemporaries of *Rock Drill:* Duchamp-Villon's *Horse Head* and Naum Gabo's *Constructed Head*. The first (Duchamp-Villon) shares the same concerns as Epstein. The components of the completed form are also gears, axles, and supports. Beyond that, the parts are inseparable from the whole. The second (Gabo) enjoys the distinction of having brought a unique gesture to British sculpture: a head tilting forward, arrogant, precise. A unique face that was linked to Epstein's work in the precious advance of a few centimeters. The first of these sculptures was done by a Frenchman, the second by a Russian.

It occurs to me that English sculpture possesses a unique character. It is difficult to find parallels outside the island geography. Its elements, its discourse are its own.

Allow me to end this section in the same way as those that precede it. Tony Cragg, the cornerstone, takes the little car of the Picasso metaphor, puts it on the floor and places another beside it, and then places several more in the opposite direction.

Perhaps in writing about the gesture of the neck tilting forward, of the found object, of the use of discovery, of color, of the fragment, of its reverse (the whole), of the ground (the supreme example of the reverse), of gravity (the ground's reason for being), of the *Rock Drill*, I may have spoken of British sculpture.

1. The Tate Gallery did not in fact divide Epstein's work. *Rock Drill* was originally conceived in 1913–15 as a full image of a man atop a drill. Epstein made the figure of the man in white plaster and joined it with an actual drill, making, in the artist's words, "a machinelike robot, visored, menacing, and carrying within itself its progeny, protectively ensconced"; see Jacob Epstein, *Let There Be Sculpture* (New York: G. P. Putnam's Sons, 1940): 49. When the sculpture was exhibited in the March 1915 London Group exhibition, it met with great criticism, especially for its machine element.

Following World War I, Epstein became wary of the machine in general and reconsidered his sculpture. He took the figure off the drill and cut it at the torso; he also trimmed one of the arms above the elbow and the other above the wrist. Smaller and more fragile in appearance, the cast bronze version of *Rock Drill* reflects little of Epstein's original intentions. This is the situation to which Muñoz referred here. —ED.

2. The exhibition that Muñoz referenced here is *Vorticism and Its Allies*, organized by the Arts Council of Great Britain and shown at the Hayward Gallery, London, 27 March–2 June 1974. For the exhibition, Ken Cook and Ann Christopher made a reconstruction of the 1913–15 original. For more on Epstein's sculpture and its 1974 reconstruction, see Richard Cork, *Vorticism and Its Allies* (London: Arts Council of Great Britain, 1974). —ED.

63

The Time of the Pose

First published as "Die Zeit der Pose,"
Durch 5 (1988): 25–27.

THE WORK OF Parmigianino does not belong to dreams. What could possibly be more realistic than to paint the space in which one is painting?

The mother in the picture *Lady with Three Children* appears not to be taking part in the scene she dominates. Each of the faces in the painting is turned toward a specific point in the salon—a corner, a wall—in which they are portrayed. The figures are intentionally presented as objects of artistic consideration, as a representation of a reality, which ends at the edge of the painting and to which the picture refers by noting its absence. A reality, perhaps, which in the final analysis is apparent neither inside nor outside the painting.

On the grounds of a certain polychrome perspective, I should like to juxtapose a photograph by Agusti Centelles from 1936 with the Mannerist work. Even beyond its suggestive parallels, however, this photograph deserves our careful scrutiny.

The license plate on the automobile on the left could indicate that the person standing in the middle has just recently made his way through the narrow streets that lead to Barcelona's main thoroughfare, the Ramblas. Perhaps it is his intention to join in one of the political demonstrations of that time. Suddenly—perhaps too suddenly for him to understand—something has changed. The figure has forgotten his part. Interrupted in his presentation, he directs a frozen stare toward the prompter. He waits for his next cue. He stands there, immobile, and does not move as the curtain falls. The prompter waits in his little box in the floor, the photographer behind his camera, and neither says a word. They simply contemplate the beauty of the moment.

Beyond their formal, indeed numerical, similarity, both works share the strangeness of the picture itself, and even that of the expressions of the people portrayed.

I said before that the expression on the mother's face in the Mannerist painting seems to reflect no participation in the represented scene. And yet, it is not without that degree of tenderness that a mother owes her children. The presence of the mother symbolizes something of a discernible tranquility. As soon as the time of the pose is over—"The Time of the Pose" might make a good subtitle for this work—the three children will return to their play. Their presence in the picture is an interruption.

Centelles's photograph presents the concept of a linear time with its irreversible and inevitable end, maintained only through the voice of the photographer: "One minute please, everybody hold still . . . thank you."

Parmigianino's work, on the other hand, seems to assume, to adopt, a circular concept of time. There is neither beginning nor end. The echo, previously a call, itself becomes a call with each repetition. The viewer's gaze, which is

Parmigianino (Girolamo Francesco Maria Mazzola), *Lady with Three Children*, 1533–35

Agusti Centelles, *Riots in St. James Square, February 17, 1936*

turned toward the family portrait, wanders ceaselessly back and forth. Like an echo, the eye returns to its starting point. It moves from the face of the boy on the left to that of the mother, then turns to the boy on the right and drops down to the hands. And the gaze flees from the center of what it sees, multiplying it. Parmigianino's work presages the world of the Baroque that will follow him.

The Mannerist painter and the Catalan photographer conjure their work into an aesthetic creation, perhaps in order to suggest that the boundaries of what is within lie beyond it.

"What is in the center of a column?" The architect Lou Kahn once asked his students this question. It may be that his disciples might have been able to satisfy him with an answer that the great Spanish mystic Juan de la Cruz suggested three hundred years earlier: ". . . the stone lies in its innermost core." The column is within its own interior.

In Parmigianino's work we find precisely this determination to describe the moment in which the viewer's gaze collapses in front of the painting (and this also includes his recognition of the image).

What does the worker see in the photograph? Only the lens? Does he stand still because he knows that whoever moves will not appear in the picture? What is essential here is that we are participating in a moment of dissolution.

Here I would ask my readers to indulge me and to play a little game. Let us pretend that the two pictures are identical.

So, let us begin.

First, we can say that the various theories that attempt to express the manifestations of that cultural epoch we call Mannerism in terms of a common denominator constantly stress the same points.

A Mannerist painting shows, as a general rule:

a) A refined selection of poses
   The three members of the *Guardia Civil*, with their dark, elaborately swirling coats, are arranged like the reflections in a triple mirror atop an Art Deco dressing table.

In another work Parmigianino had attempted to depict the riddle inherent in painting a mirror. The painting I am referring to is his *Self-Portrait in a Convex Mirror* in the Kunsthistorisches Museum in Vienna. In this picture, the artist himself is copied by his work. Perhaps there is another symbolic meaning at work here, namely that illusory nature of imitation, of copying. Only the artist's right hand, holding the brush, appears distorted in the roundness of the mirror. All the rest, his face, remains unchanged, keeps its distance, as if it wished to draw attention to its own full control.

The three *Guardias* imitate the poses in the triple mirror, while the actual (central) image is frozen and absent. Centelles's photograph imitates the mirror, which is itself imitating that reality which cannot restrain fleeting time. In the eyes of the worker this reality wants to be an illusion or to appear as an illusion.

The attempt by the Mannerist master to raise his hand to the mirror is in vain. An attempt, not as Vasari intended, a whim.

Several other concepts are also to be found among the characteristics of Mannerism:

b) The exaggeration of stylistic conventions
c) The calligraphic character of bodies
d) The love of quotations
e) The tendency to spiritualize or dramatize scenes

And yet Parmigianino emphasizes in his work two more things than his fellow artists Pontormo or Bronzino, two major aspects that will help to make the hidden thread in this meandering text clearer: secondary figures and hands.

f) Secondary figures
   Remember the *Madonna with the Long Neck*, or consider the standing figure wearing a hat, to the left of the worker. He too observes the scene. And yet how precisely he recalls the lines by Auden as he walks past us and this scene: "About suffering they were never wrong,/The Old Masters: how well they understood/its human position; how it takes place/While someone else is eating or opening a window, or just walking dully along."

g) The hands
   It would be pointless to discuss in detail the wonderful expressiveness of each individual hand in the Mannerist work. Permit me to ask just one question: What are the three *Guardias* holding in their hands? What is the worker pointing at with his right hand?

The Prompter

First published as "The Prompter," in Long Island City, N.Y., P.S.1 Contemporary Art Center, Theatergarden Bestiarium: The Garden as Theater as Museum, exh. cat. by Chris Dercon et al. (Cambridge, Mass: The MIT Press, 1989).

IT MUST HAVE BEEN afternoon, when leaning on the window, we began to speak about the city, the majestic Königsplatz and the Glyptothek.... At some moment, I no longer remember why, I referred to the importance that dwarves had in the formal courts of the period.... Sometime later, or maybe just before, I mentioned to him that that same morning I had read in the bus, while returning from the gardens of Nymphenburg ... although now that I think about it, it must have been a tram or I remember something of the rails or something particular in the stop, yes, it must have been a tram ... yes, it was then that I mentioned to him that Cuvilliés [François de Cuvilliés I; 1695–1768], the Rococo architect of the buildings that I had seen in the garden, was also a dwarf. Many afternoons have passed since that afternoon and now everything appears somewhat distorted by the whims of memory, but I think I remember that it was then that I mentioned to him a semi-circular building without doors and only one tall window through which, almost at eye level, extends a wide, long, always identical flat surface called a proscenium. We looked through a few books together, yes it must have been before the end of the afternoon when I started telling him about that house in the middle of a street.... The first thing to do was to dig a hole.... Not to lift the earth or make an opening in the ground, but to build a house-like hole.... That ... that must have been what I said, a house where there is only a hole ... and in it, living in it, a standing dwarf, immobile. I see it all and it is all in front of that hole ... on top (an immense unprotected surface where everything is feet and all the feet walk) the pride of eloquence, the delight of the romantic encounter and the warm intonation of the voice, carpets and thief-like steps. The actor stops for a moment, vacillates, unsure but indifferent he gets closer to the hole.... And in the hole: narrowness, closeness, no disappointment, nor conquests, nor landscapes in the distance.... It must have been then, at the end of the afternoon, that I mentioned to him that in the square of the Xemaa-el-Fna some storytellers say they can recite the Koran by heart.... No, it wasn't like that, now I remember.... In front of that house there is no audience nor work, there is only a spectator placed in the center of the scene, immobile, suspended, trying not to forget something.

Installation view of *The Prompter* (cat. no. 24), P.S.1 Contemporary Art Center, Long Island City, New York, 1989

On a Square

First published as "Auf einem Platz," in Krefeld, Germany, Museen Haus Lange and Haus Esters, Weitersehen (1980→1990→), exh. cat. (Krefeld: Krefelder Kunstmuseen, 1990).

THE PICTURE IS CLEAR. The lecturer's table far away. A gathering of heads together in the foreground so it was impossible to see his face. The voice of the Mexican poet Octavio Paz is telling, slowly, the story about a statue. The image of the voice is still clear. So may this circumlocution be like an accumulation of echoes resounding and dying away into something unintelligible.

In August, 1790, some street repairs were being done in the center of Mexico City. When the ground level at the Plaza Mayor was raised, a stone statue, with a height of about two and a half meters, was found under the earth.

A few years before, a large collection of plaster replicas of different Greek and Roman sculptures had been placed in the showrooms of the Royal University of Mexico. The statue of the goddess Coatlique was brought there and was placed in this unprecedented company as "a monument from the antiquity."

When a few months had passed, the doctors of the University decided that such a work among the masterpieces of classicism was an affront to the very concept of beauty. And, besides, the goddess might revive such ideas among the Indians that the viceroys thought should preferably be forgotten. Thus, the professors decided that Coatlique was to be buried again in the same hole where she had been found.

A few years later, it seems that Baron Alexander von Humboldt, during a temporary stay in Mexico, came across the notes and the description made by Antonio de Léon y Gama before the statue was again buried. Humboldt managed to have the statue unearthed once more, so he could examine it. When this was done, the statue was buried anew.

Coatlique was a stone block, vaguely resembling a human being, and she had been placed at the top of the Great Temple of Tenochtitlan. There she was anointed by the Aztec priest with blood and copal incense. She was wearing the attributes of divinity—fangs, serpents, skulls—all of it carved true to life. Bones, wood, feathers were petrified in the Mexican sculpture. "Fusion of matter and feeling" says here, exactly, the poet's voice: "the stone is idea, and the idea is transformed into stone."

Years after the independence of Mexico, Coatlique was unearthed for good. Back in the university, she was first left abandoned in a backyard; then she was placed in a passage, partially hidden behind a screen, suggesting, behind curiosity, a feeling of embarrassment and shame. Finally, after having spent some time in a small room like an object of doubtful artistic value, she was moved to occupy the central position in the main showroom for Aztec art in the National Museum of Anthropology.

From her beginning as a goddess on the top of a truncated pyramid to her present position as a masterpiece of anthropological historiography, Coatlique has remained indifferent to the plurality of interpretations made from the perspective of each period of history.

To the Catholic missionary, this stone was the very incarnation of Evil, in firm opposition to the Aztec priest who venerated it as the bearer of divine values. To them both, however, the statue in itself meant the presence of something supernatural. Coatlique was a *presence* that condensed and irradiated "a tremendous mystery." The observers able to perceive this supernatural presence in the stone figure were already gone forever when Coatlique entered the maze of aesthetic discourse towards the end of the eighteenth century and the stony paths of anthropological speculation in the twentieth.

Century upon century, what changed was not the real appearance of the statue, but the understanding of reality. And all along this road from the religion to secularization, from the Aztec priest to Humboldt and to the visitor at the Museum of Anthropology, Coatlique appeared clearly as a mystery. From its statuary autonomy, the stone of human appearance brings us back to the mystery of seeing, encompassed by our gaze. As the centuries went by, the veneration of the Aztec was joined by the horror provoked by such a buried religious legacy. And to the disdain of the aesthetes was added the curiosity of the scientists, and they all applied the same intellectual criteria.

Before this adding and subtracting of significances, before the changing ages to which each casual observer belongs, this block of stone in its immobility inspires a unique feeling: the enigma of the arousal of feelings.

Now let us take a few steps forward or perhaps aside, to add another possibility from the present time to this trail of four hundred years.

Before the Aztec statue and, forever leaving behind us so many sociology- and information-laden sculptures, it is worthwhile to turn our gaze on another statue. Any one general in the center of any square in a city anywhere, on an equally immobile horse. A statue that does not inspire us with any feeling of respect, because no one alive remembers any longer after which glorious battle this little heap of stone and bronze was placed precisely there. And we do not feel any animosity, because neither is the enemy there any longer. Neither any aesthetical fervor nor even scientific curiosity. A statue that possesses but one value: the one of not having allowed time to hide it from our eyes.

We certainly do not intend to save the image of any bronze general from oblivion, or bring back into the records of art a forgotten statue, immobile, hidden in the air in a square somewhere. Neither do we intend, by the story of Coatlique, to call attention to the fact that a block of stone can be worth a discourse on different interpretations. Because, behind all these additions and subtractions we are left with a unique understanding: we have come together only to try to grasp its presences. Thus from the present, lost in a city, crossing a square, gazing. How should we interpret this concealment?

Aztec statue of the goddess Coatlique, 15th century

Segment

First published as Segment (Chicago and Geneva:
The Renaissance Society at The University of Chicago and
Centre d'Art Contemporain, 1990).

ANDRÉ FRIEDMANN tells of how during an archaeological expedition to the Peruvian highlands, he found "in a village called Zurite, a building of uncertain origins and unknown precedent . . . genuine source of that utter enigma we call space." The details surrounding the building's construction were told to him by some Peruvian peasants through a series of interviews. Friedmann intended to publish a transcription of these conversations until his sudden death in a helicopter accident left the exploration of this building's significance incomplete.

May these notes be the payment of a debt incurred in time and a sign of friendship, or rather a certain proximity, as for years we shared identical balconies on opposite sides of the same street.

La Posa

In the Peruvian highlands one encounters a village called Zurite. Situated at an altitude of 3,391 meters, it has 3,402 inhabitants. The disparity between these two numbers prevents this normal village from becoming a perfect simile. Located on the Western slope of the Vilcabamba mountain range, it is next to a tributary of the Apurimac river. Cereals, quinoa, coca, and potatoes. Alpacas and vicunas.

Once a year, every year, and with a distance that borders on disdain, the inhabitants burn a house that they had erected shortly before at the side of the village plaza. The "posa" of Zurite, as they call this building, is constructed of long sticks, thin logs and ropes.

The posa is not of any particular design. Two walls of ordinary size slope to form a roof. On each side there is a door-like opening: an entrance and an exit used indiscriminately. There exists, perhaps, a formal peculiarity in that it completely lacks any wall covering. The vertical posts are joined to lateral crossbeams, which in turn, link smaller ones. A support structure exists. What it does not have is a brushwood covering or a roof of any kind. Just a framework. Although the inhabitants of the village define it as a house, the posa seems more like the drawing of a house.

Any one of the peasants from the village, without apparent reason, enters the building. He stays for a few seconds or for several minutes. Standing. Quiet. Motionless. After this time, he goes out. A few hours later or the next day, another passerby will, in turn, linger in it for a moment or an hour. Meanwhile, the rest of Zurite's inhabitants appear indifferent and go about their business without paying the least attention to him, even when they are but a few meters away from the posa.

The surprising thing about its construction is not the absence of functionality, but rather that its pure transparency rules out the idea of this room as shelter and lodging.

In the interviews that Friedmann conducted, the Peruvian peasants described, with absolute but paradoxical clarity, the emotions that they felt while inside it. The explanation of this experience should not be read merely for its poetic significance; neither should it be for its religious value, despite the similarity that A. Valente grants it, when he describes it as "an experience whose ultimate content is the void, inasmuch as it is negation of all content, which is opposed to the transparent state in which mystic experience is made possible." To clarify this response would be, on the one hand, in vain and, on the other, superfluous.

"What do you feel when you are inside?"

"It's like being in a dark room. That's it, standing still in a dark room."

About Living on a Balcony

Stylistically, this slight structure is above all simple. The two walls supporting each other at their highest point form an isosceles triangle with the plane of the ground as its base. Its length is approximately four meters and its height is six. It is sufficiently spacious for two men to pass each other or for three, or even four, to stand motionless. More than a house, it resembles the image of a house.

It is a construction whose forms "appear to be 'without evolution,' they simply are, as if they always were. Therefore they shun linguistic gestures. They are silent." Let this quotation of

V. Scully serve to indicate that the formal appearance of the posa duplicates—with the same detail and mystery of a mirror—the life that goes on in its interior. This room is neither majestic nor hieratic. It holds only the certainty that in it, no one will shatter a long silence.

Once inside, the passerby remains within those four meters. He may look forward or out of the corner of his eye but, in truth, while inside he will not talk. It is this state of silence that protects "this absolute enigma." The passerby, in his silence, will guard the secret of the silences that have already inhabited it.

Nevertheless, a question lingers like dust in the air after the passing of a parade. Is this place of juncture and gathering also a dwelling, a home? It cannot possibly be only a monument, a symbolic structure disguised as a house. One could infer that the momentary occupation of this uncertain passageway does not make it a dwelling. It is also true that if the Peruvian peasant had wanted to imagine a disquieting shape or a geometrically intricate box in which to perform a ceremony, he would not have chosen the image of the outline of a house, of any house, of an empty house.

In "Totality and Infinity," E. Lévinas affirms that a dwelling, "the chosen house . . . is completely contrary to a root. It indicates the nomadic condition that has made it possible." It confirms that the essential character of a house is not to take root but rather, it is that nomadic condition "that makes living possible," as Francesco Dal Co suggests. Here the passerby is not merely a window-shopper whiling away the time. Much to the contrary, upon entering the posa, the Peruvian peasant restores the dignity of being in a place where nothing happens to him and where nothing occurs.

If on the plaza in Zurite time passes over the peasant lingering inside this construction, and the occasional relief of a breeze announces this passage of time, and if nothing happens to the passerby who stays there, it is also certain that he is inhabiting this spatiality. This is the same way that one inhabits a balcony, where everything is suspended and nothing is decided. A man leaning on the railing of a balcony, abandoned to the perennial dusk, is enveloped by a spatiality that is a determined physical condition

but also by the conditions that constitute this condition. That is how the balcony, beyond being a mere place, is also a room. Also in this way, the figure who poses in this place of absolute transit inhabits it while he is there.

The Peruvian peasant, standing still and silent in the center of the posa, attentive, without future because nothing awaits him, gropes for his true center. As he enters, he knows that when he walks out of the door, everything will remain the same. Nothing will have been solved with unsuspected ease or by collusion with fate.

About Intervals
Crossroad. Place of transit. Space inscribed in its own exile. Interval. The elusive space that this house occupies summarizes and extends that other space to which Sartre once referred: "The original space that reveals itself to me is furrowed with paths and roads." The posa is not a dwelling where the traveller from far away stops to rest. Here the peasant of Zurite pauses in the midst of two actions in order to inhabit a moment of suspension. A point tangential to all roads because they meet there, this building allows its immobile occupant to be in a space of comings and goings. A center where distances cross each other. When in this place, inside this dwelling, if two or more inhabitants of the pueblo meet, neither speaks to the other. No one comes here out of curiosity, nor to listen to the drone of an insect. In this building nothing is expected, no one waits for anyone, all that happens is the conjugation of the mysteries of intersecting paths.

Geoffrey Scott, possibly speaking as Berenson's student, tried to summarize the specific values of all constructions. Scott used to say that upon entering a church and confronting a long perspective of columns from the back of the nave, the space itself suggested a forward movement towards the altar: "Because a movement without purpose, that does not lead to a culminating point, contradicts our impulses, it is not human." But also for the Peruvian peasant, each road is a trajectory toward something. It is in

that direction and because of that relation that it is a road. The approximate two meters at the center of the posa suspend the directionality of the paths that cross it. In the small area occupied by this house there is no finality. There is no offertory, only another road.

If it had been a sacred space instead of one without incident, the posa would resemble the rambling interior of an Arab mosque or the centrifugal force of a Byzantine space more so than the theatrical curves and folds of the Baroque.

Crossroad. Place of transit. Space inscribed in its own exile. House/Interval. Place that is negation of movement and at the same time generator of pathways.

About the Peasant's Voice
The voice that rises from the interviews by André Friedmann is clear and concise: "The posa is from before. It is the first house that our ancestors built in Zurite. For this reason, each year we use pieces of wood that come from our houses, which in turn came from the first one, like a seed." In answer to the question of why they remove some pieces of wood before destroying the posa, Friedmann relates that "they reuse this wood to construct walls or floors different from those they removed it from." Wood comes and goes. Whence it comes and where it goes is of no importance to the Peruvian peasant, provided that it is useful to him in his backward march toward "the first house."

"Once a year, every year, we construct the posa. Always in the same year, we destroy it." The inhabitants of Zurite apply this unwritten law with absolute precision. The tradition says nothing about whether the house should stand for one or for three hundred sixty-five days.

Each year "we build it to one side of the square." It is always constructed off the center of the square, without ever specifying whether on its right or its left side. Two walls terminating in a two-sloped roof, even halfway constructed, are immediately recognized as a house. When Friedmann interviewed some of the posa's builders, they told him the rules were passed down from parents to children, generation after generation.

No one could explain why they destroyed it each year nor why it had to be secured to "one side of the square."

About Origins
"The posa . . . is the first house."

The first grotto. The first cave, the first hut, the first house, the first place built for habitation. There are more versions of how and why the first house was constructed than historians who subscribe to each of these theories. For B. Fletcher, the house originated solely as protection against inclement weather. For Milizia, it comes from an imitation of nature. For Rykwert, it is determined by necessity. From Vitruvius's rustic to Chambers' primitive cabin (both indicate the conical form as easiest to build), arguments about the appearance of the first house are systematically and indistinctly formulated according to the same classifications: climate, materials, shelter. For all of them, the origin is simple, humble, and above all stems from the necessity of hiding from the outside.

In its transparency, the posa offers itself disdainfully to climatic changes. Its materials are the result of a partly forgotten parable rather than of the material requirements of the surrounding reality. Its function as shelter is alien to its being a threshhold. In fact, the posa appears to be related to Etienne-Louis Boullée's hypothesis, which, as a qualitative jump echoing the division Alberti establishes between concept and execution, asserts that the first humans did not construct their dwellings "until they conceived an image of them."

In his essay "Der Stil," Gottfried Semper (who revels in the glory of being Schinkel's friend) speculates that "the beginnings of construction coincide with those of woven materials." It would then be possible to affirm that, tied together with rope, the sticks and logs of the posa are the image of this first division of space invented by man: "the enclosure made of woven and tied sticks."

Only the great French historian André Leroi-Gourhan tried to see another possibility. Leroi-Gourhan argued that the first constructions and their precise circumstances, which have survived to this day, were parallel to and contemporary with the appearance of the first rhythmic markings. If successive points, alternating lines and symbolic signs were painted on cave walls—forms giving shape to mystery—then the same symbolic nature should have been carried from the cave into the first constructed dwelling.

The addition of possible archaeological certainties would justify the supposition (perhaps Leroi-Gourhan would be in complete disagreement) that: in the first houses necessity was secondary to symbolic will; rhythmic markings shaped the inside and outside appearance of the first dwelling; the braided wall (perhaps here Semper would be in complete disagreement), before becoming a wall, was a totality of knots. Origin of the labyrinth. There even exists a hierarchical order, however paradoxical it may seem, of ornament over structure. Before being a shelter, the house was a sign. Before being a dwelling, it was an interminable trickle of allegories and a lodging of the symbol. Beyond this swarm of uncertainties, it is possible to risk with unswerving conviction that "the first house," which the Peruvian peasant seeks to reconstitute in the posa, is constructed year after year as a means of alluding to something distinct from it.

About Other Ephemeral Houses
"Once a year we build the posa and always in the same year we destroy it."

Here is another quotation with a different origin but equally as precise: "The width of our churches will range from seven to eight meters. The proper proportion between their length and height will be maintained in accordance with this measurement." Beyond the moderation and humbleness of its intentions, this description of the Carmelite church, written in 1581 by Saint John of the Cross with Saint Theresa's supervision, is surprising for the exactness of its measurements. The fervent devotion of Saint Theresa, reflected in the simplicity and austerity of the convent of her mendicant order, would have been disturbed as she looked out from her expected place in heaven over the temporary church that the city of Valladolid built in honor of her canonization. In his 1615 account of ephemeral buildings, Rios Hevia writes that the Carmelites chose to found a new church for such celebrations, as they had none in the center of the city. "Taking over a street from wall to wall," a new wooden church was erected and several days later "it was taken apart with curious skill." Oddly, the width of the street was thirty-six feet, almost eight meters. This product of chance and order reached the height of its rhetoric in the façade. This was repeated on the reverse of the façade in such a way that, upon leaving the church, the faithful faced another façade identical to the one they saw as they came in.

Bonet Correa relates how eighteenth-century houses were covered with false façades. Like triumphal arches or ephemeral obelisks, they remained with the house "three, four, five, or even six days." With the exception of the Porta Nuova of Palermo or the Arco de Santa Maria de Burgos, which turned out to be permanent works, these edifices were by and large destroyed a few days after they had been erected.

The temporality of certain constructions is a symbol that varies according to historical time and geographical territory. The age of classic Japanese buildings is determined by the number of times that the parts have been substituted. Many are the coincidences and parallels that one encounters while looking for antecedents to the posa. In the course of the last thousand years, the well-known temple of Ise Shinto has been dismantled every twenty years to be replaced by an identical replica.

Of all of them, one could say that they are continuously perishing houses. As time goes by, their only permanence lies in their description.

The posa borders upon the mosaic of possibilities that adorn the Carmelite church, while it distances itself from baroque adornment or from examples of continuous renovation. Closer to its intentions are the values that African and Oceanic tribes bestow on their statues. For example, in her article "Absent

Meaning: Death and the Resurrection of the Objective Value," Susan Kuechler recounts that as Western museums and collectors acquired carved pieces and other ritual artifacts from the New Ireland tribes in Oceania, the range of forms available to reproduce was progressively reduced. She recounts how only certain members of the tribe, those who have acquired a new piece and then destroyed it, have the right to continue to reproduce it. This right is suspended as long as the object is still in existence. For the posa's builders as well, form and its destruction are also cyclical.

About Seeds
"Each year we use . . . wood that comes from our houses . . . like a seed."

How can one order the fragments that form and at the same time designate the posa? Each log is not merely an element of intersection between the surface of a wall and the point at which a wall ends. Each strip of wood has been, and will be, an exploded shape. Once the pretext for this structure no longer exists, the building itself will have to disappear. But in fact, it is impossible to destroy that which has already been dissolved.

Each one of its planks comes from many other, earlier structures. Each log will be a corner, a volume, or a point of intersection, whereas before it had been, perhaps, a railing or a wall.

It is but one of many paradoxes that questions the nature of this room that it cannot be completely destroyed but rather only reinstituted. As the new building is set on fire each year, its appearance will come to an end, but not its reason for being. As its cyclical function is completed, the flicker of its forms terminate, but not the interminable circularity of the laws that governed it. The destruction of its formal order is a dynamic reaction because the elements that constitute it as a construction were once processes of disintergration and eventually will be recomposed after its dispersal into a new fractional geometry.

The fragile weave of pieces of wood appears to suggest the unpredictability of any intention of permanence. Nevertheless,

this doubt is reiterated annually. The peasant follows a tradition of carrying from one house to another several planks that he says are seeds. But nothing in his voice indicates what appearance the posa will take, nor in which place those planks are to germinate.

How can one establish that the posa always has had the same appearance? Is it not possible that it once used to be circular, or, just two scarce groups of stakes located several meters from one another? A passageway or a mere entrance? The alley to oblivion runs parallel to the annual will to remember. In time, having turned into the sketch of a house, the posa illuminates its historic sense while at the same time signaling the impossibility of permanence. The annual rhythmic interruption of its duration is also an affirmation of the permanence of tradition.

From "the first house . . . like a seed." But when the seeds have had a part in so many stylistic and constructive changes, from the pre-Columbian epoch to the present, how did the second posa look? And the fifth? Couldn't this humble construction also be a gesture, repeated year after year, that stems from the need to remember a story, and from the suspicion of having forgotten it?

About Transparency
The Peruvian builders annually situate the posa in an undifferentiated, but not indifferent, space outside the plaza— to the side, the side of its urban condition. Nothing is exact in its positioning and yet at the same time nothing is completely arbitrary. Tradition dictates that the posa should be placed away from, although not too distant from, the place that it occupied the previous year. Someplace by the side of the plaza. That is all.

This almost entirely translucent, almost transparent house does not have a hall or a waiting room. It has no corridor since it is, in its entirety, a threshold. It has no windows because no space lies beneath where these windows should be. It hides nothing and conceals no one. It is startling because it embodies the

mystery of perfect symmetries. By entering it, the space is bifurcated. Two new possibilities surge that did not exist before: the entrance is an exit and at the same time a mirror-like double.

One might add that a fundamental conquest of this dwelling is the excessiveness of its placement. The posa is constructed next to and therefore outside of the plaza of Zurite, yet it is still within the center of urban activity. This is so in order to better articulate its extraterritoriality and to underline its distance from the plaza. If, as Heidegger says, only "that which is itself a place can concede space," reminding us that "the things that by their position concede space we call buildings," then it is possible that the posa is just a place occupied by something transitory, that before and after this duration, this building is an accurate demonstration of the "boundless impotence of shelters masquerading as homes," to which Massimo Cacciari alludes.

Before the Autonomous Image 1
An archipelago of symbols, this house spends the night alone. It lives as swiftly as the aperture that produces the photograph that now, at the end of the afternoon, justifies it. A lateral portrait. Nothing here is sepia. Tumultuous matter of time. Suddenly disappeared. Nothing is nostalgia here.

Before the Autonomous Image 2
The posa is barely a few sticks chosen by chance and without exact measurement. A few unmeasured sticks chosen by chance serve to conjugate a space absorbed in itself. A place almost chosen by chance where, for a moment, all beliefs are suspended. Nevertheless, also, a place where a man dwells and where time does not run backwards and the floor is swept mercilessly.

About the Autonomous Image
The peasants who appear to be moving away from the edge of the photograph are possibly the destroyers of the posa, or maybe its builders. The suspicion arises that, like those that inhabit the novels of Flaubert or Tolstoy, these peasants are

characters who will never recognize the stories in which they are protagonists. Novalis used to say that "the poet does not do, but permits that it be done." Octavio Paz would respond: "Who then is the one that does?" But when the inhabitant of Zurite stands still in the interior of the posa, nothing happens to him. If he does nothing then who is the doer?

The Peruvian peasant must know that upon entering this dwelling he carries the act of dwelling to its extreme. At some point, even with different words, he must truly intuit that when he occupies this dwelling he places himself in the very center of space itself, in order to affirm from this space and with this space an experience that an inhabited space cannot accommodate: that of the void. When he stops beyond this threshold, he must know that there is no vanishing point nor vantage point. And if that other place from which to focus does not exist here, how is it possible to distinguish the one who sees from what is seen?

Once again, a man crosses the plaza. He goes toward the posa. He enters. He stops a moment inside it. He leaves. Walks away. This house, this room remains empty. Perhaps it preserves the absence of the former presence. The hours go by. Perhaps another peasant walks through. Someone must be near, but who it might be is not discernible. The posa offers itself as the center of attention. In its transparent interior, without apparent reason, the absence of a human presence prolongs itself. In its interior, this place accommodates the tension between the suspension of the human presence and its possible appearance. Between its leaving and its possible return.

Let us permit ourselves for one last time an image. The image of a peasant who walks around the plaza. Hands in pockets. He walks through the door of the posa. He stops. He stays still for a moment. Maybe he takes his hands out of his pockets. His fingers are long. He leaves by the opposite door, which was once an entrance and is now an exit. The narrow space of this structure has received the meticulous pause.

Let us remember the response enunciated at the beginning: "It is like being in a dark room. That's it, standing still in a dark room."

About the Fire
Place of transit. Crossroad. Space inscribed in its own exile. Interval. "Place of absolute summoning," as J. A. Valente said of the Xemaa-el-Fna, also called, at the dawn of the Moroccan language, the Plaza of Destruction. The Plaza of Marrakesh as simultaneous summons of both multitude and emptiness. In its etymological sense, it is the place of annihilation. What annihilation? It is the same in the Peruvian plaza; the posa is set on fire and destroyed. Where does this drive towards extinction come from? Truthfully, it does not matter. This building—the sum of pauses, of interruptions, of interstices inhabited by an interlude—is, by the very essence of its nature, provisional.

To burn the posa is to confront any possible nostalgia with the evidence of distance. When it is destroyed, and this is done with a gesture of near indifference, there is no empty space left nor does its burn leave a scar. At some moment the following year, without an exact date, without an exact place, it will be rewoven. This house without educational vocation, indifferent to the multiple meanings of its obstinate geometry, is burned and destroyed out of necessity and without compassion.

By distancing itself from other ritualistic constructions it offers its destruction not as a prerogative of the rite's temporality, but rather in dialectical opposition to the house as a place of possible nostalgia. In the rest of Zurite's buildings desires are superimposed on abandoned efforts until the walls are covered with customs and habits. The annihilation of the posa is thus a gesture of affirmation, capable of signifying force as it confronts the continuity of the years with the evidence of distance.

"Once each year it will be constructed and in the same year it is destroyed," says the tradition. It is such that any morning, in any month, the peasant who wanders along this corridor, which they call the posa, realizes that upon entering he only repeats a gesture. Perhaps he senses that when he goes in or comes out all that is happening to him is what is normal. That by this repetition, he distances himself from all the other times that he has entered. It separates him from what happened or what did not happen there. So maybe some morning one or another of the Peruvian peasants notes that one or another time he passes alongside the posa because he no longer feels it necessary to pass through its interior. And another of them may also discover that it has been days or months since he has gone through this corridor, the same corridor that he, himself, had constructed.

One day, without ceremonies and without councils, some of them speak among themselves about how no one wanders across that threshold any longer. Then they decide to remove some of the sticks that have made up the building. One or several of them approach and without any ceremony at all burn the remaining pieces of wood. The destruction is fast and without preambles. A few flames and some figures, their backs turned, moving away.

Epilogue
Through the days and, by chance, the relentless pursuit of the years, the same stories come back in the conversation. Captain Giovanni Drogo facing the Tartar desert. Second Lieutenant Grange facing the Ardennes. Sentinels of battles both feared and desired. Autonomous figures facing an empty desert.

In the face of desire, from time to time, there arises the possibility of constructing a room where the next moment is eternally delayed, indefinitely postponed. A room where a future, forever to come, never takes place.

Another room. Another place where something vertiginous might occur. In The Metropolitan Museum of Art in New York there was once a room that has since been dismantled. May the photograph of that indefinitely suspended moment serve as part of the universe of the possible.

A Drawing-Room Trick

First published as "A Drawing-Room Trick," in Pittsburgh, The Carnegie Museum of Art, Carnegie International 1991, vol. 1, exh. cat. by Lynne Cooke et al. (Pittsburgh and New York: The Carnegie Museum of Art and Rizzoli, 1991).

THE FIGURE IS CUT from twelve pieces of cardboard and when complete should stand about ten inches in height. The pieces are the head, the trunk, two upper arms, two lower arms, two legs (hip to knee), two calves, and two feet. All these should be joined together in the proper places, either by threads knotted at the back and front or by wires, in such a manner that they will work freely.

The constructor, after taking a seat facing the audience, attempts ineffectually three or four times to make the figure stand upright between his feet, which are far enough apart to give it plenty of room. Each time the figure collapses and falls to the floor, the constructor then blows a whistle, and the figure rises part way up and remains a few seconds, as if listening, and then drops back again. Finally, a long blast on the whistle brings the figure up standing. The constructor only now begins to whistle a song, and the figure executes a dance keeping time to the music. When the sound ceases it stands for a few seconds and then collapses as before.

Lastly, the constructor picks up the figure and passes it to the spectators, who fail to find any "deception" about it. The secret is quite simple. A thin black silk thread passes from one of the constructor's legs to the other at the height of the figure's head; the figure is attached to this. As he keeps time to the music with his heels the figure is made to dance.

The length of the thread is determined by experiment, and it should have a black pin bent into a hook attached to each end. The thread should pass along the back of the calves and be fastened to the outer seam of the trousers, as this permits greater ease in walking and is less liable to "give away" the method by causing the trouser legs to vibrate during the dance. This manner of attaching the thread also makes it possible for the figure to rise part way up and then fall back as described above. This is done by unhooking one of the pins after the figure has been attached to the thread and manipulating it by hand while the constructor bends forward to watch the figure's movements, keeping the hand

behind the calf of the leg to mask its movements.

The method of attaching the figure to the thread is by cutting little slits in the cardboard at the sides of the head and bending them backwards, thus forming little hooks which at the proper time engage the thread.

Adapted by the artist from a book found in the Lincoln Center Public Library, New York, call number MZC-75.623.

The Prohibited Image

*First published as "*A imagem *proibida/*La imagen *prohibida/The Prohibited* Image," *in Porto, Fundação de Serralves,* Julião Sarmento: 21 de Maio a 28 de Junho 1992, *exh. cat. by Michael Tarantino (1992).*

MY SEARCH has not come to an end. . . . An investigation inspired by the words of E. H. Gombrich that leads to repeated visits to the Warburg and Courtauld Institutes in London reaches a partial conclusion in a book or manuscript that may never have existed.

In the preface to *Legend, Myth, and Magic in the Image of the Artist,* by Ernst Kris and Otto Kurz, as it appears in the 1982 Cátedra edition published in Madrid (a fact I mention because if I had consulted the 1979 Yale University Press edition or the original 1934 Vienna Krystall Verlag edition, my investigation would have been just as unproductive, but, for what it is worth, shorter), Gombrich writes that the Viennese historian Otto Kurz dedicated his last years to "a major work relating to the prohibition of images in various religions and cultures."

Born in 1908, Kurz died in 1975 in London, where he lived and worked as Director of the Warburg Institute Library. His bibliography includes highly unlikely essays, such as "Four Forgotten Works by Agostino Carraci," "The Romantic Tree in Johan Dahl," or "A Mexican Charm Against Kidney Pain," in which he explains how the true etymology of the word "jade" derives from "hijada" or kidney stone, which the ancient Mexicans carried as a charm against gallstones.

Among the hundreds and hundreds of pages that remain of Kurz's writing, the supposed text Gombrich mentions on the prohibition of images is not to be found. Nor are there any references to it in the manuscripts that Kurz, because of time, the need to revise, or death itself, left unpublished.

However, there does exist an indication, a clue. Not just a broken branch, but the remains, the ashes, the evidence that someone along the way has made a fire.

In the stacks of the Warburg Institute, among the infinite folders leaning one against another, dossiers full of writings and letters by an equally infinite number of historians that relate moments in the lives of Renaissance artists or the infinite wanderings of scholars devoted to aesthetics, there exists a file, 80 centimeters long (by 12 x 8). On top of that file, there is another file, and yet another, reaching a total of six files filled with small pieces of cardboard.

Each piece measures approximately 10 x 6. They are covered with notes, half-finished reviews, and references to pages or lines read in other books. Some of those books are in the stacks, not far from these files, barely a few meters away. Others are on the floor below, where studies on Greek statuary or the origins of architecture are lined up. File after file divided into sections according to headings such as "Medical Instruments" or "Judaic Iconography."

In minuscule print and in several languages, Kurz wrote hundreds of unconnected notes under the heading "Prohibited." Like topographical records, these notes must have allowed Kurz to trace out a detailed map of the prohibition of images in the history of representation. Possibly, like the other texts by this meticulous Viennese art historian, this book that never existed could have consisted of a continuous, precise, and exact footnote. Each note accompanied by a year of publication and a page number. Each line dedicated to the geometric design of Arabic ornamental calligraphy lucidly written to show that this vegetable script does not correspond to the world of nature.

The absence of that "major work" referred to by Gombrich—which the new librarian at the Warburg Institute does not recall his predecessor ever having mentioned—leads me to conclude that its potential author renounced it.

The reason for this is to be found both in the project's hugeness and difficulty and in that Old Testament story, that during the short period man lived in the perfection of paradise, his time was shared and perhaps complemented by the singular presence of an absent and incomprehensible prohibition.

A question: In the infinite multiplicity of shared and complementary images, which is Julião Sarmento's prohibited image?

The Face of Pirandello

First published as "El rostro de Pirandello/The Face of Pirandello," in Urban configurations, *by Gloria Moure (Barcelona: Ediciones Poligrafa, 1994).*

—And who are you?
  What do you want?
—We've come in search of an author.
—An author? What author?
—Any author, sir.
—Well, there's no author here because we're not rehearsing any new play.
—Better still, sir. Then we can be the new play.

ALLOW ME AN IMAGE: the image of the face of Luigi Pirandello. Now allow me a second image that might explain the first: the image of a man who over a period of months buys several books by Pirandello. At first, he does so just to browse through his dramatic works. Later he purchases a few more books, this time not by Pirandello but about Pirandello. Perhaps to eye the framework. As the weeks go by, every time he takes one of the books from the shelf or puts it back, he stares for a few seconds at the face on the front and back covers of the books. As he goes from the shelf to the table and back again, his attention begins to become fixed, time after time, on the hat the Italian playwright wears in all his photographs.

One day, the man enters a bookshop and buys yet another volume. When he arrives home, he does not open it. He places it on the table next to the others. One photograph after another. Front and back covers of books bought at random. Portraits of Pirandello. It should be said that in none of the photographs does the playwright smile. No smile to mitigate the discomfort of the moment. Better to stare and then leave. Even though he is from Rome and 69 years old.

On the left-hand side of the table, the black-and-white face on the back cover of *Sei personaggi . . .*, published by Monthuen. The face, in black and white, of a man, first of all: elegant. The moustache and the goatee, both white. The goatee cut slightly to a point, like a walking-stick. It begins just below the lower lip. Well trimmed. It is possible to see his care before the mirror, on certain mornings. The black-and-white face staring fixedly at the camera. A white hat on his head. A hat with a wide sash of black silk. Below: the eyes. Yes. The eyes are always

the problem. Wide, rounded below by impeccable round, dark rings. Like the eyes that so attracted Pontormo. Lengthened downwards. In order to be able to trace, from the end of the ring to below the eyebrow, an ellipse in which to situate the forever disconcerted iris. Attentive. Intact in its fascination.

Not Giacometti. Giacometti would have traced the line on the horizontal in order to mark first the cut of the eyelid. The lower eyelid. Twice, with two strokes. The lower one pressed harder, blacker. And next a vertical cut to mark the space between the eyebrows. Not Pontormo. Pontormo would have drawn Pirandello's eyes in one stroke, hastily. An ellipse embracing the whole contour of the eyelids. The iris floating halfway between and upwards.

On the table. From left to right: the back cover of Methuen Drama. To its right, Mondadori's 1986 edition entitled *Maschere nude*. Further to the right, Querci's essay "The Inconsistency of Objectivity." Here the hat appears grey, or perhaps it is just that the photograph is grey. Almost in the center of the table another Mondadori edition with its photo caption: "Roma 1906." The hat is wide brimmed. The left hand inside the pocket of the overcoat. The right cut by the edge of the photo. The moustache and the goatee still black. Just beginning to go grey. The hat. Always the hat as if it were raining. As if it were going to rain.

In this photograph from 1906 the look is still affable. We must wait a few years before the lower eyelid becomes an immense ring. Only a few years. "Ogni forma non deve essere ne antica ne moderna, ma unica." A face like an almond. The goatee below, carefully trimmed. The hat. And the rain. Perhaps the hand near the cheekbone on the cover of Borsellino's essay. But this is anecdotal. Only the rain. The hat. Because it is raining. It is always raining. It is difficult to know how long this heavy, torrential rain has persisted. Perhaps since forever. Falling on an indifferent conversation. It is not raining a little. No. It is raining everything. It is raining an everything that falls hour after hour. Throughout the night on that conversation that is unaware of it. But it is also true that the rain that beats down insistently is indifferent to the conversation. It just falls and falls.

For this reason the hat, "Un capello di feltro," in order in appearance to give shade to this face as long as an almond. A hat that traces a shadow over eyes that are all rings.

Let us begin once again. This room. The chair. The table. Ahead, the faces that are front and back covers of books purchased at random, slightly at random. Time and again the face of Pirandello covered by a hat. In this room, it is raining. Over these books, although they are not wet to the touch, it is raining.

Nothing of fiction. I am speaking of a sleepless rain that falls day and night on a normal conversation. An immutable, fundamental rain, without interpretations. Falling on the shoulders, on the sleeves, towards the hands of a figure who asks another: Have you got the time? A rain that falls on a hat that does not console, but deceives. "I love the moments in which nothing occurs, when for instance a man asks: Have you got a light? This type of situation interests me enormously. Or: What would you like to eat?" Buñuel spoke without hope of absolution. I wanted to make a room like this. Without hope, full of an irrefutable rain. Falling on an indifferent conversation.

Dusk

First published as "Anochecer," in Santiago de Compostela, Spain, Centro Galego de Arte Contemporánea, Medardo Rosso, exh. cat. by Gloria Moure (1996).

ALLOW ME AN IMAGE. The image of an inaccessible moment. It is dusk. A seated man, slightly bent over a table, is writing. Hours have passed; the light coming through the window has crossed the table and reached the floor. The furnished room grows darker and darker, and the words the man writes, once he inscribes them on the paper, already seem remote. The image he is writing about is a face that observes the room through a curtain. No shoulders, no arms. Actually, not a real face. Just a slight pressure pressed on wax. A face in waiting, timeless, tilted to one side in the dark. The minutes pass, and the meager light in the room fuses with the shadow. The light in the room is faint. The man writes, and as he writes, an invisible grayness slowly covers the table. The man grows impatient and, as the moments pass, thinks there will not be enough time to finish before both the room and the paper will become too dark. From time to time, when he tries to reread his own writing, it seems that some of the words have dissolved in the gray of the paper. Even so, he can still understand them. He feels he is wandering. As he goes on writing and looks back at what he has written, he senses there are more sentences that are incomprehensible than sentences he can decipher. The man is within himself. When he comes outside to read what he has written, he finds it difficult to make out the shapes on the paper. Words that evoke something, a face, a shadow. Perhaps a shadow or a face that evokes a word. The ink that draws the sentences merges imperceptively with the darkening gray of the paper. The man looks toward the window and tries to imagine that moment when the pressure of a thumb shapes a hollow which is also an eyelid. When the edge of the mouth is indistinguishable from the lips, when the forehead does not meet the eyebrow. Everything happens within. The man writes quickly, believing that the best words are those worn away at the edges. He searches for expressions that have linguistic form and can describe the form of a cheekbone. From within the shadows and the writing, he thinks he recognizes a face that immediately disappears.

He pauses for a moment and imagines that if he turned on the light, he would have to decipher the meaning of the sentences he wrote barely half an hour ago, sentences coming one after another that he has forgotten. He is surprised to observe that on one of the sheets of paper, where there is an "o" and an "i," he finds an "r" and a tilted "e." He is surprised because he does not remember writing the sentence that surrounds the word, and now, in the half light, he cannot make it out. He waits a moment and writes two almost identical sentences. Barely seeing them, he draws a line through both. He goes on smiling, thinking how he will be able to write something very quickly about something very mute. The man leans back in his chair thinking about the moment when the light was a bridge almost imperceptibly crossing the room, the light which has now gone. While staring at the table, the man falls asleep. After a while, he awakens to the sound of his daughter and a friend playing at the other end of the hall. The entire room is dark. The man turns on a lamp. He looks at the pages on the table and thinks he should write the text he promised to write about Medardo Rosso.

A Standard Introduction to Lectures

First published as "A Standard Introduction to Lectures," Gagarin 1, no. 1 (2000): 3–4.

1.

I would like to begin with a story, or, perhaps, with a fictitious encounter between the man that I am now, in this late summer afternoon, and the man that I am not yet, but will be when I read aloud these very same words. I have stopped and I have looked to the top of the page. I have scratched a line. I rewrite: I will begin with a story. An encounter between the man who is now sitting at this table, writing, waiting, listening to Schumann on the radio, and the man who will read these lines aloud.

I know that both of them will have an encounter, not fortuitous, but certainly brief, in two weeks' time, in the same room where I will be reading this lecture. Now, seated here behind my desk, I want to imagine that room. The room where I will pronounce these very same words. Where I will hear my own voice, reading aloud the lines that I am writing now.

Certainly I will make mistakes, but departing from this subtle fact, I begin to write . . . to speak.

Allow me to imagine this room.

A rectangular room, spacious, extended towards the back, with various narrow windows. Various rows of chairs, arranged with military precision. Just in front of me, there, where I will be standing, is a wide wooden table. With a microphone atop, always uncomfortable. Maybe the walls are white and the ceiling is delicately covered with tiny filigree. And that very table where I will read these lines, perhaps will have rounded edges, like my table. And nevertheless, sitting here, I know that I will not succeed in imagining the arabesque of the ceiling, the color of these walls. If the door is to the right or at the back. If it is open or closed. This room does not yet exist in my mind.

2.

I have stopped writing. Today is today. I have looked out of the window. To the branches of the poplars.

In front of me. To the table where I am writing now. Where I can also hear my voice, but differently, dwelling inside itself, muted, still. Just in front of me, simply framed, there is an early print of the Guarana River designed by Yago Levinas around 1550. There, where the Guarana finds the Ocean, there are tiny sailboats strolling indifferently along the Seadragon. The river sides are covered with exotic plants and the trees, meticulously drawn, are covered with schematic clouds that indicate the direction of the winds. Every time I get bored, or lose myself in thought, I look at that river and follow it, from its beginning to its mouth emptying into the Ocean.

3.

I remember having read in one of his books that Robert Louis Stevenson, who was capable of imagining Treasure Island while he was sitting in front of a child's cartography, that in the room where a writer works, there should always be one table covered with maps, plans, and travel books. A second table where he writes, and a third one that should always remain empty.

If the last will of all metaphors is to establish an analogy, draw a resemblance, reproduce in the mirror of words a similarity that allows one to forget that the image is only an image, then it would be possible to state that each of those three tables has an analogy beyond itself. Let me explain myself. The second table that Stevenson mentions: a table of Work, this is right now. The room where I write. Where I narrate and contradict myself. Where I attend to the mechanisms of creation, like a witness. The third table: the empty table, then, would be where I will speak in two weeks. An empty room that today does not exist as yet. Both tables, both rooms exist in an identical space and at the same time distant from one another. The last of the three tables is the first that Stevenson mentions. The one that is covered with topographical plans, with maps, with travel books. A table that in a certain way is a metaphor of itself. In chess terminology, it would be like a castling position. A table that is a stage constructed solely for disappearing. As if it were a magic trick. A disappearing act. He who sits there, is no longer there.

This table covered with maps, then, would be, in this play of analogies, the theme of this lecture: "The space between the man that I am, and the one that I am not yet."

Plates

Spiral Staircase, 1984, cat. no. 2

PAGE 82:

Juan Muñoz's studio, Madrid, 2001

Untitled (Balcony on Orange Paper), 1984, cat. no. 3

Untitled (Balcony on Orange Paper with Steps), 1984, cat. no. 4

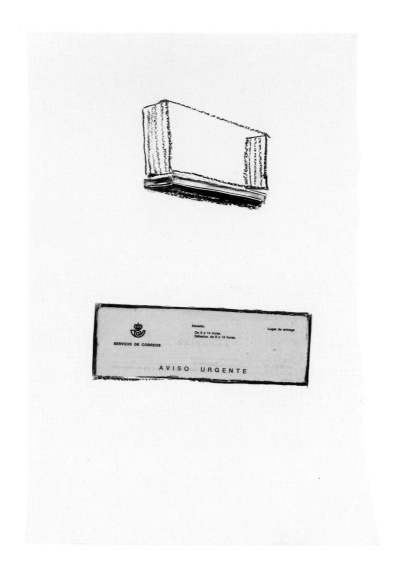

Untitled (Balcony with Death Notice), 1984, cat. no. 5

Untitled (Balcony with Fire), 1984, cat. no. 6

Untitled (Balcony with Smudged Right Side), 1984, cat. no. 7

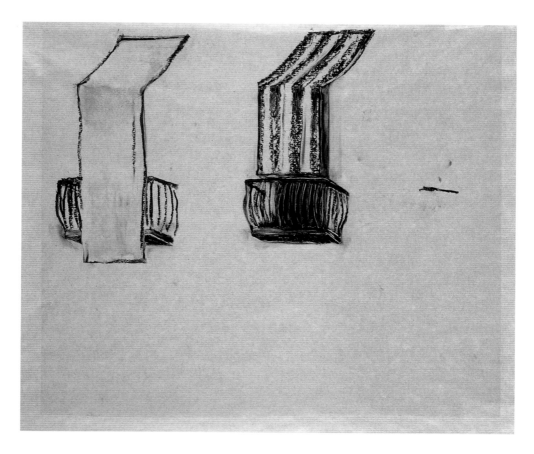

Untitled (Double Balcony with Blinds), 1984, cat. no. 8

Untitled (Double Side-by-Side Balcony), 1984, cat. no. 9

Untitled (Triple Balcony), 1984, cat. no. 10

If Only She Knew, 1984, cat. no. 1

Used Balcony (Small Balcony with Figure), 1984, cat. no. 11

Minaret for Otto Kurz, 1985, cat. no. 12

PAGES 94–95:

Hotel Declercq I–IV, 1986, cat. nos. 14–17

Double Balcony, 1986, cat. no. 13

PAGES 96–97:

The Wasteland, 1986, cat. no. 19

One Month Before, 1986, cat. no. 18

The Prompter, 1988, cat. no. 24

Dwarf with Three Columns, 1988, cat. no. 22

I Saw It in Marseilles, 1987, cat. no. 20

The Other Banister, 1988, cat. no. 23

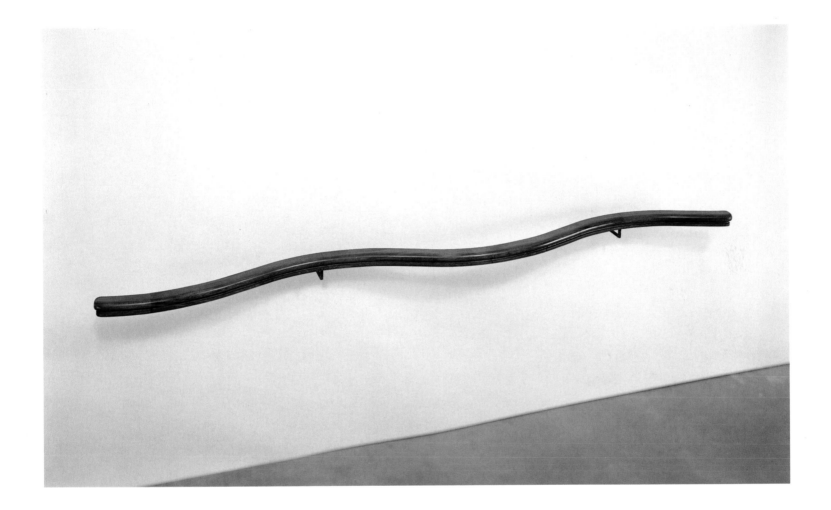

De Sol a Sol, 1990, cat. no. 33

Banister, 1991, cat. no. 35

Untitled, 1987, cat. no. 21

Ventriloquist Looking at a Double Interior, 1988

(second version, 2001), cat. no. 26

Raincoat Drawing, 1990, cat. no. 34

Raincoat Drawing, 1991, cat. no. 42

Raincoat Drawing, 1991, cat. no. 43

Raincoat Drawing, 1988, cat. no. 25

Raincoat Drawing, 1989, cat. no. 28

Raincoat Drawing, 1989, cat. no. 29

Raincoat Drawing, 1989, cat. no. 27

Raincoat Drawing, 1989, cat. no. 31

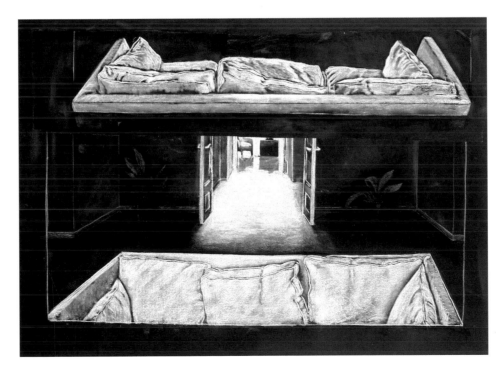

Raincoat Drawing, 1991, cat. no. 41

Raincoat Drawing, 1995, cat. no. 52

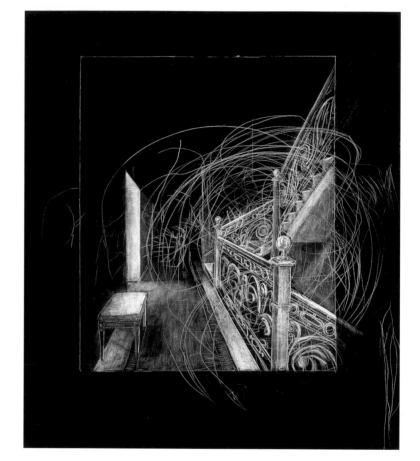

Raincoat Drawing, 1989, cat. no. 32

Raincoat Drawing, 1992, cat. no. 46

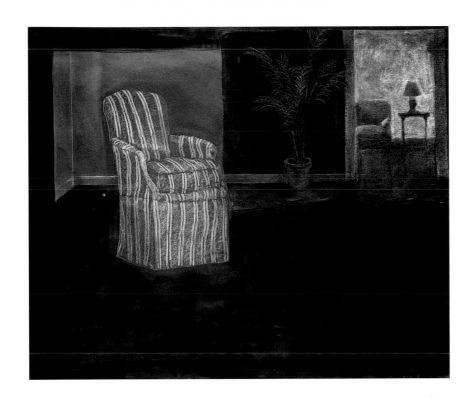

Raincoat Drawing, 1995, cat. no. 51

Raincoat Drawing, 1994, cat. no. 50

Raincoat Drawing, 1989, cat. no. 30

Raincoat Drawing, 1992–93, cat. no. 47

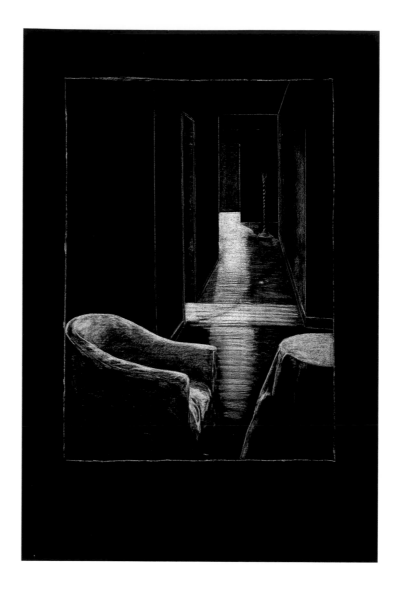

Raincoat Drawing, 1991, cat. no. 44

Window Shutters with Hinges, 1991, cat. no. 45

PAGES 120–21:

Conversation Piece I–V, 1991, cat. nos. 36–40

Stuttering Piece, 1993, cat. no. 48

Living in a Shoe Box (For Konrad Fischer), 1993–95, cat. no. 49

Elevator, 1996, cat. no. 53

PAGES 128–29:

Five Seated Figures, 1996, cat. no. 54

Loaded Car, 1998, cat. no. 56

Towards the Corner, 1998, cat. no. 57

PAGES 134–37:

Many Times, 2000, cat. no. 58

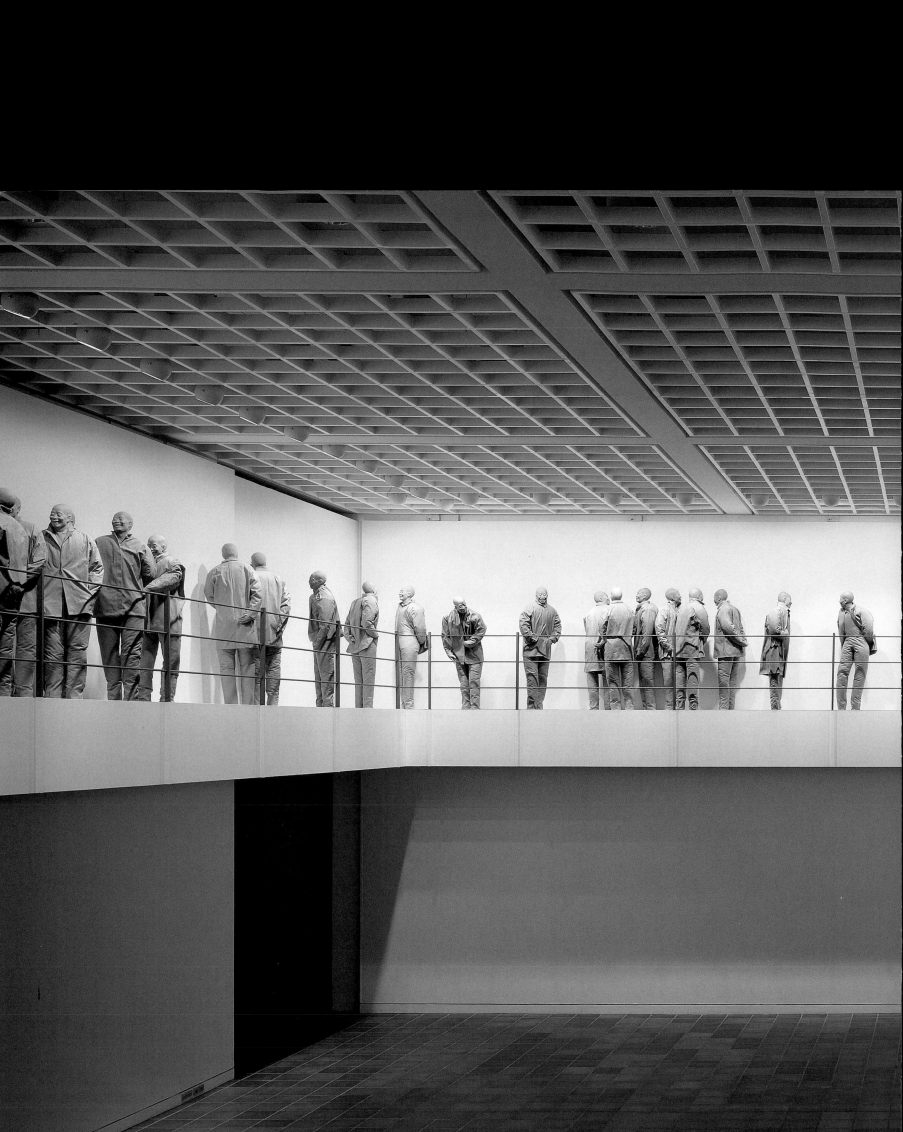

Figure Hanging from One Foot, 2001, cat. no. 59

Hanging Figure, 1997, cat. no. 55

Catalogue
of the Exhibition

1. **IF ONLY SHE KNEW**
    1984
    Iron, stone, and wood
    69^{1}/$_{2}$ x 13 x 13 in. (176.5 x 33 x 33 cm)
    Private collection, New York
    (Page 90)

2. **SPIRAL STAIRCASE**
    1984
    Iron
    18^{1}/$_{4}$ x 6^{3}/$_{4}$ x 7 in. (46.4 x 17.2 x 17.8 cm)
    The Art Institute of Chicago, Fractional
    Gift of the Neisser Family, Judith
    Neisser, David Neisser, and Kate Neisser,
    and Stephen Burns in memory of
    Edward Neisser
    (Page 84)

3. **UNTITLED (BALCONY ON
    ORANGE PAPER)**
    1984
    Oilstick on plastic film on paper
    19 x 23 in. (48.3 x 58.4 cm)
    The Art Institute of Chicago, Margaret
    Fisher Endowment
    (Page 85)

4. **UNTITLED (BALCONY ON
    ORANGE PAPER WITH STEPS)**
    1984
    Oilstick on plastic film on paper
    19^{1}/$_{2}$ x 20^{1}/$_{2}$ in. (48.9 x 52.1 cm)
    Courtesy of the artist and Marian
    Goodman Gallery, New York
    (Page 85)

5. **UNTITLED (BALCONY
    WITH DEATH NOTICE)**
    1984
    Oilstick on plastic film on paper
    27^{1}/$_{2}$ x 19^{5}/$_{8}$ in. (69.9 x 49.9 cm)
    Courtesy of the artist and Marian
    Goodman Gallery, New York
    (Page 86)

6. **UNTITLED
    (BALCONY WITH FIRE)**
    1984
    Oilstick on plastic film on paper
    24^{1}/$_{2}$ x 18 in. (62.2 x 45.7 cm)
    Courtesy of the artist and Marian
    Goodman Gallery, New York
    (Page 87)

7. **UNTITLED (BALCONY
    WITH SMUDGED RIGHT SIDE)**
    1984
    Oilstick on plastic film on paper
    22 x 17^{1}/$_{2}$ in. (55.9 x 44.5 cm)
    Courtesy of the artist and Marian
    Goodman Gallery, New York
    (Page 87)

8. **UNTITLED (DOUBLE
    BALCONY WITH BLINDS)**
    1984
    Oilstick on plastic film on paper
    18^{3}/$_{8}$ x 26^{3}/$_{4}$ in. (46.7 x 68 cm)
    The Art Institute of Chicago, Margaret
    Fisher Endowment
    (Page 88)

9. **UNTITLED (DOUBLE
    SIDE-BY-SIDE BALCONY)**
    1984
    Oilstick on plastic film on paper
    18 x 27 in. (45.7 x 68.6 cm)
    Courtesy of the artist and Marian
    Goodman Gallery, New York
    (Page 88)

10. **UNTITLED (TRIPLE BALCONY)**
    1984
    Oilstick on plastic film on paper
    27^{9}/$_{16}$ x 19^{11}/$_{16}$ in. (70 x 50 cm)
    Private collection
    (Page 89)

11. **USED BALCONY (SMALL
    BALCONY WITH FIGURE)**
    1984
    Steel and wood
    37 x 19^{7}/$_{8}$ x 7^{1}/$_{4}$ in. (94 x 50.5 x 18.4 cm)
    Collection of Marilyn Oshman, Houston
    (Page 91)

12. **MINARET FOR OTTO KURZ**
    1985
    Iron, wood, and rug
    47^{1}/$_{4}$ x 11^{13}/$_{16}$ x 15^{3}/$_{4}$ in. (120 x 30 x 40 cm)
    Collection of Francis de Beir
    (Page 92)

13. **DOUBLE BALCONY**
1986
Iron
Top balcony: $20^1/2$ x 36 x $7^7/8$ in. (52 x 91.5 x 20 cm); bottom balcony: $16^{15}/16$ x $36^1/4$ x $8^1/4$ in. (43 x 92 x 21 cm)
Collection Fondation Cartier pour l'art contemporain, Paris
(Page 95)

14. **HOTEL DECLERCQ I**
1986
Iron
$39^3/8$ x $27^9/16$ x $27^9/16$ in. (100 x 70 x 70 cm)
Collection of Marvin and Elayne Mordes, Baltimore
(Pages 94–95)

15. **HOTEL DECLERCQ II**
1986
Iron
$39^3/8$ x $27^9/16$ x $27^9/16$ in. (100 x 70 x 70 cm)
Collection of Eddy de Jaek
Exhibition copy
(Pages 94–95)

16. **HOTEL DECLERCQ III**
1986
Iron
$39^3/8$ x $27^9/16$ x $27^9/16$ in. (100 x 70 x 70 cm)
Collection of Linda and Jerry Janger, Los Angeles
(Pages 94–95)

17. **HOTEL DECLERCQ IV**
1986
Iron
$39^3/8$ x $27^9/16$ x $27^9/16$ in. (100 x 70 x 70 cm)
Collection of Mimi Dusselier, Belgium
(Pages 94–95)

18. **ONE MONTH BEFORE**
1986
Wood, stone, and terracotta
$41^3/4$ x $20^7/8$ x $11^{13}/16$ in. (106 x 53 x 30 cm)
Collection of Carol and Arthur Goldberg
(Page 98)

19. **THE WASTELAND**
1986
Bronze, steel, and linoleum
Dimensions variable
Collection of Marvin and Elayne Mordes, Baltimore
(Pages 96–97)

20. **I SAW IT IN MARSEILLES**
1987
Wood and metal
$5^1/8$ x $64^{15}/16$ x $2^3/4$ in. (13 x 165 x 7 cm)
Collection of Pepe Cobo, Seville
(Page 101)

21. **UNTITLED**
1987
Wood and metal
$5^1/2$ x $57^1/16$ x $4^5/16$ in. (14 x 145 x 11 cm)
Carlos and Rosa de la Cruz Collection
(Page 105)

22. **DWARF WITH THREE COLUMNS**
1988
Terracotta
$92^1/2$ x $59^1/16$ x $78^3/4$ in. (235 x 150 x 200 cm)
Rubell Family Collection, Miami
(Page 100)

23. **THE OTHER BANISTER**
1988
Wood and metal
$4^5/16$ x $86^5/8$ x $5^1/2$ in. (11 x 220 x 14 cm)
Private collection, Madrid
(Page 102)

24. **THE PROMPTER**
1988
Papier-mâché, bronze, wood, linoleum, and steel
Dimensions variable
Collection of the artist
(Page 99)

25. **RAINCOAT DRAWING**
1988
Mixed media on fabric
$55^1/8$ x $39^3/8$ in. (140 x 100 cm)
Collection of the artist
(Page 110)

26. **VENTRILOQUIST LOOKING AT A DOUBLE INTERIOR**
1988; second version, 2001
Resin, motor, silicone, wood, and mixed media on fabric
Drawings: 58 x $39^3/8$ in. (146.5 x 100 cm) each; figure: $24^{13}/16$ x $9^{13}/16$ x $9^{13}/16$ in. (63 x 25 x 25 cm)
Collection of the artist
(Page 107)

27. **RAINCOAT DRAWING**
1989
Mixed media on fabric
$55^1/8$ x $70^7/8$ in. (140 x 180 cm)
Bouwfonds Kunststichting, Hoevelaken
(Page 112)

28. **RAINCOAT DRAWING**
1989
Mixed media on fabric
$55^1/8$ x $39^3/8$ in. (140 x 100 cm)
Collection of Marsha Fogel
(Page 110)

29. **RAINCOAT DRAWING**
1989
Mixed media on fabric
$59^1/16$ x $78^3/4$ in. (150 x 200 cm)
Collection of Lena and Bernard Dubois
(Page 111)

30. **RAINCOAT DRAWING**
1989
Mixed media on fabric
$45^{11}/16$ x 38 in. (116 x 96.5 cm)
Private collection
(Page 116)

31. **RAINCOAT DRAWING**
1989
Mixed media on fabric
$39^3/8$ x $55^1/8$ in. (100 x 140 cm)
Collection of the artist
(Page 112)

32. **RAINCOAT DRAWING**
1989
Mixed media on fabric
$55^1/8$ x $39^3/8$ in. (140 x 100 cm)
Collection Raymond Learsy
(Page 114)

33. **DE SOL A SOL**
1990
Wood and metal
4 x $104^1/8$ x $12^1/4$ in. (10.2 x 264.5 x 31.1 cm)
The LeWitt Collection, Chester, Conn.
(Page 103)

34. **RAINCOAT DRAWING**
1990
Mixed media on fabric
$59^1/8$ x 48 in. (150 x 121.9 cm)
Collection of Anita and Burton Reiner
(Page 108)

143

An Interview with Juan Muñoz *Paul Schimmel*

Juan Muñoz spoke with Paul Schimmel on September 18, 2000.

PAUL SCHIMMEL When did you become interested in art?

JUAN MUÑOZ When I was about fourteen, my father hired a private teacher for my brother and myself named Santiago Amón. He taught Latin at our school and, as it happened, he was also the art critic for *El País*, the Spanish daily newspaper, and *Nueva Forma*, an important art journal.

PS Who were the artists who were your teacher's passion?

JM The Dutch Neoplasticists—artists such as Piet Mondrian and Theo van Doesburg. I came to admire Mondrian's deep belief in and passion for art. I was in awe of it.

PS Was going to museums a part of your life?

JM No. In fact, I didn't want to be an artist. My brother was a very skillful draftsman, and he took painting classes at home. But he gave it up.

PS You ran away from home when you were seventeen and went to London. Had you finished high school?

JM Yes. I was going to study architecture at university in Madrid. I did it for about two months and then gave it up. Spain at that time, about 1970, under Franco, had a very repressive culture.

PS How long did you stay in London?

JM About five years.

PS When you were there, did you go to the museums and galleries?

JM Not much in the first few years, and only on Sundays because I worked during the week. But the training I had received at fourteen, fifteen, sixteen—both in school and privately from Amón—was immense. I was incredibly lucky to receive that knowledge at that time in my life.

PS Did you go to school in London?

JM Later. I spent a year in Stockholm, where I had very left-leaning friends. I was very close to left-wing politics at the time. Afterwards, I came back to London and received a British Council scholarship to study printmaking. I later got a Fulbright to study printmaking at Pratt Institute in New York.

PS Your first show wasn't until 1984, was it?

JM Yes.

PS So you weren't on the fast track.

JM I was very slow. I spent one year in New York, and I made one drawing.

PS Between 1975 and 1980, did you know that you were an artist?

JM Yes, but I could not convince myself that what I did was of any importance.

When I started making the architectural maquettes, I began to realize there might be something that belongs to me.

PS I was looking at your work from 1984 to 1986. The trajectory is laid out right there. There are certain kinds of relations to architecture, there is the use of the figure, there is the willingness to deceive the viewer. Something must have been building up until 1984, because you have a complete repertoire within the next two years.

JM As I said, I spent one whole year in New York, and I made one drawing. I would walk through the streets scanning every image. I would go endlessly to shows and libraries. But I just didn't see work that I could relate to. From the age of seventeen to twenty-seven, I traveled a lot and produced very little. Much later, in 1982 or '83, when I returned to Spain, I stopped traveling and finally set up a studio. That's when I started making objects.

PS Of the generation of sculptors who are now in their mid-forties, you seem to have been the first, before Robert Gober, Charles Ray, Kiki Smith, Stephan Balkenhol, or Thomas Schütte, to work with the figure. Between 1985 and 1990, there was a shift toward the figure. When you first made figurative work in 1984, what precedents were you looking at?

JM I was looking at the world, trying to feel the reverberation of images outside of me that I could establish a connection with. I think that every artist goes through a time of flipping through the pages of the newspaper, hoping that an image will resonate. There was one event that was very important to me in this respect. After I moved back to Spain, there was this man near my house who sold garden sculpture. I didn't consider him a sculptor. I liked this contradiction because I was a sculptor who couldn't make a sculpture, and this man, whom I didn't consider a sculptor, considered himself a sculptor, and he produced a lot. He made cement lions and other statues for gardens. I bought a couple of things from him and cut and destroyed parts of his work to manufacture a work of my own.

PS That work was also conceptually driven. You took some work of his, cut it off, removed it from its original context, and relocated it to a new one.

JM I had studied art history, and this man knew nothing of art history. He just made these things in cement for the garden. But nevertheless, he had a conviction, and I loved that. I was very jealous of his capacity to assume that he was a sculptor when, in fact, I was spending years trying to make sculpture and couldn't figure out how to do it. So I took part of his language and destroyed it in order to formulate my own language. Soon thereafter I began to concentrate on the balcony sculptures.

PS The balconies are absolutely full-grown, mature works. They presume a figurative element, and they manipulate architecture in a very theatrical way. They activate space by transforming its scale. By putting a balcony on the wall, you change its scale. All of a sudden, the room becomes the sculpture. That has a precedent in Minimalism and Conceptual art.

JM I don't think I was aware of what was happening; I just knew that I had the need to start constructing figures. People were very reluctant to accept figurative sculpture at that time, which was very strange because painting and photography were nearly always figurative.

PS To do figurative work, you had to go against the tide.

JM My figures—the dwarves, ventriloquist's dummies—were, from the beginning, always conceptually oriented. I use architecture to give a "theatrical" frame of reference to the figure. I think we use the word "theatrical" to describe something that doesn't necessarily deal with theater itself. I don't remember having gone to the theater more than ten times in my life.

PS In this regard, I think of your willingness to call the objects you make statues instead of sculptures and to embrace the notion of spectacle and effect.

JM I remember being called a storyteller in the early 1990s, and therefore being accused of not really being an artist. But there's nothing wrong with being a storyteller.

PS Many of your works are in fact experienced like stories in which the spectator is choreographed in a very manipulative way. You're very clear about drawing them in, moving them around the spaces along a prescribed plan. I see that as part of your sculpture.

JM I am basically against interactive approaches to modern art. The idea of touching art seems to me completely wrong. For me, a good sleight-of-hand trick requires that you have the spectator in front of you. He cannot be behind you because he will see the trick. I do want the spectators to move in a certain direction, but that's so that the trick will be effective and so that the spectator can see the wonder of it and not get involved with the mechanisms.

PS Don't you see, Juan, that this can drive the more classically oriented modernist crazy? That you could call a sculpture a "trick" I find fascinating in itself. The radicalism of how you can embrace theater on the one hand, figuration on the other. A sleight of hand is a very beautiful thing, but should a sculpture be a sleight of hand?

Page 144: Juan Muñoz in a performance of *A Man in a Room, Gambling*, BBC Studio One, London, 1997

JM I think that a great painting is also a great fabrication. What you're looking at is an illusion. Beginning in the Renaissance, the great masters invented something that did not exist in space. And I think that marks the big change from Giotto to us. This is our great tradition: the creation of space in painting. Historically, sculpture has suffered tremendously because it has not activated space in the way that painting has. It's only with modernism, and with artists such as Robert Smithson and Richard Serra, that sculpture finds its central voice, because space is activated. The idea of going around and around in circles, as in Smithson's *Spiral Jetty*, so that you might not be so sure where you are at any one time, is a wonderful trick. It's like a labyrinth, but one without walls. From that moment, sculpture became central to modern art. The difference between these artists and myself is illustrated by Frank Stella's famous remark, "What you see is what you see." For me, what you see is not what it seems to be.

PS From Jannis Kounellis you learned about the column.

JM From Kounellis I learned that the repertoire should be extremely open— that you should not exclude anything to create the illusion. Kounellis is very theatrical. I also share with him this sense of being embedded in history.

PS You did a piece about card tricks. This seemed like a very autobiographical work. It's as if you were confirming that you embrace sleight of hand.

JM A collector once told me that I was a trickster. And I felt that there was nothing wrong with being a trickster. In a way, that's great.

PS But being a trickster has such negative connotations, which you work apart. Your card tricks and your sleights of hand—this is your language, the edginess that counters the beauty of your work.

JM For years I used to carry a switchblade in my pocket wherever I went. I'd have my hand in my pocket and I would be touching this knife. It was about an inner violence that I always had inside. I eventually stopped carrying this knife because I realized that it was getting a little neurotic, and I shifted to a deck of cards. I don't know if I'm answering your question.

PS You are. That certain kind of violence that you describe is a subject you keep coming back to. It's a muted violence. Figures who can't walk, see, or speak.

JM I grew up in an environment no more violent than that of my friends. But I realized later that violence was coming into the work. The violence has to do with my memory and with my fascination. People who have experienced violence are activated by violence.

PS In some ways, the violence balances the beauty of your work, your wonderful way of touching things. Dealing with rather tough subjects in a very beautiful way somehow makes the work tougher.

JM Yes. I had great difficulty convincing myself, for example, that I could make the ballerina. I was frightened by making such a romantic figure. But I felt like there was this inherent violence in the piece. The ballerina was muted and bound, forever moving and forever going nowhere.

PS These are all uncanny figures. They cannot do what they're supposed to do.

JM They tell you that they wish they could do more than they do. I don't think that my figures are so mute. I think that they are trying to articulate things.

PS You create a very twisted beauty. This has a long tradition in Spanish painting— Diego Velázquez's dwarves, Francisco de Goya's hollowed-out eyes.

JM I try to make the work engaging for the spectator. And then unconsciously, but more interestingly, I try to make you aware that something is really wrong. When I started making the smiling Chinese statues, I had two assistants who told me that they didn't like to be left alone at night in the studio with all these figures.

PS I want to ask you about installation art, because from the beginning your sculpture has always existed within an environment. Its ideal setting seems to be architectural. You were going to study architecture.

JM That's true. I still try to read about architecture whenever possible.

PS When I first met you, you had figured out how to control the environment in which your sculptures would be viewed by conceiving them as part of an architectural space.

JM The architecture behaves as a backdrop to the figures. For example, I learned from Carl Andre that the floor was important in the activation of space. But I make optical floors because they help me to magnify the inner tension of the figure. They create a psychological space for the figure that permeates the spectator's perception.

PS These floors are very psychologically disorienting.

JM They are make-believe. With the optical floors, you feel that your eye is fooling you. They construct a mise-en-scène that tells you that you shouldn't trust your eye, that calls into question the act of looking, that makes you uncertain of what you see—and who you are.

PS That's the real honesty of the work. You say that you are playing a trick.

JM And I'm explaining the trick. The explanation has as much wonder as the trick itself.

PS "A Place Called Abroad," your 1996 exhibition at Dia in an industrial warehouse in New York, was by far the most complex and theatrical series of installations you've ever made.

JM For Dia, I was invited to develop the floor plans for my installation. I decided to incorporate but also to cut through the architecture of the preceding exhibition, which had been devoted to Dan Flavin. The emphasis on complete freedom in modern art—the idea that you can do whatever you want—I find very boring. I like the idea of doing something for a given problem. To pick up on something you were saying about the Dia project, presenting the devices of the trick is part of the artwork itself.

JM Probably not. I'm very suspicious of those who try to prove their "manliness." As they say in Spain, the barking dog is the one that doesn't bite. I'm always suspicious of this outspoken physicality.

PS But every time you push your work in the direction of illusionism, you run the risk of being criticized as a prop man. That's been one of the hallmarks of the generation of artists that includes you, Gober, Ray—artists who take on the monumental heroism Serra still represents.

Three-Card Trick, 1995

PS That's the theatrical aspect of your work, and it's very interesting. The notion of the architecture as a prop. The manipulation of light in a very theatrical, chiaroscuro way.

JM I'm trying to open sculpture to a larger frame of reference by including optical illusions. It seems necessary to me in order to reject the obsession with the physical object. For example, I know that I can make a sculpture that appears to weigh one ton out of ten pounds of Polyester resin.

PS That's right. But that's a gutsy thing to say in an era still dominated by that type of sculpture. Sculpture forged in the belly of the beast. None of these tricks with light and space. That's not "manly" sculpture.

JM What is important is that each generation learns from the previous one. But what you learn might not be what you have been taught to learn.

PS You take their spiritual reverence toward space and turn it on its end by turning it into a set.

JM Yes. I was never interested in the physical form and the formal problems of sculpture as such. For example, I'm much more interested in what Donald Judd did at Marfa than in his sculpture. His final and most important creation was not rectangular sculptures placed in the middle of a museum. It was this gigantic environmental display. In the same way, what you learn from a Smithson is how to use mirrors and how a spiral jetty can become a neo-Romantic presentation of landscape.

PS In *Spiral Jetty* and at Marfa, the viewer is manipulated as a performer within a larger set.

JM That's exactly right. That's what I learned from them. American Minimalism was my perfect inspiration—an epistemological obstacle that I needed to grow strong.

PS The artist I keep thinking about in relationship to theater and also to the idea of the trickster is Yves Klein.

JM He was a wonderful artist.

PS He was very manipulative of the notion of theater. He wasn't so much a sculptor as a painter.

JM We've been talking about figurative presence. The feel of the way Klein imprints the woman's body into the canvas is wonderful, although Rauschenberg achieved similar results earlier. I still find Willem de Kooning's *Women* more poignant. Nonetheless, the physical outcome of Klein's performance is still brilliant.

PS You've also always had a strong interest in both words and sounds.

JM Yes, but I shifted. For years I used to write, though I have written very little in the last four or five years. I have written only one thing—"A Standard Introduction to Lectures." It's about the difference between the moment of writing and the moment of knowing that you will hear yourself speaking these words that you are writing now.

PS We were talking earlier about the difference between a statue and a sculpture. You have said that you want to make an autonomous statue.

JM I have always liked the dichotomy established in what has been considered one of the first modern sculptures, *Balzac*, by Auguste Rodin. There is one cast installed permanently outdoors in Paris, and most people pass right by it without paying any attention. It inhabits this place of transition—the street. I find this anonymity of the figure fascinating.

PS We have a certain reverence for sculptures that we don't have for statues.

JM As I told you earlier, when I started making sculpture in Spain after all the years of traveling, I used the works of a man who made garden statues and considered himself a sculptor. I think this is an interesting dichotomy.

PS As a sculptor, you seem to be consistently concerned with the boundaries of your own medium to the degree that you're trying to bring a kind of installation environment to the traditions of sculpture and statuary. You're constantly bumping up against the limitations of being a sculptor.

JM I would like to retain the illusionistic elements of painting and photography for my sculpture.

PS Regarding the notion of illusionism, you've mentioned on several occasions the Baroque architect Francesco Borromini.

JM I think he was the great master of the Baroque in that he was very aware of the intellectual implications of drawing a straight line. He was a master of deception. There was this sense of dislocation in his architecture that I admire. My floors also owe a debt to Italian Baroque architecture.

PS Looking and framing are consistent interests of yours, whether it's the framing of a floor, a window, or a door. When I walked through the Dia project, I kept thinking of Giorgio de Chirico—his emphasis on freezing time, which is a theme you've dealt with in your sculpture.

JM In de Chirico, the statue plays the role of frozen time—the indifference to time of those statues of public figures, generals, poets, and so on, in the middle of the square. He is an artist that it will be necessary to return to again and again. The way he can compress time and space and make it uncanny. He's unique in the history of modern art.

PS Did the Surrealist movement have a place in your early training?

JM No. I was always much more interested in and emotionally drawn to de Chirico. In my education, I remember that Naum Gabo was absolutely important. I would go to the Tate almost every weekend when I was in London and look at *Constructed Head*, his large sculpture. But, like de Chirico, I never felt very comfortable with the Surrealists. What the Surrealists brought about is the collision of two unfriendly objects in the hope that a dialectical crash would produce a new image. For me this seemed very unproductive. I never felt any real interest in Salvador Dalí or Joan Miró, and they're both Spaniards. But de Chirico was about the suspension of the moment of looking, about an indifference to reality that the Surrealists didn't have. De Chirico was more interested in this solitary moment. He freezes and crystallizes a moment in time and space.

PS You say that you have not been interested in Dalí or Miró. You are a Spanish artist, but, in some ways, you have no historical allegiance to Spain.

JM I was born in Spain, and I live there, but I don't feel any historical allegiance. Any artist of my generation in America has a whole history to trace back over the last forty years. I don't have that history, but instead a European history that is broken down. I therefore feel that displacement has always been my condition, my only state of being. I have always felt outside of the mainstream. But this has given me a lot of freedom to create my own language. When I came back to the very isolated landscape of Spain in 1982, when nothing was happening there, I was able to construct my own images in solitude. And to relate back to the international art world.

PS Your work is built on a foundation of your manipulation of Minimalism and on your interest in figuration, which, as you pointed out, was reemerging in painting in the 1970s and '80s, but was nowhere to be found in sculpture. Does that make you a postmodernist?

JM I don't think so. Postmodernism has always existed as a critique of modernism, and I have no critique. I am perfectly embedded in the same history that the modernist artists are. I can go back to Edvard Munch, just as I can to Jasper Johns. And, like Johns, I can travel from the clock to the bed and back again.

PS You identify with the bastard modernism that connects de Chirico with Alberto Giacometti.

JM As many other artists have always been, I have been sidetracked along the central journey.

PS When you say that Judd's work, at least as it's realized in its most perfect form at Marfa, is theater, isn't that a heretical remark? A postmodernist approach to his classic modernism?

JM Judd saw in an artist like Kazimir Malevich a formal problem—squares and other geometric shapes but never any symbolic value. He took from Malevich only what he was interested in. The black square had a symbolic value, but Judd did not want to look at it. I can take from Judd what I want and what I need, in the way he did with Malevich. I was more interested in the presentational devices of his work at Marfa than in the formal problem.

PS You may see something in Judd's work that he would deny, but it's still there and informs your work.

JM You don't reject the generations before you. You use them to your own advantage.

PS Many of your figures tend towards the exotic—dwarves, aliens, puppets, ballerinas, actors, Chinese figures. As the spectator, we are looking at the Other. We do not see ourselves.

JM My characters sometimes behave as a mirror that cannot reflect. They are there to tell you something about your looking, but they cannot, because they don't let you see yourself.

PS You are dealing with types, but not in a clinical and scientific way. Somehow your types are characters but they're not human.

JM Maybe without realizing it, I used the word "character." But then if I did so, it was more in the Pirandello sense—you know, the famous play *Six Characters in Search of an Author*. My characters are more in search of an author.

PS You talk a lot about Pirandello.

JM He had this wonderful thin, long, narrow face. But I don't go to the theater. Maybe we should be using the word "effect" instead of "theatricality."

PS Your interest in exoticism is what unites all these different characters together. We are unable to relate to them on a personal basis. They become like props. They stand in for the figure, but you don't read them emotionally. You do not connect to them on an intimate basis.

JM They don't try to coexist in the same space as the spectator. They are smaller than real figures. There is something about their appearance that makes them different, and this difference in effect excludes the spectator from the room they are occupying.

PS The spectator becomes like a prop.

JM At one moment this is the means of reversal that has taken place. The spectator becomes very much like the object to be looked at, and perhaps the viewer has become the one who is on view.

A Winter's Journey (detail), 1994

Sound, Sight, Statuary

Michael Brenson

I. SOUND

In Juan Muñoz's work, silence rules yet the presence of sound is inescapable. Sound seems to be in the pores of the silence, to permeate and consolidate it, disturb and inflict it. Muñoz's figures are preternaturally alert to sound. So are his walls, streets, and sofas, which are infused not only with a need to listen but also with a will to be heard. In the chambers, corridors, and courtyards of silence to which Muñoz's figures find themselves sentenced, the desire for—and *of*—sound provides evidence of cries and whispers, fortitude and dread, suppression and survival. The persistence of sound within this kingdom of silence gives Muñoz's sculptures, drawings, and installations a perpetual yearning and utterance.

In his introduction to *Juan Muñoz: Monologues and Dialogues*, James Lingwood, one of the artist's most devoted and articulate supporters, emphasized this paradoxical relationship between silence and sound. He referred to Muñoz's "muted world" and declared that his art is distinguished, "most particularly of all," by "the absence of sound."[1] Then Lingwood went on to describe all the sounds with which the book, and, by implication, the work, "resonate," including "the sound of the figure in the room" and the sound of "the artist laughing." In the interviews that follow, references to silence and stillness are as prevalent as they are in the rest of the Muñoz literature. But Muñoz acknowledges that creating an experience of inaudible sound is one of his ways of mobilizing stillness and silence. Referring to his 1994 "conversation piece" in a courtyard in Dublin (fig. 1), with its cliques of agitated figures, some trying to get their bearings, like villagers in the aftermath of a shooting, Lingwood said that "the whole arena of the work" seemed to have been "animated" by "perhaps one sound, a sudden noise." Muñoz responded: "A non-existent sound became the reference point. We used something invisible to organize what it was not possible to see."[2] Inaudible sound both animated and deepened the silence; the force of the silence, in turn, communicated the urgency of the inaudible organizing sounds.

Muñoz has planted evidence of sound everywhere. Since he was a child, he has made drawings and sculptures of ears. He has also made drawings and sculptures of mouths—detached from the eyes and face, open in ways that suggest talking, jeering, screaming, laughing, or perhaps just trying to remember, after speechless years, how the tongue is used. He has modeled and cast many figures in "conversation." One of his signature images is the ventriloquist's dummy in his 1986 *The Wasteland* (see cat. no. 19). Facing us from across the floor, this odd, sexless man-child sits alone on a ledge. The ventriloquist—the dummy's voice, its potential for sound—is gone, deported, or banished forever. In some of Muñoz's sculptures, lips move. In *Shadow and Mouth*, in the last room of the 1996–97 installation "A Place Called Abroad" at Dia Center for the Arts in New York, a figure sat by a wall, his mouth incessantly opening and closing, his body as intent as that of a fretful sinner talking into the partition of a confessional (see Benezra, fig. 19b). His silent speech suggested delirium, madness, or perhaps a mumbling monologue that was the only communication his situation permitted. Like the other figure, sitting erect at a nearby table, the entire large room, as stark as an asylum or interrogation chamber, seemed fixated on his inaudible chattering.

154

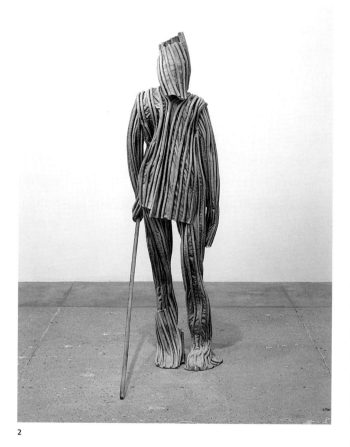

2

Silent speaking focuses many of Muñoz's other spaces as well. In his 1994–95 "conversation piece" just outside the Hirshhorn Museum and Sculpture Garden in Washington, D.C. (fig. 8), the private exchange among three clustered figures seems to have the power to decide the fates of the two solitary figures trying frantically to get access to what is being said. In Muñoz's 1999 installation *Blotter Figures* at New York's Marian Goodman Gallery (see fig. 2), a polyester resin figure pushed a stick ahead of him as if it were a shuffleboard cue, but the cue also suggested a blind man's cane, and

his path was determined by the silent conversation between two other figures just like him, their heads, legs, and arms also implied but invisible beneath their pleated, pajama-like clothing. Since the path of the figure with the cane was going to skirt them, the assumption was that he heard their conversation. In this installation, too, the composition was determined by sounds we could not hear, to whose vibrations the figures outside the conversation were as attuned as bats.

The spell of these silences is unbreakable. In most of Muñoz's work, actual sound is an unpardonable offense. Where there are instruments of sound, there is usually violence. Muñoz has been drawn to the minaret, which, he has said, "is the place of song, the dwelling place of the voice."[3] He has included objects, like drums, that symbolize emphatic sound, uninhibited noise. But the four-foot-tall minaret in his 1985 *Minaret for Otto Kurz* (cat. no. 12) is tipped and disabled: no one could sing on it or use it to call people to prayer. And his 1988 yellow *Wax Drum* (fig. 3) has been stabbed with a scissor. The message is clear: if you disobey the silence, you will be silenced. The desire for sound may seem irresistible but the prohibition against it will not be transgressed.

The sources of sound are multiple and surprising. The figures may need and want to speak and listen, but so do the environments in which they find themselves. While some figures converse and others don't, almost all the walls in Muñoz's installations seem to have the capacity to speak and listen. The chattering figure in "A Place Called Abroad" could be understood as talking *with* the wall. He may have been speaking to it incessantly because of his confidence it was listening. The other figure would probably not have been watching so intently if he had not believed he was in the presence of an actual exchange. Muñoz embedded in the experience of the work the sensation that the wall had ears, that it could communicate, and that it held essential information. Not only could the wall speak and listen, but it knew more than the figures. As a result of this silent conversation, all the walls in the stark interiors and street of this installation seemed invested with the power of speech and knowledge. The experience of its sound gave legitimacy both to the paranoia that seems

3

4

same; the threat is therefore always from an insider, even a family member. Because the figures in his "conversation pieces" tend to lean close and whisper, their interactions imply not the trusting exchange implied by the word "conversation" but something illicit. Muñoz's figures tend to be so self-absorbed, so indifferent to everything around them except information only they can hear and see, that what they exchange seem to be lethal secrets. Since these silent exchanges never involve all the figures, they usually seem to be at someone's expense. Betrayal and malice are the rule. The divisions between insiders and outsiders can make the sculptural spaces between and around the figures seem like precipices or trenches.

Everyone has good reason to be suspicious. It is not just that signs of terrorism are everywhere but that the border between play and torture has dissolved. In Muñoz's 1986 *Jack Palance at the Madeleine* (fig. 4), a weird little toy-like staircase seems to have been guillotined and a switchblade jammed into each of its two sections. In the 1987 *First Banister* (fig. 5), a knife is attached to the back of an object of architectural support on which the middle-aged and elderly at some of their most tired and vulnerable moments depend—suggesting a crueler version of the kind of trick kids might play on the old guy upstairs who yelled at them for making a racket. In the 1996 *Square (Madrid)* (see Benezra, figs. 18a–b), in the midst of the crowd of laughing, well-dressed Chinese men, as confident and cheerful as company families at the boss's exquisitely catered cocktail party, was an open area that suggested a space in which people they didn't like would be made to disappear. While these

to be the condition of many of Muñoz's figures and to their eagerness to be part of the conversation.

Muñoz was born in Madrid in 1953. He grew up during the waning years of the Spanish dictator Francisco Franco (1892–1975), under whose rule conspiracy and surveillance were commonplace, innumerable stories were repressed, and people who expressed themselves openly could indeed vanish. In his artistic world, suspicion is rampant, and everyone understands the danger of leaving tracks. Since almost all the figures in a given work have the same head, friend and foe look the

FIG. 5 *First Banister*, 1987

5

figures bring to mind the smugness of dictatorial regimes everywhere, in any era, the toy-like sedan tipped on its side in the 1998 *Loaded Car* (cat. no. 56) suggests acts of vandalism or civil disobedience by groups intent on defying the state. Violence is everywhere. Any act can be punished. Everything we say will be held against us sooner or later. It is hard to imagine anything, including laughter, that does not have a cruel or sinister edge.

Even when Muñoz includes actual sound in his work, silence rules. He may identify sound with the promise of acceptance and understanding, as well as with betrayal and malice, and his figures may be convinced that if they can finally enter the conversation, their exile will end, but when a work includes actual sound, it only reinforces the authority of the silence. In the 1993 *Stuttering Piece* (cat. no. 48), two small figures sit on resin boxes, condemned to listen again and again to a snippet of absurdist conversation, recorded in a café or bar.

"What did you say?"
"I didn't say anything."
"You never say anything. No. But you keep coming back to it."

Muñoz's 1992 BBC radio performance, *A Man in a Room, Gambling*, consisted of ten five-minute radio segments in which the artist, accompanied by music, or, on one occasion, by street sounds in Seville, explained card tricks. These explanations of magical acts that depend upon looking—and yet partly depend for their pleasure on their ability to undermine confidence in visual observation—were absurdist skits. They were broadcast just before the 11 pm news, the last news of the evening, the kind of program that gives a sense of normalcy to many people's lives. But these explanations of magic, spoken in a Spanish accent on a bastion of the English cultural establishment, just appeared one night and therefore seemed themselves to have magically materialized out of nowhere. In addition, the explanations promised transparency and then were so transparently manipulated to fit the theatrical conventions of five-minute radio presentations that the segments seemed doubly elusive. Matter-of-fact discussion led to punch lines to jokes no one seemed to have scripted. For example, in one segment, a Japanese man seemed to be trying simply to repeat the explanations in order to learn them, but sometimes he couldn't:

"Little finger."
"Little finger."
"Ring finger."
"Ring finger."
"Thumb."
"Little finger."

In the end, the explanations of tricks seemed themselves tricks, and the absurdity seemed to be at someone's expense, or at many peoples' expense, but whose?[4]

So when Muñoz's work does include sound, it does not lead to acceptance and understanding but to riddles that no one even knows how to ask. In the end, everyone is absurd and everyone is someone else's toy, cut off from the rules of the game, without access to the real language. Even when power seems right there, with the figures, as in *Square (Madrid)*, Muñoz lets us know that it is ultimately elsewhere. The laughing men have no feet. Like the solitary outsiders nearby, the members of the inner sanctums in the "conversation pieces" have small heads with disjointed arms and hands that often seem stuck on with sadistic casualness, and torsos made from sacks stuffed with cloth. Anchoring their bodies, in place of legs and feet, are big bulbous bases. These figures, like Muñoz's dancers, have been promised and then deprived of movement. They are doubly captive—within their immobile and ungainly bodies and within an environment infinitely more aware of them than they are of it. In Muñoz's world, every figure is outside the loop. Everyone is a victim of black magic or black humor, and no one knows where or what the real joker or magician is. The real conversation is always elsewhere. It is taking place somewhere—surely it is, it must be—but it cannot be heard.

II. SIGHT

Muñoz is an artful and mischievous storyteller. The instant we meet and are met by his sculptures or drawings, we enter a distinct world. His silences speak of juicy tales of punishment and intrigue. With his cast of misfits, his array of body parts, his bag of diabolical tricks, and his bizarre and expectant crime sets from which the author, and sometimes even the victims, have vanished, he is a master of the picturesque. But for all its narrative immediacy, his work is also distant, detached. Muñoz was a child under Franco, who pretty much obliged Spaniards to be hyper-conscious of their words and acts. He came into his own as an artist during a postcolonial, postmodern moment defined in the West, in part, by distrust of all systems of authority, including aesthetic systems, and by respect for the legitimacy of multiple perspectives. Muñoz does not want to let anyone take his or her response, gaze, or identity for granted. So even as he lures us in, he pushes us back. While we glance, stare, peep, and scrutinize, he, like his eminent compatriot Diego Velázquez, wants us to look at ourselves looking and consider the complexity and repercussions of the act of looking. Just as important, he wants us to know that as we are looking, we are always, in a sense, being looked at.

Muñoz is no less ingenious at provoking a hyperattentiveness to sight and consciousness than he is at provoking a hyperattentiveness to sound. When he turns an object we depend on, like a banister, into a site for a cruel prank or a terrorist act, he makes us look more closely at all sorts of everyday objects on which we depend. When he invites us to walk across floors whose dizzying patterns confuse figure and ground in ways that make the floors seem both vast and insubstantial— in effect, anti-floors—he also arouses greater consciousness of unavoidable aspects of our architectural environment about which we almost never think.

Muñoz is fascinated by narcissism. His images of figures preoccupied with their appearances both dramatize the impact of our obsessions with our own images and accentuate the distinction between looking and consciousness. Sara, the dwarf in high heels and dress, revels in her feminine grace in the 1996 *Sara in front of a Mirror* (fig. 6). The standing man with the hideously laughing or horrified face in the 1998 "Streetwise" installation in Santa Fe stood so close to his image in the mirror that he seemed on the verge of being devoured

158

6

by it. The eight-inch-tall figurine with the statuesque Playboy body and see-through skin-tight corset in the 1999 *Crossroads Cabinet October* (fig. 7) is so concerned with herself in the mirror that she does not even notice the well-dressed men in her presence. All of these figures are so fixated on their mirror images that they are oblivious to everything else, including their fixation.

Muñoz implicates us in this magnetic attraction and then makes us uneasy with it. The infectious self-absorption of his figures makes us want to look at ourselves in the mirror, but, like Edgar Degas and, even more, like Édouard Manet (for example, in his 1877 *Nana*, or, most famously, in his 1881 *Bar at the Folies-Bergère*), Muñoz often incorporates mirrors at such odd angles, and of such an uncomfortable size, that any desire to trust the authority of our own image is thwarted. For example, the small mirrors in which the sexy figurine is absorbed with her image on two of the ten shelves in *Crossroads Cabinet October* are arranged so that we can barely see ourselves in them, even when they are at eye height, and what we do see—fragments of our faces— seems so grotesquely oversized in relation to her eight-inch-tall body that the proportions of our "normal" body can seem as peculiar as a dwarf's. In *Sara in front of a Mirror*, Sara turns and looks at herself in a full-length mirror that seems way too large for her, and, as a result, our image beside hers in that mirror does not look right either. Our body seems every bit as strange as hers. Muñoz makes it impossible for us to see ourselves as we want to. Like Sara, we can never see ourselves apart from our desire. His sculpture compels us into con- sciousness and yet also lets us know that it has limits. In Muñoz's work, neither looking nor the consciousness of it is ever "natural."

Through narcissism, Muñoz emphasizes the role of point of view in what and how we see. In the penulti- mate room of "A Place Called Abroad" (see *Five Seated Figures*; cat. no. 54), one of the seated figures seemed to have just turned around and noticed himself in a large mirror tilted down toward him. He, too, was mesmer- ized by his image and by the act of looking. The mirror had such a grip on him that we wanted to look in it as well, but from our upright position we had to struggle to see ourselves in it, and we could not see ourselves from exactly his position. We could not see what he saw. It was hard to be unaware of the unbridgeable gap between our point of view and his.

There is still another eye in these works, and another point of view, and they are every bit as impor- tant as those of the viewers and figures. Muñoz's walls

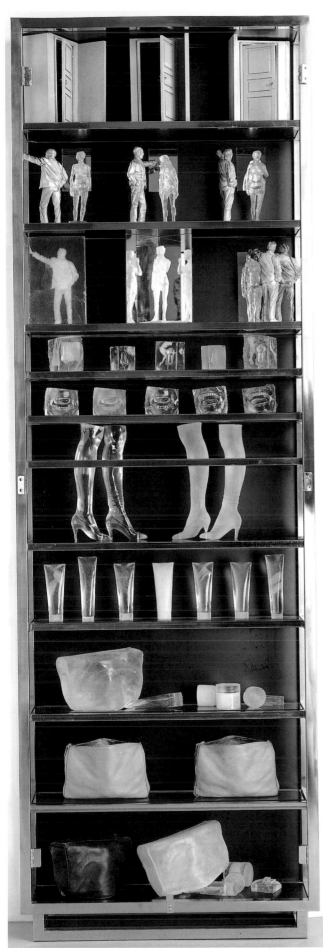

7

see as well as hear. And they see—as well as hear—differently and *more* than the figures. In "A Place Called Abroad," the intensity with which that seated figure jerked around his greyish, sandblasted body to look at himself in the clean square mirror and the discipline with which he held himself in that twisted position implied that something had communicated to him that he was being observed. It couldn't have been the four other seated figures, none of whom were looking at him or the mirror. So it must have been the looking glass, or the wall behind it, that was both looking at him and letting him know he was under observation. With one subtle device—in this case, a figure suddenly, inexplicably captured by his own image—Muñoz instilled a sense that the entire environment, including rooms and street, was ceaselessly looking, and that everyone within it was under surveillance. The stucco architecture, with its blank walls and its unfinished, sealed-off, or blind windows, seemed not only more aware than he or we but more aware than he and we can ever be. The figure turned, looked, and froze. He looked but could not see or recognize what was observing him. Looking and consciousness, looking and knowing, were distinct. Within the architecture, however, with its intense focus on the figures—its evident ability not only to look at them but also to know them—looking and consciousness seemed fused.

In Muñoz's outdoor "conversation pieces," whether the site is a Dublin courtyard or a Washington, D.C., lawn, the environment is also vastly more conscious than the figures in its midst. Because of the intense inwardness and sculptural concentration of the figures, because their disjointed, herky-jerky bodies are smaller and more vulnerable than those of most of the human beings who roam around them, and because some of them already seem subjugated by something invisible in their vicinity, the walls and windows and even the air around them seem to have been invested with the power to see and know. The environment seems to lean into the figures, thereby creating a sense that the pressure against them is being created by a concentrated awareness embedded in the architecture but not confined to it. This attention on the figures seems, in effect, the pressure of consciousness itself. The figures are always seen more than they see, more known then they know. Even as Muñoz insists on the necessity of human consciousness, he evokes an omniscient, godlike consciousness of which the consciousness of any human being is just a pitiful fragment—a consciousness so vast and pervasive that we, like the figures, will always be seen more than we see, more known than we know.

How do we characterize the consciousness permeating the architectural and environmental spaces in Muñoz's work? Is it still or simmering, good-natured or vindictive, tolerant or wrathful? Or all of this together? Certainly it is looking that truly sees—that knows—that everything in its midst. It is looking that puts the figures in their places and exposes their vulnerability and mortality and the limits of human perception. If this consciousness suggests a deity, is it an offspring of the New Testament Christ of universal brotherhood, forgiving and forgetting and encouraging peace on earth and good will toward everyone? Or is it rather an Old Testament patriarch, who, like an emperor or dictator, gets his kicks by taunting family and neighbors and devising jokes and traps with which to amuse himself and make his populace sufficiently appreciative of his desire to command and laugh? Is the supreme Muñoz consciousness, rather than being uncontaminated by human vanity, perversity, longing, and need, embedded in them? Is it perhaps even their source? And does it see—is it conscious of—itself? Muñoz's aesthetic space asks questions art does not usually ask: if there is a supreme consciousness that exists apart from human beings, out there somewhere, what is its identity? What

is its relationship to our desires and acts and to the consciousness of which we are capable?

III. STATUARY

Probably no single word could provide the key to art as intelligent and multi-layered as Muñoz's, but if there were one, it might be "statuary." Muñoz has used the word "statue" with a frequency and affection almost unheard of among modern and contemporary artists. Statuary *has* maintained a formative presence in modern and contemporary sculpture: the work of Constantin Brancusi, Julio González, Alberto Giacometti, David Smith, Louise Bourgeois, Tony Smith, George Segal, Magdalena Abakanowicz, Giovanni Anselmo, Richard Serra, Joel Shapiro, and Tony Cragg is hard to imagine without it. But this presence is so rarely acknowledged that "statuary" has been a largely forgotten word in twentieth-century aesthetics.[5] Certainly it conjures up the dreaded word "monument," which implies academic authority and official values. Throughout much of the post-World War II era, the gravity, mass, and labor identified with statuary have been widely accepted as enemies of sculpture that had to be overcome if it was going to be able to compete with the freedom and speed of painting and meet the challenges of industrial and technological upheaval and transformation. The frequency and affection with which the word is used by Muñoz, one of the most artistically and historically aware artists of his generation, is therefore not only personally but also historically revealing.

"Statue" is often assumed to be a synonym for "sculpture." In *Webster's New World College Dictionary*, sculpture is defined as (1) "the art of carving wood, chiseling stone, casting or welding metal, molding clay or wax, etc. into three-dimensional representations, as statues, figures, forms, etc.," and (2) "any work of sculpture, or such works collectively." "Statue" has different roots. The same dictionary indicates that it comes from the Latin words *"statua"* and *"statuere,"* which mean to set or place, both of which are forms of the Latin word *"stare,"* meaning to stand. So "statue" implies more than its dictionary definition as "the figure of a person or animal, or an imagined or abstract form, carved in stone, wood, etc., modeled in a plastic substance or cast in plaster, bronze, etc., esp. when done in the round rather than in relief."[6] A statue is firmly situated or planted. Its etymology suggests standing presence and with it a sense of place. While a statue does not have to be freestanding, it is most a statue when it is freestanding. So while a statue is a sculpture, "statue" and "sculpture" are not synonymous.

The statuary of ancient Egypt, Archaic Greece, ancient China, ancient India, and Olmec and Aztec Mexico is more idealized than naturalistic: if the statue is based on an actual person, that person is usually represented in an ennobling and often a heroic manner. Statuary tends to be economical and geometric; often its form suggests the cubic block from which many statues were carved. It is invariably monolithic: its closed, self-contained mass contributes to its aura of assurance and permanence. It is often frontal, which makes it seem as if the statue is facing visitors even as it retains its distance, looking at them but also through and beyond them. So while statues may resemble us, await and even desire us, and be made of earthly materials we encounter and use every day, like stone or wood, they seem more concerned with something else. In the process of acknowledging our presence and our needs, yet answering to a reality beyond us, statuary maintains the difference between mortality and immortality, temporal and eternal, human and divine.

Although the statues of ancient Egypt and Archaic Greece, in particular, have shaped my discussion of statuary here, any thorough consideration of a sculptural concept even more indestructible than any monument to a pharaoh or king—and of the place of statuary in Muñoz's work—must recognize the importance of those sculptural manifestations in which statuary and sculpture do seem synonymous. Think of ancient Roman sculptures like the *Augustus of Primaporta*, with its small striding legs that make the Roman emperor seem mobile and human, and yet a torso and head that seem to lift him above human behavior. Or of Republican paterfamilias portraits, so naturalistic that they look like men we meet in our homes and offices, yet seemingly in the grip of a supra-human authority.[7] Like the Augustus, they seem both controlling and controlled, both intellectually agile and puppets of something

about which they will never have more than limited information. No artist blurred the line between sculpture and statuary more profoundly than Michelangelo. His seated Moses, one of the most emblematic of all sculptures, is hyper-aware and an embodiment of dramatic emotion and potential action. But he is also a container of irresistible and forbidden energy that not even he can control, that threatens to burst the marble skin and punish the earth.[8]

In his interviews, Muñoz occasionally does make "statue" and "sculpture" synonymous, but when his uses of these words are examined together, it is clear that they have different meanings for him and that his idea of statuary depends in part on the monumental sculptures of religious civilizations. For example, he describes statuary as hieratic and frozen in time. "With one figure, nothing much is happening because nothing much can happen, and there's nowhere to go," he told Lingwood. "Time is moving, and then at a moment, it stands still. The figures are like statues, not sculptures. It's always about a position: the statuesque."[9] Speaking of the work of Georges Seurat, an early modernist admirer of Egyptian art, Muñoz said, "everyone is standing so still . . . and each one seems to be occupying a space of silence"—an image that evokes the motionlessness quiet that is a condition of the stone statuary of ancient Egypt, Sumeria, and the West.[10]

Muñoz wants his sculptures to communicate the sense of internal energy and self-containment that characterizes great statuary. "I wanted the figures to be very concentrated as if their strength came from inside," he said.[11] When he told Lingwood, "I want to make an autonomous statue but I don't seem to be able to," he revealed his desire to make a sculpture that, even as it may seem to be waiting for us and need us, preserves its independence from anyone in its presence, as well as his inability to make a sculptural figure that is not part of a tableau.[12] Again and again he comes back to this desire to make sculpture that will not seem dependent on the viewer. "I like to believe that the best work can exist without a spectator," he told Lingwood.[13] Speaking of the figures in the "conversation pieces," he said, "the fact that they are indifferent to the presence of the person who's in the room is very important to me."[14]

Again, "It should also remain separate from you. So no matter now much you look at it, it's still outside you."[15]

On occasion, Muñoz has identified this separateness and independence with the sensation of sound. The sound he imagines is not that of a sculpture talking because it is so lifelike, a fantasy or dream that has haunted sculptors since ancient Greece. (For example, Donatello and Michelangelo expected sculptures of theirs to talk.)[16] It is a different sound, more pervasive and sustained than speech. "You think of great pieces in great museums—whether there's anyone there or not, they keep emanating an incredible energy, visual energy," Muñoz has said. "I would like to make a humming sound in one of the pieces, only to be switched on at night when everybody's gone. Have it working only at night, then the moment you open the door, the piece stops humming."[17] The implication is that after his piece stops actually humming, not only it but every other sculpture in the room, perhaps even the room itself, would seem to vibrate with its absent presence, like a room just after a parent or lover has left.

In another interview with Lingwood, Muñoz returned to the idea of an internal hum, this time identifying its inner intensity with the blindness that he believes to be one of the conditions of figurative sculpture. He accepts the impossibility of creating a figure that seems actually to see. A number of his figures, like the ventriloquist's dummy in *The Wasteland*, or the dwarf in the 1988 *Dwarf with Three Columns* (cat. no. 22), do seem to be intently looking at us, and their look helps to pull us in, but as we approach them that look deadens and they seem self-absorbed. "It's always been said that statues are blind," Muñoz said. "You cannot represent the gaze convincingly in a three-dimensional way. Even in France in the eighteenth century when they made the most elaborate cuttings of the iris in the stone, the statues still seemed blind. When you look at these classical pieces from a certain distance, you might think for a second that the statue is looking, but it never does. The acceptance of this condition of blindness is important to the pieces. They are looking inwards, and that looking inwards automatically excludes the receiver, the person in front. The most successful statues give the impression that they are humming inside even though you can't hear them."[18]

The best statuary does seem to be humming. The impression depends upon a tension between a sculpture's desire to reach out and its inability actually to do so. With ancient Egyptian and Archaic Greek statues, the sculptural vitality of volume, surface, and light, and the feeling for the mobility of the face, particularly the mouth—the orifice that releases the voice into the world—make it seem as if the self-contained sculptural mass not only has its own life but also a need and will to speak. Yet this will, which becomes will by the force with which light grips the surface, thereby drawing out the sculptural interior, is so rigorously restrained within the geometrical block, and so inverted by the blindness of eyes that want to engage the world outside the sculpture but can't, that it seems both irresistible and imprisoned. Since the hum suggests an inner purr within the closed authority of the monolith, it gives the masculine authority of the statue a touch of softness, of feminine receptivity. It suggests a maternal engine confined within the stony patriarchal mass. The inner sound holds within it the promise of an exchange that could, in theory, take place, but never will. It makes immanence, perhaps incarnation, a reality, even while asserting religious and sculptural limits that cannot be transgressed.

In the 1990 "On a Square," one of his wryest and most evocative literary concoctions, Muñoz underlined the difference between statuary and academic sculpture and suggested statuary's radical potential.[19] Affirming its historical connection to ritual, and with it to the human capacity for revelation and repression, he underlined its ability to connect people to their deepest terrors and hopes. His focus was a more than two-meter-tall stone statue of the goddess Coatlique, which had once crowned "the Great Temple of Tenochtitlan," where an Aztec priest had ceremonially anointed it with blood and copal incense. "Found under the earth" in 1790, the statue was deposited in the showrooms of the Royal University of Mexico alongside "a large collection of plaster replicas of different Greek and Roman sculptures" that had been installed there a few years earlier. To the "doctors of the University," when situated "among the masterpieces of classicism," the statue "was an affront to the very concept of beauty." It was also politically dangerous: "Besides,"

FIG. 8 *Last Conversation Piece, 1994–95*

8

Muñoz wrote, "the goddess might revive such ideas among the Indians that the viceroys thought should preferably be forgotten."

Unlike the classical sculpture, the statue of Coatlique possesses a power and poetry to which no one is indifferent. For both the Catholic missionary, for whom the stone goddess was the "very incarnation of Evil," and the Aztec priest, for whom it was "the bearer of divine values," the statue represented "tremendous mystery" and "the presence of something supernatural."

In secular settings different from those for which it was made, the statue continues to ignite thoughts and feelings about life and death, although they are thoughts and feelings to which it now seems aloof. The statue of Coatlique also "remains indifferent to the plurality of interpretations made from the perspective of each period of history." Near the end of the essay-story, Muñoz wrote, "its immobility inspires a unique feeling: the enigma of the arousal of feelings." In the secular worlds of galleries and museums, far from the ritual sites for which it was created, statuary can seem both immediate and removed. The language of statuary can therefore arouse profound and visceral responses and yet leave them in a suspended state where it is possible to examine them and think about the sculptural conditions that make certain kinds of thoughts and feelings possible.

The traditions of statuary must now include Muñoz's work. His figures look human, and some seem to be eyeing us, on the lookout for us; yet they are ultimately unapproachable. The environments in which we meet them may look familiar, like our streets or homes, yet they are realms of silence and stillness in which sacrifice, and with it unnamable acts and rites, seem imminent. Figures, objects, and the spaces themselves seem inhabited by pleas, prayers, curses, and spells. Everywhere the figures turn, they encounter thresholds they cannot cross, mysteries they cannot solve, domains they cannot enter. In Muñoz's world, human desire is so pervasive that it seems palpable, but it is always subordinate to other desires, and greater wills, to which human responses can be as amusing as mice to cats.

While Muñoz has incorporated many statuesque elements, however, his work leaves no doubt about the irreconcilable differences between ages of religious statuary and the contemporary world. For example, traditional statuary is usually frontal. A statue may ask us to walk around it, but it has one predominant point of view, and since it greets viewers from that point of view, it is invariably authoritative and often confrontational. The conviction of this frontal perspective reflects the power of a unified, totalizing society and the control of its political and religious systems. Muñoz avoids frontality and insists on multiple points of view. He

invites us to walk through and around his tableaux and encourages us to look up and down and around their sides. He wants us to feel free to reply to his enigmas any way we choose. "They don't take that frontal position that demands a response," Muñoz said. "Maybe we are all tired of having to answer back all the time to things that are displayed in front of us."[20]

Statuary communicates certainty and normality. Don't worry, it says. Everything has a place, everything is in its place, and as long as you accept this order, nothing will happen to you. Some of the most effective statuary expresses sympathy with human needs but is so sure of itself in the great scheme of things that it lets us know it knows what it is, has what it wants, and is beyond earthly desire. It knows what it is waiting for; it has been visited before and it has no doubt it will be again. Its restraint reflects the conviction that everything exists for a reason and that if true believers accept the same religious and political order, they, like the statue, will be able to bathe in the light of the Word. At the same time, because of the statue's enormous compressed power, this self-containment and restraint effectively warn those who are not of the faith, and who do not accept its normality and order, that they can be effortlessly repressed. Everything is under control, even the unknown. Obedience is expected, no questions asked.

In Muñoz's work, there is no certainty or normality. Every sign of the familiar, even the furniture, halls, and doorways that reek of European bourgeois normality in the "raincoat drawings" from the late 1980s and early 1990s, seems arcane and dysfunctional. Every room, or place, is a site of unpredictability, an arena of the unnatural. Certainty and normality did seem to have existed, but black magic and black humor, or postmodernity, or something else, took over. Now we know only that something happened and the order that was taken for granted has been undone. The figures and furniture remember that order and expect that one day it will return. Although confident that they will be revisited by a consistency and truth religious statues took for granted, they also seem to know deep down that such stability is gone forever, which helps explain the anxious edge of Muñoz's pranks and laughter. Traditional statuary assumes that desire is always manageable and that if you follow the right directives it can always be satisfied. In Muñoz's tableaux, desire is never manageable, and it and consciousness are caught in a Shakespearean—or a Laurel and Hardy-like—farce without beginning or end.

Muñoz's work sometimes seems like a detective story that could have been co-written by John le Carré, Luis Buñuel, and Samuel Beckett. Someone is always trying to come in from the cold. The sculptures, like the interiors in the "raincoat drawings," suggest crime scenes in which someone has just been hunted down and taken away or some kind of unspeakable act is about to occur, and the décor itself is waiting either to bear witness or to be exonerated. Many of Muñoz's rooms, like those at Dia, seem both stripped clean by criminals who cannot be found and like cells in which the criminals will get their comeuppance. Like the counselor reveling in offering clues to a murder mystery to enthralled teenagers by the campfire, Muñoz loves providing clues to mysteries and then waiting for the laughter or gasps—only there is no resolution to his narrative that will put everyone to sleep with a smile, and he wants his audiences to know that the stories they invent are as valid as his. Yet no one should be misled by his cleverness and wit. The force of the Muñoz silence; the poignant forsakenness and inadequacy of his figures; the hint there really is something else out there, something bigger than us, that knows us more than we know it; and the clear belief that transgression is not an aesthetic convention—not just a figure of modernist speech that gives artists license to do whatever they wish—but a serious breach, reveal the gravity of his vision and the urgency of his questions. His work is filled with laughter, but it is a hard laughter, uproarious and convulsive and occasionally a bit mad. It is not unlike the feral and scandalous laughter that might greet us at the threshold of the sacred.

NOTES

1. James Lingwood, "Monologues and Dialogues," in Zurich, Museum für Gegenwartskunst Zürich, *Juan Muñoz: Monologe und Dialoge/Monologues and Dialogues*, exh. cat. by James Lingwood (1997): 17. Revised reprint of Madrid, Museo Nacional Centro de Arte Reina Sofía, *Juan Muñoz: Monólogos y diálogos/Monologues and Dialogues*, exh. cat. by James Lingwood (1996).

2. Juan Muñoz, "A Conversation, January 1995," interview by James Lingwood, in Museum für Gegenwartskunst Zürich (note 1): 123.

3. "A Conversation between Juan Muñoz and Jean-Marc Poinsot," in Bordeaux, Capc Musée d'Art Contemporain, *Juan Muñoz: Sculptures de 1985 à 1987*, exh. cat. by Jean-Marc Poinsot (1987): 43.

4. For a full explanation of this work, see Gavin Bryars, "A Man In a Room, Gambling," *Parkett*, no. 43 (March 1995): 52–55.

5. Probably no contemporary sculptor has done more in his work and writings to insist on the continuing vitality of statuary than Alain Kirili. See his *Statuaire* (Paris: Editions Denoel, 1986).

6. *Webster's New World College Dictionary*, 3rd ed. (MacMillan USA, 1997): 1208 and 1310, respectively.

7. The gesture of Augustus is very similar to that of one of the well-dressed nine-inch-tall men, each part detective, part voyeur, part suitor, in Muñoz's *Crossroads Cabinet October*.

8. Kenneth Gross concluded his book *The Dream of a Moving Statue* (Ithaca and London: Cornell University Press, 1992) with a thoughtful discussion of this work that was inspired by Sigmund Freud's essay on Michelangelo's Moses.

9. "A Conversation, January 1995" (note 2): 125.

10. Ibid.: 66.

11. Ibid.: 153.

12. Ibid.: 63.

13. Ibid.: 125.

14. Ibid.: 153.

15. Ibid.: 124.

16. Gross (note 8): 179.

17. Juan Muñoz, "A Conversation, September 1996," interview by James Lingwood, in Museum für Gegenwartskunst Zürich (note 1): 40.

18. Ibid.: 155.

19. Ibid.: 112–13.

20. Ibid.: 128.

Suspicions of the Gaze

Olga M. Viso

"Images tell us something and, if possible, something other than that which meets the eye."[1]

—Juan Muñoz

JUAN MUÑOZ FREQUENTLY OPENS his texts with a humble request. "Allow me an image," he has implored, asking his readers to indulge him in moments of eloquent and concise description. Painting pictures in the "mind's eye," Muñoz conjures up images that engage his audience and draw it into the internal structure of his prose. Setting the mood and context for a possible story, the author constructs visual metaphors carefully. He develops unlikely, even unexpected, associations between subjects or objects and evokes complex meaning, often by challenging conventional modes of interpretation. In the text "Also a Metaphor,"[2] Muñoz opposed two images, one, a building cornerstone, the other, a keystone, architectural elements that constitute the beginning and the end of the construction of a cathedral. For Muñoz, these essential structural components—in their place and function within the monumental edifice—embody the totality and unity of sculpture. In the "The First/The Last" (see pp. 58–59), the author compared paleolithic cave paintings to modern art. Rather than reinforcing the modernist vision of the "primitive," Muñoz's comparison focuses on mysterious aspects of the prehistoric sensibility and underscores contemporary humanity's inability to grasp fully how ancient cultures perceived themselves and their various realities. Similarly, in "On a Square" (see pp. 67–68), the author contrasted the lasting power and intrigue that

surrounded an Aztec statue of the goddess Coatlique with the obscure and ineffectual character of less memorable forms of commemorative public sculpture created over the last two centuries. And, in "La Posa," from his text *Segment* (see pp. 69–75), Muñoz fictionalized an anthropological account of a curious dwelling in the Peruvian highlands in order to effectively deconstruct that "utter enigma we call space."[3] Muñoz's texts consistently challenge readers to put themselves in places outside accepted frames of reference and, as a result, question the very nature of vision and perception.

Muñoz's fascination with the mechanics of vision and the complexities of human perception can be traced throughout his career. In both his written and sculpted works, he contrasts the power of images with the creative potential of the human imagination. Knowing that human perception is tied to the desire to make meaning from images, Muñoz appreciates that what we see is often not what we perceive. His "suspicions of the gaze"[4] and his interest in the distance between vision, knowledge, thought, and perception are among the most potent subjects of his art. The artist has explained, "You just have one material world to explain another material world, and the gap in-between is the territory of meaning."[5]

Evoking images in his writings as well as his installations, Muñoz "sets the stage for signification"[6] in his art. Creating room-sized environments and stagelike settings populated by anonymous figures, the artist has sometimes drawn on the language of theater to make his art. In *The Prompter* (1988; cat. no. 24), for example, the sculptor used the metaphor of the theater

2

and constructed a stage platform that, in its original installation, stretched the entire width and depth of the space. Unlike in conventional theater, where a narrative is played out before the audience, Muñoz's stage is empty; no action takes place or is suggested by the visual cues provided by the artist. Only the prompter, a dwarflike figure, is present, standing quietly in the dialogue prompter's box, ready to feed an absent actor his or her forgotten lines. In this, as in many of Muñoz's mise-en-scènes, the artist "evoke[s] only to thwart the potential for narrative,"[7] effectively making the viewer the protagonist of his quiet, disturbing dramas. Even in his two-dimensional works, such as the "raincoat drawings" (1989–95; see cat. nos. 25, 27–32, 34, 41–44, 46–47, 50–52), narrative remains completely suspended; here, we are given intimate access to a variety of domestic interiors where the human figure is absent and essentially nothing happens. The "raincoat drawings" give the spectator the impression that he or she has arrived on the scene too late—either immediately before or after the occurrence of some unspecified event. What remain

are the silent charge of mystery and potential narratives pregnant with possibility.

Muñoz's references to the theater have often been discussed in terms of the twentieth-century playwrights Luigi Pirandello and Samuel Beckett, authors admired for their efforts to defy theatrical and narrative conventions in their plays. Pirandello's classic construction of a "theater-within-a-theater" in his best-known drama, *Six Characters in Search of an Author* (1921), innovatively challenged the expected role of the actors as well as the audience. By presenting simultaneous realities and blurring the boundaries among the personalities on stage, the theater director, the "lost" characters from another play, and the spectator, Pirandello's stage seeks to bring the experience of theater closer to life.[8] Similarly, the disconnected narratives and frustrating failures of communication between the characters in Beckett's dramas suggest parallel moments from everyday life, where actions and events rarely have such clear and timely resolution.

The "unscripted" narratives evoked in Muñoz's two- and three-dimensional works also engage the viewer, only to confuse, disorient, and transgress his or her expectations. Although the artist resists overemphasizing associations either to the above-mentioned playwrights or to the concept of theater in general as it relates to his artistic language, the notion of humanist theater as a "common beholding place"⁹ seems especially relevant to discussions of his work. The understanding of theater as a space where individuals gather to temporarily observe fictional narratives and contemplate experience and knowledge has obvious parallels with art in its current installation-based context. Indeed, the contemporary exhibition site, or temporary environment constructed within the space of the gallery or museum, constitutes a comparable type of "common beholding place"—a space the artist can demarcate in the world where the ordinary rules of activity are suspended and replaced by strategies of observation and interpretation. It is a place, like the theater, where the artist can "reduce the confusion of phenomena into an ordered whole."¹⁰

What obviously separates Muñoz's works from the conventions of traditional theater is the direct physical engagement he encourages between the work of art and the viewer. Inviting the audience to enter into and occupy his spaces, allowing them to walk across, stand in between, and pass through his figures and constructions, Muñoz closes the distance between architectural space, the work of art, and the spectator. In the text "Notes on Three" (see pp. 56–57), he expounded upon his fascination with this triangle of vision and perception. His preoccupation with the role of the observer and his interest in mining the interstices between illusion and reality are concerns shared by a number of artists of his generation, among them Robert Gober, Katharina Fritsch, Thomas Schütte, Miroslaw Bałka, and Mona Hatoum. While these artists' various approaches to space and their interest in the place of observer have precedents in art of the postwar period, these issues became central themes for artists active in the late 1980s and throughout the 1990s—the period in which Muñoz emerged as a sculptor internationally and in which visual theory and the place of the observer were at the critical forefront of contemporary art-historical discussions. A review of both the artistic and critical

explorations surrounding the place of the viewer in Western art not only will help broaden the understanding of this dimension of Muñoz's work, but will also provide a context for understanding the diverse influences and interests that converge in his art.

Since the development of one-point perspective in pre-Renaissance Italy, the dominant mode of vision and visuality in the art of Western culture has centered the visible world on the eye of the beholder. Positioning observers at the very center of vision, artists arranged compositions for their benefit. In a fifteenth-century view of an ideal city painted by a follower of the Italian Renaissance master Piero della Francesca (fig. 2), the artist carefully structured the painting to conform to this ocularcentric perspective. Making a clear distinction between the place of the viewer and the space of the work of art, the Renaissance approach to vision effectively distanced the spectator, placing him or her squarely outside the space (or universe) delineated by the artwork. The notion of a "supreme" spectator outside the picture frame or beyond the space of the pedestal predominated until the eighteenth and nineteenth centuries, when artists began to rigorously question the viability of this monocular type of vision and became increasingly concerned with the role of the observer.

According to many visual theorists, the development of the camera in the early decades of the nineteenth century challenged the existence of the "absolute" spectator by providing access to unconventional views and introducing artists and the audience to alternative modes of vision.¹¹ Fragmentary compositions in which objects and figures were cut off by the picture frame and arbitrary cropping of subject matter created a more radical, "uncomposed" approach to vision that contributed to many of the artistic innovations of the late nineteenth and early twentieth centuries, most notably Impressionism. The modernist approach to vision afforded by the camera thus began to move artists away from the illusionistic tradition of painting and toward interpretations presumed to be closer to reality. At the same time, the observer was effectively displaced from a position of centrality and

FIG. 3 Diego Velázquez, *Las Meninas*, 1656

to the revolutionary ways of seeing the world in the modern era was the evolution of physiology in the eighteenth century. This branch of biology, which sought to explain bodily phenomena, afforded a greater understanding of the mechanical processes of vision and humanity's capacity to misperceive. What emerged in the twentieth century, then, was a more subjective approach to vision in which the observer had a "productive new role" as well as a considerable amount of "perceptual autonomy."[12]

170

3

Yet, in the view of many contemporary art historians, artists attempted to cross the hallowed space between the work of art and the viewer even before many of these modern scientific and technological advances occurred. In *Ways of Seeing* (1972), John Berger, a friend of and sometime collaborator with Muñoz, suggested that the tradition of the nude in Western painting had already initiated the process by introducing a more "performative" role for the spectator.[13] In Berger's view, the observer, in his or her contemplation of the nude, became a protagonist, and the nude became a projection of the viewer's perception. Art historian Norman Bryson has also suggested that the fracturing of visual space and the significant break with Renaissance perspective happened "upon the entry of the body in painting."[14] For him, vision became especially "performative" in the Baroque period, when artists such as Caravaggio forced the viewer into surprising and uncomfortable perspectives of spectatorship that essentially rendered him or her witness to dramatic narratives of saintly martyrdom. Perhaps one of the most compelling examples from the time is Diego Velázquez's *Las Meninas* (1656; fig. 3). Here Velázquez used a mirror to create an enigmatic composition that is a fascinating meditation on the nature of vision and beholding. In *The Order of Things: An Archaeology of the Human Sciences* (1970), French critic Michel Foucault articulated a complex circularity of vision in *Las Meninas* among the Infanta Margherita (who looks outward, presumably toward the viewer), the King and Queen of Spain (whose gazing images appear only as a reflection in the mirror depicted in the background of the painting, implying that their position coincides with the spectator), the painter (who glances outward to the monarchs), and the viewer (who is confused about

propelled into a new role that was no longer passive or absolute. Édouard Manet's unidealized nudes in *Olympia* and *Luncheon on the Grass* (both 1863), for example, aggressively engaged the viewer as never before in the history of painting. Staring back at the spectator unabashedly, Manet's subjects implicated the viewer in a process of vision that significantly altered the face of painting from that moment forward. Also contributing whose eye or point of view the painting depicts). Foucault's analysis suggests that the focal point of the painting might be the invisible space outside the painting between the viewer and the image.[15]

Still, according to art historian Michael Fried, the beholder's presence before painting emerged as "a problematic for painting as never before" in mid-eighteenth-century France.[16] In *Absorption and Theatricality: Painter and Beholder in the Age of Diderot* (1980), Fried credited the French painter Jacques-Louis David with significantly opening up painting to alternative points of view by shifting the viewer away from the center of vision to the left-hand side of the painting in *Belisarius* (1781–85).[17] Fried also argued that in the *Raft of the Medusa* (1819) by Théodore Gericault, the struggling figures on the raft were oriented not to the front of the painting and the viewer but to the tiny ship in the distance.[18]

Although contemporary visual critics have disputed a number of points surrounding the moment artists first demonstrated a significant interest in activating the space and position of the beholder, their arguments make clear that vision is extremely complicated and that the history of the relationship between the viewer and the work of art is equally complex. As Norman Bryson explained in *Vision and Painting: The Logic of the Gaze* (1983), vision is neither direct nor absolute. Mediated by social codes, artistic vision is filtered first by the artist, then by the spectator, and ultimately by society.[19] Each member of this equation brings to the experience of viewing his or her own set of values, expectations, and social and historical contexts. For Bryson, as for many contemporary historians writing in the 1980s and first half of the 1990s, Western art had historically labored under the misconception that art was an illustration of nature and that all viewers were the same. Throughout this period, the politics of viewing and issues of spectatorship in the history of art became topics of considerable critical and scholarly debate. The volume *Vision and Visuality* (1988) documents a series of important dialogues between noted contemporary critics, including Bryson, Jonathan Crary, and Rosalind Krauss, who examine the various dimensions of vision in the modern era.[20] Another significant volume of essays published in those years was *Vision and Textuality* (1995), which contains a number of important investigations related to vision and issues of gender, social class, privilege, and prestige.[21]

THESE THEORIES OF VISION and perception serve as a backdrop for approaching Juan Muñoz's art. Maturing as an artist in the early 1980s, Muñoz emerged at a time when vision and visuality, as well as the role of the spectator, were topics of special concern in the cultural arena. Revisionist approaches to art history, which were being written and debated with tremendous vigor, were no doubt of interest to Muñoz, an avid reader and intellectual who began his career as a curator. As an aspiring artist, Muñoz was also contending (as were many of his peers) with the legacy of Minimalism and the new demands that Minimalist sculpture had placed on the viewer. Challenging the "placelessness" of modern sculpture and the self-contained nature of the modernist art object, Minimalist artists in the 1960s such as Donald Judd, Robert Morris, and Carl Andre discarded the notion that sculpture should be relegated to a base.[22] They believed that sculpture should exist in spatial relation to the spectator and include the viewer in its own ambience rather than reside in an ideal space separate and distinct from the beholder.[23] The situational context of a sculpture—its relationship to its surroundings, to architecture, to other manufactured objects from everyday life, and to humanity—was thus a primary concern among these Minimalist artists in America as well as post-Minimalist artists such as Bruce Nauman and Richard Serra, the latter of whom took a more critical position toward the act of viewing and spectatorship. Developments in performance art and video in the 1970s continued to locate the responsibility for viewing with the beholder by energizing the audience to respond to or interact directly with the performer or images projected.

By the 1980s, the active and critical role of the spectator in the experience of viewing was indeed a given. It was, however, a condition in need of revitalization and rethinking, particularly since the resurgence of painting in the late 1970s and early 1980s had revived such modernist themes as narrative, metaphor, and expression, creating a series of uncertainties for the direction of contemporary sculpture. That Muñoz was grappling with these and other issues is clear. His writings and notes from the period reveal explorations into the debates surrounding Minimalism and the social and critical positions of American artists such as Morris and Serra as well as Tony Smith and Robert Smithson. These texts also demonstrate his fascination with historical and anthropological approaches toward physical space and visual perception both inside and outside the immediate scope of art history. Indeed, throughout his career, Muñoz has pursued his topical interests in an ahistorical and cross-disciplinary fashion. Anthropologist Marc Augé's analysis of the contemporary sense of the "other" and his notion of "non-places" in late-twentieth-century global culture, for example, have served as important resources for Muñoz,[24] whose sculptures and installations of the 1990s have often addressed the isolation of the individual in familiar, collective contexts.

Muñoz's admiration for the Baroque has been another important topic of consideration throughout his career. Indeed, aspects of the Baroque approach to vision were an important early concern for him as well as the subject of one of his essays, "Borromini-Kounellis: On the Brilliant Opacity of Signs" (see pp. 60–61), first published in 1985. Celebrating the multiplicity of vision evidenced by the churches of Francesco Borromini, the young artist clearly respected the Baroque architect for his ability to create complex spatial relationships charged with mystery, light, and movement. In his essay, Muñoz compared Borromini's work to the sculptural installations of the Greek-born contemporary

4

artist Jannis Kounellis. The uncertainty instilled in the viewer and the desire to represent the unrepresentable were concerns Muñoz shared with these very different artists. Elements of Baroque sensibility and design have, at times, provided the artist with rich subject matter. *Baroque Exercise* (1984; fig. 4), which was included in the artist's first solo exhibition, at Galería Fernando Vijande, Madrid, consisted of two bird forms mounted on iron stands that spelled the title of the sculpture at the base. The birds (found plaster garden ornaments) were positioned with their heads turned and facing a metal spiral inserted at the birds' eye level into the wall. With their vision fixed on the spiral—a quintessential motif of Baroque architecture and design—the birds were engaged in a hypnotic trance that was punctuated at once by the desire for stillness and focus and the realization of that impossibility.

Another early work, in which the artist's interest in the complexities of vision and perception is perhaps most explicit, is the large floor sculpture *Portraits B* (1986; see fig. 5), which was included in Muñoz's third solo exhibition, at Galerie Joost Declercq in Ghent. The installation was inspired by a story about the Mannerist painter Parmigianino that Muñoz recounted in two essays of the same period, "Notes on Three" and "The

173

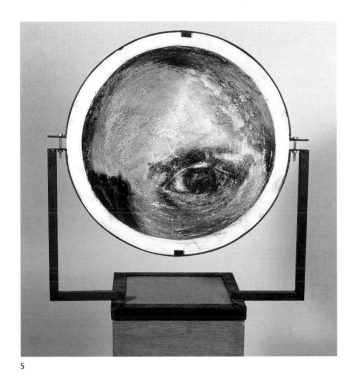

5

6

Time of the Pose"(see pp. 64–65). These narratives
centered on Parmigianino's execution of a self-portrait
reflected in a mirror (1524; fig. 6). As Muñoz retold
the story, Parmigianino commissioned a lathe worker
to make a wooden sphere the same size as the mirror,
which he then split in half in order to paint the portrait
on the convex side. Inspired by the account, Muñoz
created a series of five hollow half-spheres mounted on
pedestals that were deployed in a spatial grouping.
Painted on the convex and concave surfaces of the
spherical halves are distorted details of eyes and noses,
presumably taken from Parmigianino's self-portrait.
What is immediately apparent when comparing Muñoz's
study with Parmigianino's is that the optical distortions
in the face depicted by Muñoz are absent from the

Mannerist painter's rendition, where only the hand
of the artist is elongated by the mirror. In the original
painting, Parmigianino's face remains curiously legi-
ble and intact; no natural distortions are recorded.
According to Muñoz, Parmigianino's lack of attention
to factual detail reveals the "illusory nature of imitation,
of copying."[25] The notion of art as illusion, which was
being rigorously challenged by art historians at the
time, seems commensurate with Muñoz's earliest sculptural investigations.

Other works from the same period, such as *Spiral
Staircase* (1984; cat. no. 2) and a series of welded iron
balconies, minarets, and watchtowers (see cat. nos. 1,
3–13, and Benezra, fig. 7) confirm that Muñoz's interest
as an artist was not in the depiction of static objects

to be viewed by the spectator but in the effects of spatial manipulation on both the object and the viewer. Using the architecture of the space and placing the viewer in a critical role within it, Muñoz's first mature works, such as *Spiral Staircase* and the balcony sculptures *Hotel Declercq I–IV* and *Double Balcony* (both 1986; cat. nos. 13–17), were not functional imitations of existing forms put in the service of the artist for the sake of illusion. Reduced in scale so that they were engulfed by space, or placed high on the wall as if viewed from a distance, these sculptures reverse the terms of normal stairs and balconies. Both dysfunctional and distorted, the balconies serve as metaphors for the experience of viewing and spectatorship. They are, as the artist explained, "set where walking and watching intersect."[26] Similarly, the spindly legs of the various sculptures Muñoz made of watchtowers and minarets collapse regular vision to create a feeling of instability and a sense of disorientation.

A strong correlation may be observed between many of Muñoz's early metal works and the bronzes of the Swiss modernist Alberto Giacometti. Like Muñoz, Giacometti was immensely interested in problems of perception and, in particular, how figures were viewed across space. In *Four Figurines on a Base* (1950–65; fig. 7), Giacometti recorded his impression of four nightclub singers seen on a stage from a great distance. Here, the thin, elongated figures register the strain of vision as well as the inevitable distortions of memory. Mounted on bases that are incorporated into the sculptures themselves, the human form in Giacometti's art is typically situated in defined spaces, as in several of Muñoz's early sculptures, such as *If Only She Knew* (cat. no. 1),

7

a towerlike structure framed in metal and filled with wood and stone figures clustered together under a peaked roof that was exhibited at Galería Fernando Vijande in 1984. For Giacometti, the "gulf between the seer and seen" was critical to representing the full reality of a subject's humanity, and he sought to capture and preserve this "unbridgeable" divide in his art.[27] While the human figure, as well as the conventional base, temporarily disappeared as essential elements in Muñoz's early sculptures (such as in the figureless balconies), he did simplify the human form (almost to the point of abstraction) and use the base as a container or house in *If Only She Knew* to locate the figures in space. Yet in another work in the same installation, *General Miaja Looking for the Guadiana River* (1984; see Benezra, fig. 7), Muñoz liberated the figure from the confining pedestal. Here, Muñoz mounted empty balcony forms above the spectator on several existing columns that

8

floated in the middle of the space. Though the figure was absent from this and subsequent works, its presence was nonetheless implied by the viewer, who was invited to project him- or herself across the space and into the elevated balconies or, perhaps, imagine others who might inhabit the same perceptual realm. Although the human figure reappeared in Muñoz's work in 1986 in *The Wasteland* (cat. no. 19), its function had now changed dramatically. Acting as a foil rather than as a traditional subject, the human being in Muñoz's art had, in the words of Portuguese art critic Alexandre Melo, been "wrested from its role as subject to be subjected to the effects of spatial manipulation."[28] This statement also describes the parallel experience of the spectator encountering Muñoz's art.

Increasing the scale of his sculptures in 1986, Muñoz ventured more aggressively into the area of installation by creating platforms for the viewer to traverse both mentally and physically. In *Jack Palance at the Madeleine* (1986; see Brenson, fig. 4), commissioned for an exhibition at the Abbaye Royale de Fontevraud, site

175

of a former prison hospital in France, Muñoz provided two human-scaled stairway fragments, one mounted on the wall and the other placed directly across from it on the floor. While physical passage was not encouraged, viewers could not help but project their bodies between the two spaces. Two switchblades placed on the side panels of two steps also lent an eerie and disturbing dimension to the sculpture that invited a number of narrative associations related to violence and criminal activity. In *Balcony on the Ceiling of a Basement* (1986; fig. 8), the balcony form was also enlarged, but this time raised to the ceiling and tilted overhead, with the platform tipped at an angle to the floor. Viewers were overcome by a disorienting feeling of collapse and slippage as they walked below, particularly the first time this piece was exhibited, on the basement level of a domestic building. The same year, Muñoz also began to make a series of sculptures inspired by the form of a banister or handrail. This was a subject he would continue to explore throughout the early 1990s (see cat. nos. 20, 21, 23, 33, and Brenson, fig. 5). Like the balconies, the banister shapes are at times whimsical and are often perversely distorted, not unlike Robert Gober's "sink" sculptures from the same period. In *Untitled* (1987; cat. no. 21), for example, the rail follows alongside a wall like a conventional banister, except at one end, where it curves abruptly into the wall. *The Other Banister* (1988; cat. no. 23) swells gradually into the wall, inhibiting the steady grasp of a hand seeking balance and support for the body.

In the floor pieces such as *The Wasteland*, Muñoz further complicated the space between the art and

FIG. 9   *Neal's Last Words*, 1997

9

176

the viewer. Urging his viewers to cross over the patterned floor of the installation and enter into the physical environment of the work, he coaxes them to take what might be perceived as a calculated risk. The geometries of the floor, which appear to undulate before the viewer, were inspired by Baroque trompe-l'oeil floor designs and create the illusion that the space delineated by the artwork is unstable and constantly in motion. Muñoz has referred to the black shapes in the floor patterns as "black holes" that create a sensation in the viewer of infinite vastness below.[29] A bronze ventriloquist's dummy, which sits on a ledge beyond the floor and looks out toward the spectator, seems to bridge the uneasy distance. Yet rather than provide comfort as a kind of surrogate beholder (who shares the same space as the viewer), this anonymous figure curiously displaces the observer, forcing him or her into the uncomfortable space between. The same awkward sensation— of familiarity and distance—accompanies the contemplation of the artist's "raincoat drawings," which were begun in 1988 with *Ventriloquist Looking at a Double Interior* (second version, 2001; see cat. no. 26). Given voyeuristic access to these rooms, spectators find themselves vacillating between imagining themselves and imagining others inhabiting the mysterious, private domains.

In *The Prompter* (1988; cat. no. 24), the spectator assumes the central role of actor (or subject) in Muñoz's art. Even though the dwarf dialogue prompter (who is encased in the theatrical stage box and turns away from the audience) seems at first to fill this role, the viewer quickly discovers that the prompter is merely a bystander, albeit a critical one, ready to provide his

services if needed. Uncertain of the scene or action suggested by the empty stage ahead, the beholder of this artwork feels stranded and alone in the space. What is especially disturbing to the viewer in this and subsequent works, such as the dwarf sculptures, floor installations, and "conversation pieces" of the late 1980s and early 1990s, is the realization that their subjects have been left unspecified. In *Dwarf with Three Columns* (1988; cat. no. 22), three freestanding columnar forms emphasize the small stature of the man who stands between them. Is the figure here the primary focus of the artist's curious study? Is this a portrait of a specific individual? Or is the artist's (and the viewer's) discomfort with the dwarf's meager scale, relative to the onlooker and the implied architecture, the real topic of consideration?

It is important to note that Muñoz's figures, such as the dwarves, ballerinas, and "conversation piece" characters, rarely, if ever, return the viewer's gaze. Instead they are typically withdrawn, engrossed in thought, or completely uninterested in the presence of the spectator. Their status as anonymous or socially marginalized individuals further reinforces the perceptual distance. Caught in a space between thought and action, the beholder of Muñoz's art seems abandoned and open to the uncertain gaze of others. Yet, as Lynne Cooke so aptly stated, the spectator in Muñoz's art is not exposed to the uncompromising look of others as much as he or she is subjected to a more disturbing process of introspection—what Cooke described as the "specularity of the divided self."[30] Acting as a type of mirror that reflected the viewer's psyche, Muñoz's installations of the 1990s propelled the subject, as well as the viewer's gaze, inward and outward, stimulating an endless cycle of vision and perception that began and ended with the viewer (see fig. 9). Whether left completely alone, as in *No. 9* (1994; fig. 10), or accompanied by a large group of figures, as in *Many Times* (2000; cat. no. 58), the spectator in Muñoz's art remained distant and vulnerable—susceptible not only to the artist's calculated shifts in physical and perceptual space but also to the powers of the beholder's own anxieties and imaginings.

Muñoz's gamesmanship with the viewer is indeed both subtle and complex. On occasion his provocations have been imbued with a considerable amount of playfulness and humor, as in the curious audio-enhanced mousehole installation *Waiting for Jerry* (1991; see Benezra, fig. 21), as well as poignancy, as in *Towards the Corner* (1998; cat. no. 57). Upon first encountering the latter work, spectators see a grandstand with seven figures—one standing, the others sitting with their backs toward them. As they move through the space and around to the front side of the bleachers, viewers discover that the men are laughing, some quite hysterically. At first, viewers might chuckle, joining in the surrogate audience's curious revelry—until they realize that the joke is perhaps on them. Have they been duped? Has the artist turned the mechanisms of spectatorship around, making them the unknowing subject of someone else's, even his own, ridicule? Or, has he temporarily reversed the gaze to demonstrate what it feels like to be considered "foreign" or "other"? The artist's intentions are not clear, and it is this ambiguity that keeps viewers questioning this disturbing turn of events.

In "A Place Called Abroad" (1996; see Benezra, figs. 19a–b), the unknowing viewers similarly journeyed into a maze of uncertainties. The multi-level street construction, made specifically for Dia Center for the Arts in New York, occupied nearly 7,500 square feet of gallery space and presented a series of encounters for the viewer. Traveling through the mock urban environment, spectators happened upon figures engaged in both private and public moments of intimacy and conversation. Privy to these social interactions as well as to the crude internal structure of the architecture (which was often left exposed), observers were granted access to a place they recognized but could never fully grasp and in which they could never really participate. Even though Muñoz's street scene was literally a composite of architectural features (windows, door frames, moldings) derived from buildings surrounding the Dia Center, which is located in the Chelsea neighborhood of New York City, it seemed to conjure up, rather, humanity's perception of a foreign place, a romantic evocation of the notion of a place called "abroad." The artist's interpretation was obviously filtered through his own experience, through his understanding of European (particularly Spanish) pedestrian life as well his awareness of the urban American landscape at hand. Working as a foreigner in the United States on this project, Muñoz was also keenly aware of American society's nostalgic romanticization of Europe and, conversely, the expectations Europeans themselves bring to their conceptions of America.

The artist's fluid dialogue between individual and universal values in the Dia installation has many affinities with the approach of Jorge Luis Borges, the Latin American poet and author renowned for weaving labyrinthine tales of human existence that also hover between fiction and reality, local concerns and broader human themes.[31] Seeming to share in Borges's conviction that concrete reality consists only of mental perceptions, Muñoz created an unsettling realm of memory and imagination at Dia. There, the sculpture, architecture, and observer became indistinguishable elements of the same story and the space between the art work and the viewer folded in on itself repeatedly, at once collapsing and reinforcing familiarities and distances and interminable disjunctions between reality and perception.

177

FIG. 10 *No. 9, 1994*

178

10

Muñoz's ambitious installation for the Turbine Hall of Tate Modern, London, in 2001 (see pp. 216–28) further revealed the artist's consummate skill at enlivening the often unfathomable divide between the space of art and the beholder. The challenges of this endeavor were made all the greater by the sheer vastness and monumentality of the hall, which is 500 feet long and 115 feet high and contains nearly 36,000 square feet of public space. Faced with the overwhelming dimensions of the building as well as the reality of the thousands of visitors who attend the Tate daily, Muñoz set out to accomplish one thing. His goal, above all else, was to make possible the experience of viewing. By giving the individual observer a private encounter that brought the scale of the architecture down to a human level, he provided the possibility for a more intimate and personal engagement to take place. Muñoz achieved this objective by charting a journey of discovery for the spectator.

Extending the floor between the central bridge (or observation platform) of the building across to one end of the Turbine Hall, the artist created a deep geometric landscape for the eye, and, by extension, the body to traverse. The black-and-white patterned floor, which could be viewed but not walked on, recalled the design of Muñoz's earlier optical floor installations, such as *No. 9*. At the far end of the hall, two functioning freight elevators could be seen slowly scaling the height of the museum in a calculated, even, syncopated rhythm. At times, the elevators—which were designed by the artist and closely resembled the tiny elevator in the Dia installation (see cat. no. 53)—mysteriously disappeared into the "black holes" of the floor, which here were more than mere optical illusion. While at Dia the elevator was seen through a small, shaftlike opening that was visible only to the highly perceptive and inquisitive viewer, at the Tate the elevators were considerably larger, dominating the viewer's visual field.

Journeying by foot to the bottom level of the museum in search of what might lie within these consuming voids in the floor, curious visitors discovered a series of holes, or shafts, that pierced the floor level above. As they approached each shaft, they peered inside to discover the existence of a wholly independent world that seemed to be functioning within the floor of the building.[32] The nearly life-sized, resin sculptures that inhabited these secret domains were engaged in a variety of activities. Gazing upwards into the rafters, conversing and conspiring, Muñoz's figures comfortably scaled the seemingly vast interior network. For the viewers, who were enthralled by this discovery, the internal structure (and indeed the life) of the building suddenly was revealed as more intricate and complex than the monumental edifice that provided the outer shell. Giving surprising scale and dimension to the space between the ceiling and the floor above, Muñoz effectively reversed the terms of viewing and, indeed, the spectator's understanding of this enormous space. In retrospect, his approach at the Tate seems not unlike the one he

took in creating many of his early sculptures, such as *Spiral Staircase* and the series of balconies. While these metal works of the 1980s are small and modest in comparison with the grand scale of this major architectural intervention, the effects of spatial manipulation on the viewer are no less revealing and dramatic.

Throughout his career, Juan Muñoz has sensitively bridged a series of uneasy distances in his art. Giving substance to the fragile incongruities between vision, knowledge, thought, and perception, and the often impenetrable gaps between the space of art, the object, and the viewer, the artist has brought to life many sensations that are generally intuited or processed at a subconscious level. In his sculptures, installations, and more recent architectural environments, he has created spaces of common beholding that are set apart from the rest of the world and subject to their own rules of engagement. It is here that images can readily appear and alternative modes for perceiving the world can be expressed and imparted to the viewer. For this reason the artist has been aptly described as a dramatist of human perception.

179

1. "A Conversation between Juan Muñoz and Jean-Marc Poinsot," in Bordeaux, Capc Musée d'Art Contemporain, *Juan Muñoz: Sculptures de 1985 à 1987*, exh. cat. by Jean-Marc Poinsot (1987): 43.

2. "Allow me an image" is from "The Face of Pirandello" (pp. 78–79). The alternative translation "Permit me an image" has also been published. This expression in Muñoz's texts seems to have evolved from his reading of Paul Klee's writings. In a speech Klee gave in Jena, Germany, in 1924, the artist used the phrase "Permit me an image, an image of a tree"; see Alexander Klee et al., *Paul Klee in Jena 1924: Der Vortrag*, Minerva, Jenaer Schriften zur Kunstgeschichte, vol. 10 (Jena and Gera: JENOPTIK AG/Druckhaus Gera, 1999). For "Also a Metaphor," see *Domus* 659 (March 1985): 77.

3. See p. 69. Muñoz credited this phrase to a fictional character, André Friedmann.

4. Artist in conversation with the author, January 14, 2001.

5. "A Conversation, September 1996," in Madrid, Museo Nacional Centro de Arte Reina Sofía, *Monólogos y dialogos/Monologues and Dialogues*, exh. cat. by James Lingwood (1996): 159.

6. New York, Dia Center for the Arts, *Juan Muñoz*, exh. cat. by Lynne Cooke (1999): 8.

7. Ibid.: 9.

8. See Jana O'Keefe Bazzoni, "Seeing Double: Pirandello and His Audience," *Review of National Literatures* 14 (New York: Griffon House Publications, 1987): 160–83.

9. William N. West, "The Idea of a Theater: Humanist Ideology and the Imaginary Stage in Early Modern Europe," in *The Space of the Stage*, edited by Jeffery Masten and Wendy Wall, vol. 28 of *Renaissance Drama* (Evanston, Ill.: Northwestern University Press, 1999): 247–49.

10. Ibid.: 250.

11. According to art historian Jonathan Crary, who has examined the role of the spectator in nineteenth-century art, the shift in vision, in which a different emphasis was placed on the observer, began to occur well before the 1840s with the popularization of the camera obscura in the seventeenth and eighteenth centuries. In his view, the camera obscura—a device in which light from external objects enters a darkened enclosure to form an image of the objects on an opposite surface—initiated the demise of the inner-/outer-world structure that had existed between the spectator and the artwork since the early Renaissance. See Jonathan Crary, "Modernizing Vision," in Hal Foster, ed., *Vision and Visuality*, Dia Art Foundation Discussions in Contemporary Culture, no. 2 (Seattle: Bay Press, 1988): 29.

12. Ibid.: 35.

13. John Berger, *Ways of Seeing* (New York: Viking Press, 1972). See Chronology (pp. 184–85) for information on collaborations between Berger and Muñoz.

14. Bryson in conversation with Martin Jay, in Foster, ed. (note 11): 25.

15. Michel Foucault, *The Order of Things: An Archaeology of the Human Sciences* (London: Tavistock Publications, 1970): 3–15. Such gamesmanship with the viewer was evidenced during the Baroque period not only in painting but also in sculpture. Gianlorenzo Bernini's *The Ecstasy of Saint Theresa* (1645–52), designed for the Cornaro Chapel in the church of Santa Maria della Vittoria in Rome, fused architecture, sculpture, decoration, painting, and natural light to create a dynamic *concetto* of religious mystery. Here, Bernini struggled to eliminate the barrier between the work of art and the spectator by creating a virtual threshold between the imaginary space of heaven (symbolized by the rays of light that bathe the central figure as well as the ceiling of the entire chapel) and the physical space of earthly existence (inhabited by the viewer and the marble statues of members of the Cornaro family). The portraits of the patron's family, which were placed in balconies resembling opera boxes on either side of the chapel, extended the central action (between the Saint and the angel) into the space of the viewer. This illusionistic effect drew the spectator into the dynamic sphere of the work.

16. Michael Fried, *Absorption and Theatricality: Painting and Beholder in the Age of Diderot* (Los Angeles: University of California Press, 1980): 92.

17. Challenging the assumption that the observer stood before the canvas, David installed the "source of beholding or spectatordom" behind the figure of the soldier, which Fried described as a type of "surrogate beholder." Ibid.: 158.

18. Essentially escaping the viewer's gaze, these compositions support Fried's notion of "absorption" and illustrate what the critic describes as the "supreme fiction of the beholder's non-existence." Creating a paradoxical relationship between painting and beholder, artists at this time (according to Fried) sought at once to engage and "negate" the beholder's presence in order to "establish the fiction that no one is standing before the canvas"(ibid.: 108).

19. Norman Bryson, *Vision and Painting: The Logic of the Gaze* (London: MacMillan Press, 1983).

20. See Foster, ed. (note 11).

21. Stephen Melville and Bill Readings, eds., *Vision and Textuality* (Durham, N.C.: Duke University Press, 1995).

22. American artists associated with Pop Art in the early 1960s, such as Andy Warhol and Richard Artschwager, also liberated sculpture from the traditional pedestal, by placing objects directly on the floor.

23. Andrew Causey, *Sculpture since 1945* (New York: Oxford University Press, 1998): 124. This

volume is an excellent resource for a general summary of the growing concern of artists with the place of the viewer in art made during the second half of the twentieth century.

24. See Marc Augé, *Non-Places: Introduction to an Anthropology of Supermodernity*, trans. John Howe (London: Verso, 1995), and *A Sense for the Other: The Timeliness and Relevance of Anthropology*, trans. Amy Jacobs (Stanford, Calif.: Stanford University Press, 1998).

25. Juan Muñoz, "The Time of the Pose" (see pp. 64–65).

26. "A Conversation between Juan Muñoz and Jean-Marc Poinsot" (note 1): 43.

27. Causey (note 23): 33.

28. Alexandre Melo, "Some Things That Cannot Be Said Any Other Way," *Artforum International* 27 (May 1989): 121.

29. Artist in conversation with the author, January 19, 2001.

30. Lynne Cooke, "Juan Muñoz and the Specularity of the Divided Self," *Parkett*, no. 43 (March 1995): 23.

31. Acknowledging Borges as an influence, the artist has explained, "I am trying to create work that is a little foreign, that has what Jorge Luis Borges called 'otherness.'" See Juan Muñoz, "Juan Muñoz: 'O jogo é entre a consciência e a impossibilidade,'" interview by Alexandre Melo, *Journal de Letras* (19 March 1985): 12.

32. This architectural form is reminiscent of the Spanish term *entresuelo*, which describes a typical feature in Spanish architecture. This term has no direct corollary in the English language. The *entresuelo* may be best described as a type of landing or mezzanine-level space between two stories—between the street level (typically occupied by a store or commercial business) and the actual first-floor living area of a home. Muñoz evoked the *entresuelo* here, in keeping with his interest in exploring the thresholds between perception and experience.

Stephanie D'Alessandro

Documentation

Chronology

John Berger and Juan Muñoz in a performance of
Will It Be a Likeness?, Frankfurt, 1996

1953

Born 17 June in Madrid, the second of seven children, to Vicente and Hermenia Muñoz.

1966–70

Sent to boarding school briefly after being expelled from grade school, 1966–67. Attends Colegio Alameda de Osuna in Madrid, where he is taught by Santiago Amón, editor of *Nueva Forma* and art historian and critic for *El País*. Amón also tutors Muñoz and his brother, Vicente, privately at their home.

1970–75

Briefly studies architecture at the University of Madrid. Moves to London with Vicente in October 1970. Travels widely in Europe and lives in Stockholm for fourteen months. Briefly considers pursuing filmmaking; in Madrid, makes a short, 16-mm film documenting public sculpture.

1976–77

Receives a British Council scholarship and attends Central School of Art and Design, London (now known as Central Saint Martins College of Art and Design); awarded a Special Advanced Studies in Printmaking (lithography) certificate. Experiments with sculptures that involve sound, tape recorders, moving audiotape, body imprints, and weight and balance.

1979–80

Receives another British Council scholarship and attends Croydon School of Art, London (now known as Croydon College), where he completes coursework in advanced printmaking. Meets Spanish art student Cristina Iglesias, whom he later marries. In Malaga, erects a makeshift temporary minaret in the Plaza de Toros.

1981

Attends Pratt Graphic Center, New York. Receives a Fulbright Fellowship through the North American Spanish Committee. Serves as artist-in-residence at P.S.1 Contemporary Art Center, Long Island City, New York. Conducts interview with Richard Serra.

1982

Lives in Torrelodones, northwest of Madrid. Curates the exhibition "Correspondencias: 5 arquitectos, 5 escultores"; for the exhibition's catalogue, publishes his first essay, "Notes on Three" (see pp. 56–57; for a complete list of writings by the artist, see pp. 194–95).

1983

Curates a second exhibition, "La imagen del animal: Arte prehistórico, arte contemporáneo." Abandons curatorial work to concentrate on sculpture. Makes his first welded-metal sculptures.

1984

Makes his first balcony and staircase sculptures. First solo exhibition, "Juan Muñoz: Últimos trabajos," is held at Galería Fernando Vijande, Madrid. (For a complete exhibition history, see pp. 186–93.)

1986

Exhibits sculpture *North of the Storm* (see Benezra, fig. 10) in the Aperto 86 section of the Venice Biennale, along with a 45-rpm recording of the same title he created with his brother-in-law, composer Alberto Iglesias. Makes *The Wasteland* (cat. no. 19), his first work to feature a floor element with a human figure.

1987

First solo museum exhibition, "Juan Muñoz: Sculptures de 1985 à 1987," is held at Capc Musée d'Art Contemporain, Bordeaux.

1988

Makes *Dwarf with Three Columns* (cat. no. 22), his first sculpture to include a dwarf. Makes his first "raincoat drawings."

1989

Makes his first bronze sculptures, a series of ballerinas. Collaborates with the Belgian architect Paul Robbrecht on *A Room for a Doctor of Pain*, an installation at Galería Marga Paz, Madrid, 14–19 April, that features an actual-sized reconstruction of the waiting and surgical rooms of a Belgian doctor.

Page 182: Juan Muñoz's studio, Madrid, 1999

1990

First solo museum exhibition in the United States is held at The Renaissance Society at The University of Chicago; in lieu of an exhibition catalogue, *Segment*, the artist's longest essay to date, is published (see pp. 69–75). Daughter, Lucia, is born.

1991

Makes first "conversation piece" sculptures. Creates illustrations for an edition of Joseph Conrad's *An Outpost of Progress*, the studies for which are exhibited in 1992 at Frith Street Gallery, London. Moves to Rome and rents a studio in Trastevere.

1992

Lives in Rome. Receives commission for two works from James Lingwood of Artangel, London: *Untitled Monument (London)*, a temporary outdoor monument on the South Bank of the River Thames, and *A Man in a Room, Gambling*, a series of ten five-minute sound works made in collaboration with composer Gavin Bryars and conceived for the late-night listener. *A Man in a Room, Gambling* is broadcast on public radio stations in Great Britain, Canada, Germany, Austria, and Scandinavia. Muñoz receives commission from Gloria Moure for the Olimpíada Cultural Barcelona '92, for which he creates *A Room Where It Always Rains*, a permanently sited outdoor sculpture at the Plaça del Mar, Barcelona. Makes sound tape *Third Ear* (with critic Adrian Searle) for radio broadcast by the BBC. Invited by the BBC to participate in *Building Sites Europe*, a television series devoted to contemporary architecture in Europe; selects José Rafael Moneo's Museo Nacional de Arte Romano in Merida to discuss on the show. Makes the sound tape *Building for Music* with Alberto Iglesias.

1993

Completes *Two Figures for Middelheim* (see Benezra, fig. 1), for the Openluchtmuseum voor beeldhouwkunst Middelheim, Antwerp. Makes *Stuttering Piece* (cat. no. 48), his first figurative sculpture to include sound. The sound tape *Building for Music* is broadcast on the radio during the 1993 exhibition *Sonsbeek 93*, in Arnhem, The Netherlands.

1994

Solo exhibition at Irish Museum of Modern Art, Dublin, features *Conversation Piece (Dublin)* (see Brenson, fig. 1), the artist's largest outdoor sculpture (with twenty-two figures), and the sound piece *Doors of My House*; in conjunction with the exhibition, the museum later publishes *Silence please!: Stories after the Works of Juan Muñoz* (1996), with short stories by John Berger, William Forsythe, Dave Hickey, Patrick McCabe, Alexandre Melo, Vik Muniz, Quico Rivas, Luc Sante, Adrian Searle, Lynn Tillman, and Marina Warner.

1995

Serves as artist-in-residence at Isabella Stewart Gardner Museum, Boston.

1996

Two major solo exhibitions open: "Juan Muñoz: Monólogos y diálogos," organized by James Lingwood, at Palacio Velázquez, Museo Nacional Centro de Arte Reina Sofía, Madrid (travels in 1997 to Museum für Gegenwartskunst Zürich), and "A Place Called Abroad," at Dia Center for the Arts, New York (travels in 1998 to SITE Santa Fe, New Mexico, as "Streetwise"). Muñoz directs *Will It Be a Likeness?*, written and performed by John Berger at Theater am Turm, Frankfurt; the performance is broadcast by Hessischer Rundfunk and other German radio stations (winning "Hörspiel des Jahres 1996" for best radio program in Germany) and by the BBC (transcript published with illustrations by Muñoz in John Berger, "¿Será un retrato?," *Arte y parte*, no. 32 [April–May 2001]: 36–49). Son, Diego, is born.

1997-99

Gavin Bryars Ensemble performs *A Man in a Room, Gambling* in public concerts at BBC Studio One, London, September 1997. In the same year, these sound works are released on compact disk. Muñoz collaborates with Berger on *A Correspondence about Space*, a lecture and performance at the Geheimnisse der Raumproduktion, Hamburg, May 1998. *Will It Be a Likeness?* is performed at Thik Theatre im Kornhaus, Baden, Switzerland, November 1999.

2000

Awarded the Premio Nacional de Artes Plásticas by the Spanish government. Receives commission in The Unilever Series for work in the Turbine Hall, Tate Modern, London.

2001

Public performance and radio play of Muñoz's *A Registered Patent*, with music by Alberto Iglesias and the voice of John Malkovich. In June, *Double Bind*, Muñoz's commission for the Unilever Series at Tate Modern, London, is unveiled.

Alberto Iglesias and Juan Muñoz, Madrid, 2000

Gavin Bryars and Juan Muñoz, London, 2001

Exhibition History

Exhibitions are listed chronologically within each year; exhibitions for which dates are unknown follow alphabetically at the end of each section.

SOLO EXHIBITIONS

1984
Madrid, Galería Fernando Vijande, *Juan Muñoz: Últimos trabajos*, 7 November–7 December. Exh. cat.

1985
Lisbon, Galeria Cómicos, *Retrato de um homem em pé de Pontormo*, 7–30 March.

1986
Ghent, Galerie Joost Declercq, *Juan Muñoz*, 28 November 1986–24 January 1987.

Madrid, Galería Marga Paz, *Juan Muñoz*, 11 December 1986–20 January 1987.

1987
Marseille, Galerie Roger Pailhas, *Juan Muñoz*, 23 May–22 June.

Bordeaux, Capc Musée d'Art Contemporain, *Juan Muñoz: Sculptures de 1985 à 1987*, 25 September–22 November. Exh. cat.

London, Lisson Gallery, *Juan Muñoz*, 9 November–19 December.

Lisbon, Galeria Cómicos, *Estudos para a descrição de um lugar*, 3 December 1987–9 January 1988.

1988
Athens, Galerie Jean Bernier, *Juan Muñoz*, 26 May–24 June.

Dusseldorf, Galerie Konrad Fischer, *Juan Muñoz*, 19 October–3 December.

Paris, Galerie Ghislaine Hussenot, *Juan Muñoz*, 24 November–23 December.

1989
Madrid, Galería Marga Paz, *Juan Muñoz*, 14–19 April.

Ghent, Galerie Joost Declercq, *Juan Muñoz*, 13 May–17 June.

London, Lisson Gallery, *Juan Muñoz*, 27 October–25 November.

Madrid, Galería Marga Paz, *Juan Muñoz*, October–28 November.

1990
Athens, Galerie Jean Bernier, *Juan Muñoz*, 19 January–19 February.

Bristol, England, Arnolfini Gallery, *Vertical Balcony Too*, 9 June–15 July.

Chicago, The Renaissance Society at The University of Chicago, *Juan Muñoz*, 18 November–30 December. Traveled to Geneva, Centre d'Art Contemporain, 1 December–16 February 1991. (In lieu of an exh. cat., Muñoz's essay *Segment* [1990] was published.)

1991
Dusseldorf, Galerie Konrad Fischer, *Juan Muñoz*, 16 February–20 March.

Krefeld, Germany, Museum Haus Lange, *Juan Muñoz: Arbeiten 1988 bis 1990*, 17 February–21 April. Exh. cat.

New York, Marian Goodman Gallery, *Juan Muñoz*, 3–27 April.

Eindhoven, The Netherlands, Stedelijk Van Abbemuseum, *Juan Muñoz: Sculpturen, installaties en tekeningen*, 23 November 1991–12 January 1992. Exh. cat.

Paris, Galerie Ghislaine Hussenot, *Juan Muñoz*, 30 November 1991–8 January 1992.

1992
Valencia, Instituto Valenciano de Arte Moderno (IVAM) Centre del Carme, *Juan Muñoz: Conversaciones*, 10 April–28 June. Exh. cat.

London, Frith Street Gallery, *Juan Muñoz: Drawings and Prints*, 6 November–19 December.

1993
New York, Marian Goodman Gallery, *Juan Muñoz*, 17 February–20 March.

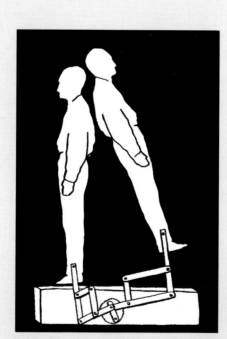

Exhibition invitation, *Juan Muñoz*, Galerie Ghislaine Hussenot, Paris, 1988

Athens, Galerie Jean Bernier, *Juan Muñoz*, 13 May–9 July.

London, Lisson Gallery, *Juan Muñoz*, 22 October–4 December.

Dusseldorf, Galerie Konrad Fischer, *Juan Muñoz*, 29 October–6 December.

1994
Nîmes, Carré d'Art-Musée d'Art Contemporain, *Juan Muñoz*, 25 March–29 May. Exh. cat.

Dublin, Irish Museum of Modern Art, *Juan Muñoz: Sculpture, Drawings and Installation*, 6 July–4 August. (In lieu of an exh. cat., the book *Silence please!: Stories after the Works of Juan Muñoz* [1996] was published.)

1995
Boston, Isabella Stewart Gardner Museum, *Juan Muñoz: Portrait of a Turkish Man Drawing*, 15 September–31 December. Exh. cat.

Santa Fe, Laura Carpenter Fine Art, *Juan Muñoz: New Work from New Mexico—Sculpture and Drawings*, 14 October–12 December.

Santiago de Compostela, Spain, Centro Galego de Arte Contemporánea, *Juan Muñoz*, 12 December 1995–25 February 1996. Exh. brochure.

1996
Athens, Galerie Jean Bernier, *Juan Muñoz*, 21 March–29 April.

Turin, Marco Noire Contemporary Art, *Juan Muñoz: Mobiliario, grabados 1996*, 10 April–7 May. Exh. cat.

New York, Dia Center for the Arts, *A Place Called Abroad*, 26 September 1996–29 June 1997. Exh. brochure. Traveled to Santa Fe, SITE Santa Fe, as *Streetwise*, 6 June–2 August 1998. Exh. brochure; exh. cat. (1999).

Madrid, Palacio de Velázquez, Museo Nacional Centro de Arte Reina Sofía, *Juan Muñoz: Monólogos y diálogos*, 25 October 1996–15 January 1997. Traveled to Zurich, Museum für Gegenwartskunst Zürich, as *Juan Muñoz: Monologe und Dialoge*, 1 February–19 May 1997. Exh. cat.

1997
Washington, D.C., Hirshhorn Museum and Sculpture Garden, *Directions: Juan Muñoz*, 6 March–15 June. Exh. brochure.

San Gimignano, Italy, Galleria Continua, *Juan Muñoz*, 22 November 1997–31 January 1998.

Paris, Galerie Ghislaine Hussenot, *Juan Muñoz*, 6 December 1997–20 January 1998.

1998
Miengo, Spain, Sala Robayera, *Juan Muñoz: Certain Drawings in Oil and Ink/Algunos dibujos en óleo y tinta 1996–1998*, July. Exh. cat.

1999
New York, Marian Goodman Gallery, *Juan Muñoz: Crossroads*, 21 September–30 October.

Athens, Bernier/Eliades Gallery, *Juan Muñoz: A Brief Description of My Death*, 25 November–22 January 2000.

2000
Humlebæk, Denmark, Louisiana Museum for Moderne Kunst, *Juan Muñoz: The Nature of Visual Illusion*, 18 March–18 June 2000. Exh. cat.

2001
London, Tate Modern, *The Unilever Series: Juan Muñoz*, 12 June–10 February 2002.

GROUP EXHIBITIONS

1979
London, Dryden Street Gallery.

London, Half Moon Gallery.

London, Morley Gallery.

1980
London, British Council, *Three Days a Week: Wolfgang Koethe, Lila Mookerjee and Juan Muñoz*, March–April.

London, Morley Gallery.

Warsaw, Museum Plaketu.

1981
Fribourg, Switzerland, *Fri-art 81*, 21 August–18 October. Exh. cat.

Long Island City, N.Y., P.S.1 Contemporary Art Center, *Room 202*.

1982
Berlin, *Büro Berlin*. Exh. cat.

1983
Madrid, Casa del Monte, Palacio de las Alhajas, Caja de Ahorros y Monte de Piedad, *La imagen del animal: Arte prehistórico, arte contemporáneo*, December 1983–January 1984. Traveled to Barcelona, Fundació "la Caixa," 22 March–30 April 1984. Exh. cat.

Madrid, Galería Fernando Vijande, *Seis españoles en Madrid*. Exh. cat.

1984
Madrid, Centro Cultural de la Villa, *Madrid, Madrid, Madrid: 1974–1984*, July–September.

1985
Eindhoven, The Netherlands, Stedelijk Van Abbemuseum, *Christa Dichgans, Lili Dujourie, Marlene Dumas, Lesley Foxcroft, Kees de Goede, Frank van Hemert, Cristina Iglesias, Harald Klingelhöller, Mark Luyten, Juan Muñoz, Katherine Porter, Julião Sarmento, Barbara Schmidt Heins, Gabriele Schmidt-Heins, Didier Vermeiren*, 24 May–30 June 1985. Exh. cat.

Madrid, Círculo de Bellas Artes, *Muestra de arte joven*.

1986
Seville, Pabellón Mudéjar, *Diecisiete artistas, diecisiete autonomías*, 28 February–6 April. Traveled to Palma de Mallorca, Mallorca, La Lonja, summer. Exh. cat.

Madrid, Sala de Exposiciones de la Fundación Caja de Pensiones, *Pintores y escultores españoles 1981–1986*, 9 April–11 May. Traveled to Paris, Fondation Cartier pour l'art contemporain, fall. Exh. cat.

Zurich, Museum für Gegenwartskunst Zürich, *Die Sammlung*, 5 May–15 September. Exh. cat.

Ghent, Museum Van Hedendaagse Kunst, *Chambres d'amis*, 21 June–21 September. Exh. cat.

Sara with Mirror, 1996

188

Contemporain (FRAC) des Pays de la Loire, *Ateliers internationaux des pays de la Loire*, November–December. Exh. cat.

Madrid, Palacio de la Moncloa, *Arte joven en el Palacio de la Moncloa*. Exh. cat.

1987

Fontevraud, France, Abbaye Royale de Fontevraud, Fonds Régional d'Art Contemporain (FRAC) des Pays de la Loire, *Lili Dujourie/Juan Muñoz*, summer. Traveled to Meymac, Abbaye Saint-André, Centre d'Art Contemporain, spring 1988. Exh. cat.

Madrid, Galería Marga Paz, *Juan Muñoz, Julião Sarmento, José María Sicília, Jan Vercruysse*, 2 October.

Paris, ARC-Musée d'Art Moderne de la Ville de Paris, *Espagne 87: Dynamiques et interrogations*, 10 October–22 November. Exh. cat.

Amsterdam, De Appel, *Nightfire*, 20 December 1987–31 January 1988. Exh. cat.

1988

Annemasse, France, Villa du Parc, Fonds Régional d'Art Contemporain (FRAC) Rhônes-Alpes, *Presentation & propositions*, 22 January–5 March. Exh. cat.

Amsterdam, Maatschappij Arti et Amicitiae, *Jan van de Pavert and Juan Muñoz*, 26 April–21 May. (In lieu of an exh. cat., the book *Juan Muñoz: Un objeto metálico/A Metallic Object* [1988] was published.)

Bayonne, France, Musée Bonnat, Fonds Régional d'Art Contemporain (FRAC) d'Aquitaine, *Richard Baquié, Pascal Convert, Juan Muñoz, Susana Solano*, 17 June–17 September.

Graz, Austria, Stadtmuseum Graz, Grazer Kunstverein, *Steirischer Herbst '88*, 25 September–3 November. Exh. cat.

1989

Long Island City, N.Y., P.S.1 Contemporary Art Center, *Theatergarden Bestiarium: The Garden as Theater as Museum*, 15 January–12 March. Traveled to Seville, Casino de la Exposición-Casino del Teatro Lope de Vega, 26 June–30 July, and Poitiers, France,

Venice, Aperto 86, XLII Venice Biennale, *Bienal de Venecia: Aperto 86—Cuatro artistas españoles*, 29 June–28 September. Exh. cat.

Zamora, Spain, VII Bienal de Escultura de la Ciudad de Zamora, *Escultura ibérica contemporánea*, 20 September–20 October. Exh. cat.

Álava, Spain, Fondos del Museo de Bellas Artes de Álava Vitoria-Gasteiz, *Generación de los 80: Escultura—Fondos del Museo de Bellas Artes de Álava*, September 1986–April 1987. Traveled to San Sebastian, Monte San Telmo, December 1987–January 1989. Exh. cat.

Lisbon, Galeria Cómicos, *L'attitude*, 16 October–22 November.

Fontevraud, France, Abbaye Royale de Fontevraud, Fonds Régional d'Art

Entrepôt-Galerie du Confort Moderne, 30 September–29 November. Exh. cat.

Brussels, Centre Albert Borschette, *Jeunes sculpteurs espagnols: Au ras du sol, le dos au mur,* 23 January–30 May. Exh. cat.

Lisbon, Galeria Cómicos, *Spazio umano,* 14–25 March.

New York, Langer and Co., *80's International,* 15 March–14 April.

Karuizawa, Takanawa, Japan, The Museum of Modern Art, *Supein aato toudi/Spain Art Today,* 29 April–12 June. Exh. cat.

Paris, Centre Georges Pompidou and La Grande Halle-La Villette, Musée National d'Art Moderne, *Magiciens de la terre,* 18 May–14 August. Exh. cat.

Amsterdam, KunstRai 89, *Before and after the Enthusiasm 1972–1992,* 24–28 May. Exh. cat.

Athens, The House of Cyprus, DESTE Foundation for Contemporary Art, *Psychological Abstraction,* 18 July–16 September. Exh. cat.

Lisbon, Galeria Cómicos, *Crise de l'objet,* 19 October–25 November.

Santiago de Compostela, Spain, Casa da Parra, *Presencias e procesos: Sobre as ultimas tendencias da arte,* November. Exh. brochure.

Madrid, Galería Marga Paz, *Complex Object.*

1990
Newport Beach, Calif., Newport Harbor Art Museum, *OBJECTives: The New Sculpture,* 8 April–24 June. Exh. cat.

Sydney, Art Gallery of New South Wales, *The Readymade Boomerang: Certain Relations in Twentieth Century Art: The 8th Biennale of Sydney,* 11 April–3 June. Exh. cat.

Madrid, Sala Julio González, Museo Español de Arte Contemporáneo, *X salon de los 16,* 8 May–17 June. Exh. cat.

Rennes, France, Galerie Art & Essai, Université Rennes 2 and Galerie du Cloître,

Ecole Régionale des Beaux Arts, Centre d'Histoire de l'Art Contemporain, *Le spectaculaire: Rebecca Horn, IFP, Niek Kemps, Claude Lévêque, Raoul Marek, Juan Muñoz, Emmanuel Saulnier, Haim Steinbach, Jan Vercruysse,* 10 May–13 July. Exh. cat.

Epernay, France, Office Régional Culturel de Champagne-Ardenne, *Sculpture contemporaine espagnole.* Traveled to Charleville-Mézières, Musée Rimbaud; Reims, Palais du Tau, Fonds Régional d'Art Contemporain (FRAC); Reims-Val-de-Vesle, Silo, Centre de Création Contemporaine; and Troyes, Musée d'Art Moderne, Centre d'Art Contemporain Passages, Cadran Solaire; summer. Exh. cat.

Ghent, Galerie Joost Declercq, *R. Devriendt, L. Dujourie, J. Muñoz, J. P. Temmerman, N. Tordoir,* 11 July–1 September.

Munich, Galerie Tanit, *Jardins de bagatelle,* 14 September–31 October. Exh. cat.

North York, Ontario, Art Gallery of York University, *Meeting Place: Robert Gober, Liz Magor, Juan Muñoz,* 26 September–28 October. Traveled to Calgary, Alberta, Nickle Arts Museum, 22 February–7 April 1991, and Vancouver, British Columbia, Vancouver Art Gallery, 8 May–7 July 1991. Exh. cat.

New York, Marian Goodman Gallery, *Group Show,* 18 October–30 October.

London, Institute of Contemporary Arts and Serpentine Gallery, *Possible Worlds: Sculpture from Europe,* 9 November 1990–6 January 1991. Exh. cat.

Krefeld, Germany, Museen Haus Lange and Haus Esters, *Weitersehen (1980→ 1990→),* 18 November 1990–27 January 1991. Exh. cat.

1991
Berlin, Martin-Gropius-Bau, *Metropolis: Internationale Kunstausstellung Berlin 1991,* 20 April–21 July. Exh. cat.

New York, Marian Goodman Gallery, *A Group Show,* 14 June–31 August.

Santa Monica, Calif., Meyer/Bloom Gallery, *History as Fiction,* 1 August–7 September. Exh. cat.

Malmö, Sweden, Rooseum Center for Contemporary Art, *Trans/Mission: Konst i interkulturell limbo/Art in Intercultural Limbo,* 27 August–27 October. Exh. cat.

Krefeld, Germany, Krefelder Kulturstiftung, Kaiser Wilhelm Museum, *Skulpturen für Krefeld 2,* 15 September–10 November. Exh. cat.

Graz, Austria, Grazer Kunstverein, *Körpe und Körper,* 6 October–14 November.

Pittsburgh, The Carnegie Museum of Art, *Carnegie International 1991,* 19 October 1991–16 February 1992. Exh. cat.

Plymouth, England, Plymouth Arts Centre, *The Poet in Paint,* 26 October–23 November.

Krefeld, Germany, Museen Haus Lange and Haus Esters, *In anderen Räumen,* 1 December 1991–9 February 1992. Exh. brochure.

Madrid, Galería Marga Paz.

1992
Lisbon, Galeria Cómicos, *Accrochage 1/92,* 17 January–21 March.

Valencia, Instituto Valenciano de Arte Moderno (IVAM), Centre Julio González, *La colección del IVAM: Adquisiciónes 1985–1992,* 7 February–5 April. Exh. cat.

London, Hayward Gallery, *Doubletake: Collective Memory and Current Art,* 20 February–20 April. Traveled to Vienna, Kunsthalle Wien, as *Doubletake: Kollektives Gedächtnis & heutige Kunst,* 8 January–28 February 1993. Exh. cat.

Seville, Salas del Arenal, Pabellón de España, Expo 92, *Los últimos días,* 19 April–12 May. Exh. cat.

Seville, Pabellón de España, Expo 92, *Pasajes: Actualidad del arte español,* 20 April–12 October. Exh. cat.

Ljubljana, Slovenia, Moderna Galerija, *Tišina: Protislovne oblike resnice/Silence: Contradictory Shapes of Truth,* 19 May–21 June. Exh. cat.

Kassel, Germany, Museum Fridericianum, *Documenta IX,* 12 June–20 September. Exh. cat.

Juan Muñoz in his studio, Madrid, 1987

Seville, Expo 92, *Fundação de Serralves, um museu português*, 26 June–15 July. Exh. cat.

Barcelona, l'Hospitalet de Llobregat, Centre Cultural Tecla Sala, Fundació "la Caixa," *Tropismes: Colleccio d'art contemporani Fundació "la Caixa,"* 11 July–15 August. Exh. cat.

Le Havre, France, Musée des Beaux-Arts André Malraux, *Ceci n'est pas une image: Les iconodules, l'image aujourd'hui.* Traveled to Darnétal-Rouen, l'Usine Fromage-École d'Architecture de Normandie, and Evreux, Musée-Ancien Evêché; 16 October–14 December. Exh. cat.

Dusseldorf, Kunstverein für die Rheinlande und Westfalen, *Jahresgaben '92: Editionen*, 3–23 November. Exh. cat.

Madrid, Sala de Plaza de España, *Artistas en Madrid: Años 80*, November 1992–January 1993. Exh. cat.

Sydney, *The Boundary Rider: 9th Biennale of Sydney*, 15 December 1992–14 March 1993. Exh. cat.

1993
Rome, Palazzo delle Esposizioni, *Tutte le strade portano a Roma*, 11 March–26 April. Exh. cat.

Albuquerque, N. Mex., The Albuquerque Museum, *The Human Factor: Figurative Sculpture Reconsidered*, 14 March–3 July. Exh. cat.

Copenhagen, Charlottenborg, *JuxtaPosition*, 29 April–6 June. Exh. cat.

Bignan, France, Centre d'Art Contemporain du Domaine de Kerguéhennec, *Domaine: L'ordre du temps*, 1 May–23 May. Exh. cat.

Arnhem, The Netherlands, *Sonsbeek 93*, 5 June–26 September. Exh. cat.

Venice, Peggy Guggenheim Collection, 45th Venice Biennale, *Drawing the Line Against AIDS*, 8–13 June. Traveled to New York, Guggenheim Museum Soho, 6–9 October. Exh. cat.

New York, Marian Goodman Gallery, *Group Show*, summer.

Antwerp, Koninklijk Museum voor Schone Kunsten, Antwerp 93, *Het sublieme gemis/The Sublime Void: On the Memory of the Imagination*, 25 July–10 October. Exh. cat.

Brussels, Galerie Xavier Hufkens, *Accrochage*, July–August.

Eindhoven, The Netherlands, Stedelijk van Abbemuseum, *Aanwinsten/Acquisitions 1989–1993*, 18 September–31 October. Exh. cat.

Beja, Portugal, Galeria dos Escudeiros, *Juan Muñoz-Julião Sarmento: Metalúrgica alentejana*, 27 November 1993–31 January 1994. Exh. cat.

Quimper, France, Centre d'Art Contemporain de Quimper, *Lieux de la vie moderne*, 17 December 1993–30 January 1994.

1994
San Sebastian, Spain, Arteleku and Fonds Régional d'Art Contemporain (FRAC) d'Aquitane, *1m = c.299792458⁴s*, 13 January–4 February. Exh. cat.

Basel, Kunsthalle Basel, *Welt-Moral: Moralvorstellungen in der Kunst heute*, 30 April–31 July. Exh. cat.

Las Palmas de Gran Canaria, Canary Islands, Centro Atlántico de Arte Moderno, *Entre la presencia y la representación*, 17 May–16 July. Exh. cat.

Bordeaux, Capc Musée d'Art Contemporain, <<*Même si c'est la nuit*>>, 17 June–6 November. Exh. cat.

Madrid, Galería Soledad Lorenzo, *Malpaís: Grabados y monotipos 1994*, 27 June–27 July. Traveled to Barcelona, Galería Joan Prats-Artgrafic, June–July 1995. Exh. cat.

Porto, Fundação Serralves, *Fragmentos para um museo imaginario*, 28 July–18 September. Exh. cat.

London, Marc Jancou Gallery, *The Little House on the Prairie*, 15 September–21 October.

London, Frith Street Gallery, *Marlene Dumas, Juan Muñoz, Thomas Schütte: Drawings*, 25 November 1994–21 January 1995.

Storrs, Conn., Atrium Gallery, University of Connecticut, *Selections from the Le Witt Collection*, 2–23 December. Exh. cat.

Hirai, Japan, Museo Marugame.

1995
Barcelona, Galeria Àngels de la Mota, *El contrato natural*, 11 February–11 March.

Helsinki, Nykytaiteen Museo-Valtion Taidemuseo, *Yksityinen/Julkinen/Private/ Public: Ars 95*, 11 February–28 May. Exh. cat.

Maastricht, The Netherlands, Bonnefantenmuseum, *Sculpture from the Collection of Marlies and Jo Eyck/Sculpturen uit de colectie var Marlies en Jo Eyck*, 11 March–3 September. Exh. brochure.

Palma de Mallorca, Mallorca, Centre de Cultura, *Arquitectures plurals*, 6 April– 25 March. Exh. cat.

Santiago de Compostela, Spain, Casa de la Para, *Incidentes*, 27 April–18 June. Exh. cat.

Lisbon, Galeria Luís Serpa, *Formas únicas da continuidade do espaço, parte 1*, 6 May–9 June.

Glasgow, Tramway Gallery, *Trust*, 7 May– 18 June.

Athens, Athens Exhibition Centre, Art Athina 3 '95, *Forms from Spain: End of Twentieth Century Spanish Art*, 9–14 May.

Luxembourg, Musée National d'Histoire et d'Art, <<Collection>>: *Art moderne et contemporain au Van Abbemuseum Eindhoven*, 13 May–25 June. Exh. cat.

New York, Marian Goodman Gallery, *Group Show*, 17 June–31 August.

Lisbon, Galeria Luís Serpa, *Formas únicas da continuidade do espaço, parte 2*, 24 June–29 July.

Hamburg, Hamburger Kunstverein, *Juan Muñoz/Henk Visch*, 7 July–27 August.

Tokyo, The Watari Museum of Contemporary Art, *Ripple across the Water*, 2 September– 1 October. Exh. cat.

Manchester, England, Rochdale Canal, *Duck not on a Pond, Ganders never Laid a Golden Egg*, 23 September–31 October. Exh. brochure.

Bignan, France, Centre d'Art Contemporain du Domaine de Kerguéhennec, *Le domaine du diaphane*, 30 September 1995–28 January 1996.

Villeurbanne, France, Le Nouveau Musée-Institut d'Art Contemporain, *Artistes/ Architectes*, 7 October–24 February.

Athens, Galerie Jean Bernier, *Andreas Gursky, Cristina Iglesias, Juan Muñoz, Eric Poitevin, Yvan Salomone, Pia Stadtbaumer and Sue Williams*, 30 November 1995–10 January 1996.

Barcelona, Museu d'Art Contemporani, *L'escultura. Creacions paral-leles. Metáfores del real*, 30 November–18 February 1996. Exh. cat.

1996
Athens, Athens School of Fine Arts, DESTE Foundation for Contemporary Art, *Everything That's Interesting is New: The Dakis Joannou Collection*, 20 January–20 April. Traveled to Copenhagen, Museum of Modern Art, spring 1997. Exh. cat.

Turin, Castello di Rivoli, Museo d'Arte Contemporanea, *Collezioni di Francia: Le opere dei Fondi Regionali d'Arte Contemporanea*, 15 February–21 April. Exh. cat.

Zurich, Museum für Gegenwartskunst Zürich, *Die Sammlung*, 5 May–15 September. Exh. cat.

Copenhagen, *CitySpace 1996: Sculptures and Installations Made for Copenhagen 96*, 15 May– 1 October. Exh. cat.

Jerusalem, Israel Museum, *Marks: Artists Work throughout Jerusalem*, 5 June–31 August. Exh. cat.

Madrid, Galería Juana de Aizpuru, *Tórridos terrenos: Colección Sibila de arte contemporáneo*, 6–26 June. Traveled to Seville, Sibila, 3–15 September; Valencia, Charpa, 19 September–19 October; and Barcelona, Joan Prats, 24 October–30 November.

Berwick-upon-Tweed, England, *Berwick Ramparts Project*, summer. Exh. cat.

Knokke-Heiste, Belgium, Crown Gallery, *Francesco Clemente, Juan Muñoz, Wilhelm von Gloeden*, October–November.

New York, Marian Goodman Gallery, *A Group Show*, 5 December–5 January 1997.

Amsterdam, Bloom Gallery.

1997
Brussels, Galerie Xavier Hufkens, *Accrochage*, 23 April–18 May.

Prague, Jiri Svetska Gallery, *United Enemies: Mannerism and Synthesis*, 4 May–22 June.

North Miami, Fla., Museum of Contemporary Art, *Tableaux*, 8 May–27 July. Traveled to Houston, Contemporary Arts Museum, 18 October–30 November. Exh. cat.

Madrid, Palacio de Velázquez, Museo Nacional Centro de Arte Reina Sofía, *En la piel de toro*, 14 May–8 September. Exh. cat.

Venice, *La Biennale di Venezia: XLVII Esposizione internazionale d'arte*, 15 June–9 November. Exh. cat.

Lyon, La Halle Tony Garnier, Musée d'Art Contemporain, *4e Biennale d'art contemporain de Lyon: L'Autre*, 9 July–24 September. Exh. cat.

New York, Marian Goodman Gallery, *A Summer Show*, July–August.

Athens, Galerie Jean Bernier, 7 October– 11 November.

Los Angeles, Margo Leavin Gallery, *Maxwell's Demon*, 8 November–20 December. Exh. cat.

Zurich, Museum für Gegenwartskunst Zürich, *Hip*, 8 November 1997–11 January 1998. Exh. cat.

Paris, Fondation Cartier pour l'art contemporain, 1: *La collection de la Fondation Cartier pour l'art contemporain*, 21 November 1997– 11 January 1998. Exh. cat.

1998
London, Hayward Gallery, *Voice Over: Sound and Vision in Current Art*. Traveled to Bristol, Arnolfini Gallery, 31 January–22 March;

Newcastle, Hatton Gallery, 4 April–17 May; and Nottingham, Castle Museum and Art Gallery, 12 September–1 November. Exh. cat.

Stockholm, Moderna Museet, *Wounds: Between Democracy and Redemption in Contemporary Art/Mellan demokrati och forlosning i samtida konst*, 14 February–19 April. Exh. cat.

Gainesville, Fla., Samuel P. Harn Museum of Art, *Inner Eye: Contemporary Art from the Marc and Livia Straus Collection*, 22 March 1998–3 January 1999. Traveled to Knoxville, Tenn., Knoxville Museum of Art, spring 1999; Atlanta, Georgia Museum of Art, summer 1999; Norfolk, Va., The Chrysler Museum of Art, fall 1999; and Purchase, N.Y., The Neuberger Museum of Art, 30 January–16 April 2000. Exh. cat.

Oostende, Belgium, Museum voor Moderne Kunst, *René Magritte en de hedendaagse kunst/René Magritte and the Contemporary Art*, 4 April–28 June. Exh. cat.

Malmö, Sweden, Malmö Konsthall, *Arterias*, 24 April–7 June.

Humlebæk, Denmark, Louisiana Museum of Modern Art, *Louisiana at 40—The Collection Today*, 18 June–30 August. Exh. cat.

Ghent, Stedelijk Museum voor Actuele Kunst, *Watou: 'Voor het verdwijnt en daarna,'* 28 June–6 September. Exh. cat.

Pontevedra, Spain, Museo de Pontevedra, *Fisuras na percepción: 25 Bienal de arte de Pontevedra*, August–September. Exh. cat.

New York, Marian Goodman Gallery, *Breaking Ground*, 25 September–7 November.

Gijón, Spain, Palacio Revillagigedo, Centro Cultural Caja de Asturias, *II trienal de arte gráfico: La estampa contemporánea*, September–November. Exh. cat.

Antwerp, Museum van Hedendaagse Kunst, *Subjective Presences: A Choice from the Collection of Fundació "la Caixa,"* 9 October–10 January 1999. Exh. cat.

Madrid, Palacio de Velázquez, Museo Nacional Centro de Arte Reina Sofia, *Dibujos germinales: 50 artistas españoles*, 14 October 1998–11 January 1999. Exh. cat.

1999
Künzelsau, Germany, Museum Wurth, *Spanische Kunst am Ende des Jahrhunderts*, 24 January–26 May. Exh. cat.

Le Blanc-Mesnil, France, Forum Culturel du Blanc-Mesnil, Département de la Seine-Saint-Denis, *Regards croisés*, 16 February–30 April.

Boston, The Institute of Contemporary Art, *Collectors Collect Contemporary 1990–99*, 31 March–28 May. Exh. cat.

Madrid, Circulo de Bellas Artes, *20 años de escultura española: Hacia un nuevo clasicismo*, 15 April–9 May.

Warsaw, Mediterranean Foundation and the National Museum, *North-South: Transcultural Visions*, 14 May–25 June. Exh. cat.

Humlebæk, Denmark, Louisiana Museum of Modern Art, *Nye Konstallationer/New Constellations*, 21 May–25 July.

London, Frith Street Gallery, *0 to 60 in 10 Years: A Decade in Soho (Part I)*, 28 May–2 July.

Cagliari, Italy, Centro Comunale di Arte e Cultura Exma, *Grabados*, 18 June–17 July.

Middelburg, The Netherlands, Zeeuws Museum, *Het betoverde plein*, 19 June–3 October. Exh. cat.

Istanbul, *6th International Istanbul Biennial*, 17 September–8 November. Exh. cat.

Liverpool, Tate Gallery Liverpool, *Trace: 1st Liverpool Biennial of International Contemporary Art*, 24 September–7 November. Exh. cat.

Athens, Bernier/Eliades Gallery, *George Lappas, Juan Muñoz, Thomas Schütte . . .*, 14 October–20 November.

Nuremburg, Kunsthalle Nürnberg, *Vergiß den Ball und spiel' weiter*, 21 October 1999–9 January 2000. Exh. cat.

Leipzig, Germany, Galerie für
Zeitgenossische Kunst, *Life Cycles*,
24 October–5 December. Exh. cat.

Krefeld, Germany, Krefelder Kunstmuseum,
C/O Haus Lange-Haus Esters, 1984/1999,
21 November–2 February 2000. Exh. cat.

Bonn, Kunstmuseum Bonn, *Zeitwenden:
Ausblick*, 4 December 1999–4 June 2000.
Traveled to Vienna, Museum moderner
Kunst Stiftung Ludwig Wien, 20er Haus and
k/haus-Künstlerhaus, 5 July–October 2000.
Exh. cat.

2000

Sydney, Art Gallery of New South Wales,
Biennale of Sydney 2000: 12th Biennale of Sydney,
26 March–30 July. Exh. cat.

Ghent, Stedelijk Museum voor Actuele
Kunst, *Over the Edges*, 1 April–30 June.
Exh. cat.

London, Tate Modern, *Between Cinema
and a Hard Place*, 12 May–3 December.
Exh. brochure.

Long Island City, N.Y., P.S.1 Contemporary
Art Center, *Around 1984: A Look at Art in
the 80's*, 21 May–September. Exh. cat.

Athens, Bernier/Eliades Gallery, 6 June–
6 July.

Las Palmas de Gran Canaria, Canary
Islands, Centro Atlántico de Arte Moderno,
Máquinas, 19 September–19 November.
Traveled to Palma de Mallorca, Mallorca,
Fundació "la Caixa," 19 December–
4 February 2001. Exh. cat.

2001

Oakland, Calif., Oliver Art Center, California
College of Arts and Crafts Institute, *A
Contemporary Cabinet of Curiosities: Selections
from the Vicki and Kent Logan Collection*,
17 January–3 March. Exh. cat.

New York, Museum of Modern Art,
Collaborations with Parkett: 1984 to Now, 5 April–
12 June 2001. Exh. brochure; exh. cat.

Installation view of "Juan Muñoz: The Nature of Visual Illusion," Louisiana Museum for Moderne Kunst,
Humlebæk, Denmark, 2000

Artist's Writings

This list represents published writings by Juan Muñoz, listed chronologically by publication date. Only the first publication of each work is included here. For a selection of writings by the artist, see "Selected Texts," pp. 55–81.

1982
"Notas afines a tres." In Madrid, Ministerio de Obras Públicas y Urbanismo, *Correspondencias: 5 arquitectos, 5 escultores*, exh. cat. by Carmen Giménez and Juan Muñoz.

1983
"Los primeros/Los últimos." In Madrid, Palacio de las Alhajas, Caja de Ahorros y Monte de Piedad, *La imagen del animal: Arte prehistórico, arte contemporáneo*, exh. cat. by Juan Muñoz. Madrid: Ministerio de Cultura with the collaboration of The British Council.

1985
"Desarrollo de la escultura inglesa actual: La palabra como escultura. Richard Long. Ian Hamilton Finlay." *Figura*, no. 4 (winter): 18–20.

"The Best Sculpture is a Troy [Trojan] Horse/Tambien metafora." *Domus* 659 (March): 77.

"Desarrollo de la escultura inglesa actual II: Hacia delante. De Richard Deacon a Anthony Caro." *Figura*, no. 5 (spring–summer): 32–33.

"De la luminosa opacidad de los signos: Borromini-Kounellis." *Figura*, no. 6 (fall): 94–95.

1986
"De la precision en las distancias." In Madrid, Palacio de Velázquez, *Piedras: Richard Long*, exh. cat. Spain and Great Britain: Ministerio de Cultura and The British Council.

"Un hombre subido a una farola (Entre la escultura britànica y la escultura a solas)." In Madrid, Palacio de Velázquez, *Entre el objeto y la imagen: Escultura britànica contemporánea*, exh. cat. Madrid and London: Ministerio de Cultura, Dirección General de Bellas Artes y Archivos and The British Council.

"El hijo mayor de Laocoonte/Laocoon's Eldest Son." In Bern, Kunstmuseum Bern, *Chema Cobo*, exh. cat. by Jürgen Glaesemer and Juan Muñoz.

1987
"Illusionismo, percepcion, proyecto." *Sur Exprés*, no. 1 (15 April–15 May): 35.

1988
Amsterdam, Maatschappij Arti et Amicitiae, *Juan Muñoz: Un objeto metálico/A Metallic Object*. (Published in lieu of an exh. cat. in conjunction with Amsterdam, Maatschappij Arti et Amicitiae, *Jan van de Pavert and Juan Muñoz*, 26 April–21 May.)

"Die Zeit der Pose." *Durch* 5: 25–27.

1989
"The Prompter." In Long Island City, N.Y., P.S.1 Contemporary Art Center, *Theatergarden Bestiarium: The Garden as Theater as Museum*, exh. cat. by Chris Dercon et al. Cambridge, Mass.: The MIT Press.

"Un texto de Juan Muñoz/A Text by Juan Muñoz/Un testo di Juan Muñoz." *Spazio umano/Human Space* 1 (March): 20–24.

"Yotsu no imeiji/Tres imágenes o cuatro." In Karuizawa, Takanawa, Japan, The Museum of Modern Art, *Supein aato toudi/Spain Art Today*, exh. cat. by Jaime Brihuega and Miguel Fernández-Cid.

1990
"Auf einem Platz." In Krefeld, Germany, Museen Haus Lange and Haus Esters, *Weitersehen (1980→1990→)*, exh. cat. Krefeld: Krefelder Kunstmuseen.

Segment. Chicago and Geneva: The Renaissance Society at The University of Chicago and Centre d'Art Contemporain. (Published in lieu of an exh. cat. in conjunction with Chicago, The Renaissance Society at The University of Chicago, *Juan Muñoz*, 18 November–30 December.)

1991
"A Drawing-Room Trick." In Pittsburgh, The Carnegie Museum of Art, *Carnegie International 1991*, vol. 1, exh. cat. by Lynne Cooke et al. Pittsburgh and New York: The Carnegie Museum of Art and Rizzoli.

1992
"A *imagem* proibida/La *imagen* prohibida/The Prohibited *Image*." In Porto, Fundação de

Serralves, *Julião Sarmento: 21 de Maio a 28 de Junho 1992*, exh. cat. by Michael Tarantino.

1994
"El rostro de Pirandello/The Face of Pirandello." In *Urban Configurations*, by Gloria Moure. Barcelona: Ediciones Polígrafa.

1996
"Anochecer." In Santiago de Compostela, Spain, Centro Galego de Arte Contemporánea, *Medardo Rosso*, exh. cat. by Gloria Moure.

"Rein, I am sitting in this train station." In Zurich, Museum für Gegenwartskunst Zürich, *Museum für Gegenwartskunst Zürich*, exh. cat. by Arina Kowner and Rein Wolfs.

1997
"Zwei in einem/Two in One." In Zurich, Museum für Gegenwartskunst Zürich, *Juan Muñoz: Monologe und Dialoge/Monologues and Dialogues*, exh. cat. by James Lingwood.

1998
"My dear friend." In *Works in Architecture, Paul Robbrecht and Hilde Daem*, by Steven Jacobs. Architecture Monographs, no. 1. Ghent: Ludion.

"Welche Bedeutung hat Picasso für Sie heute?" *du* 9 (September): 73.

2000
"A Standard Introduction to Lectures." *Gagarin* 1, no. 1: 3–4.

"Tägliches Leben in einem Mies van der Rohe-Haus/Everyday Life in a Mies van der Rohe House." In *Ein Ort der denkt: Haus Lange und Haus Esters von Ludwig Mies van der Rohe. Moderne Architektur und Gegenwartskunst/ A Place that Thinks: Haus Lange and Haus Esters by Ludwig Mies van der Rohe. Modern Architecture and Contemporary Art*, by Julian Heynen. Krefeld: Krefelder Kunstmuseen.

2001
[With John Berger.] "Una correspondencia sobre el espacio." *Arte y parte*, no. 32 (April–May): 50–61.

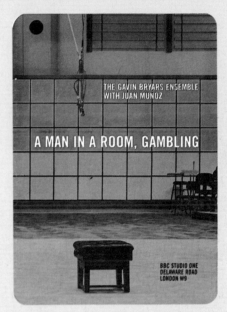

Program cover, *A Man in a Room, Gambling*, BBC Studio One, London, 1997

Interviews with the Artist

Interviews are listed chronologically by date of publication.

1984
"Fragmentos de una conversación/ Fragments from a Conversation." By Jan Debbaut. In Madrid, Galería Fernando Vijande, *Juan Muñoz: Últimos trabajos*, exh. cat. Madrid: F. Vijande.

1985
"Juan Muñoz: 'O jogo é entre a consciência e a impossibilidade.'" By Alexandre Melo. *Journal de Letras*, 19 March.

1987
"Un dialogue entre Juan Muñoz et Jean-Marc Poinsot/A Conversation between Juan Muñoz and Jean-Marc Poinsot." In Bordeaux, Capc Musée d'Art Contemporain, *Juan Muñoz: Sculptures de 1985 à 1987*, exh. cat. by Jean-Marc Poinsot.

1989
"Oscuras paternidades/Obscure Parent-hood . . ." By José-Luis Brea. In Amsterdam, KunstRai 89, *Before and after the Enthusiasm 1972–1992/Antes y despues del entusiasmo*, exh. cat. by José-Luis Brea. The Hague and Amsterdam: SDU Publishers and Contemporary Art Foundation.

1990
Interview by Maya Aguiriano. *Zehar*, no. 6 (September–October): 4–6.

Interview by Iwona Blazwick, James Lingwood, and Andrea Schlieker. In London, Institute of Contemporary Arts and Serpentine Gallery, *Possible Worlds: Sculpture From Europe*, exh. cat. by Iwona Blazwick, James Lingwood, and Andrea Schlieker.

Interview by Juan Vicente Aliaga and José Miguel G. Cortes. In *La creacíon artística como cuestionamiento/Artistic Creation at Stake*, edited by José Miguel G. Cortes. Valencia: Instituto Valenciano de la Juventud.

1991
"Fluiten in het donker." By Jan Braet. *Knack*, no. 48 (December): 111–12, 114, 118.

1992
"Mis esculturas son autosuficientes." By Octavio Zaya. *Diario 16* (Madrid), 15 May, Culture section.

Interview by Zdenka Badovinac. In Ljubljana, Slovenia, Moderna Galerija, *Tišina: Protislovne oblike resnice/Silence: Contradictory Shapes of Truth*, exh. cat. by Zdenka Badovinac.

1994
Interview by Rafael Sierra. *El Mundo* (Madrid), 4 April.

1995
"A Conversation, New York, 22 January 1995." By James Lingwood. *Parkett*, no. 43 (January): 42–47.

1996
"En la tensión del silencio . . ." By Basilica Sariláqui. *Caos* (April–May): 76–78.

"Una conversación, septiembre 1996/A Conversation, September 1996" (I and II). By James Lingwood. In Madrid, Museo Nacional Centre de Arte Reina Sofía, *Juan Muñoz: Monólogos y diálogos/Monologues and Dialogues*, exh. cat. by James Lingwood. 1996. (Translated and revised as Zurich, Museum für Gegenwartskunst Zürich, *Juan Muñoz: Monologe und Dialoge/Monologues and Dialogues*, exh. cat. by James Lingwood. 1997.)

Interview by Rafael Sierra. *El Mundo* (Madrid), 9 November.

1997
Interview by Simon Maurer. *Tages-Anzeiger* (Zurich), 3 February.

"Me and a Man in a Room, Talking." By Judith Palmer. *Independent* (London), 17 September.

1998
Interview by Gianni Romano. *Flash Art* (Italy), no. 209 (April–May): 110–13.

Interview by José-Luis Brea, Madrid, 27 September 1997. In *Servicio público: Conversaciones sobre financiación pública y arte contemporáneo*, edited by Jorge Ribalta. Salamanca and Barcelona: Ediciones Universidad de Salamanca and Unión de Asociaciones de Artistas Visuales.

1999

Interview by Walter Smerling. In Bonn, Kunstmuseum Bonn, *Zeitwenden: Ausblick*, exh. cat. by Dieter Ronte and Walter Smerling. Cologne: DuMont.

2000

"Artists on Art: Juan Muñoz on *Spiral Jetty* (1970) by Robert Smithson." By Martin Gayford. *Daily Telegraph* (London), 11 November.

A BRIEF DESCRIPTION OF MY DEATH

JUAN MUÑOZ

Exhibition invitation, *Juan Muñoz: A Brief Description of My Death*, Bernier/Eliades Gallery, Athens, 1999–2000

Selected Bibliography

Sources are ordered chronologically, and, within years, alphabetically. Interviews with the artist are listed separately, on pp. 196–97; the artist's writings are listed on pp. 194–95.

SOLO EXHIBITION CATALOGUES AND BROCHURES

1984
Madrid, Galería Fernando Vijande. *Juan Muñoz: Últimos trabajos*. Exh. cat. Madrid: F. Vijande.

1987
Bordeaux, Capc Musée d'Art Contemporain. *Juan Muñoz: Sculptures de 1985 à 1987*. Exh. cat. by Jean-Marc Poinsot.

1991
Eindhoven, The Netherlands, Stedelijk van Abbemuseum. *Juan Muñoz: Skulpturen, installaties en tekeningen*. Exh. cat.

Krefeld, Germany, Museum Haus Lange. *Juan Muñoz: Arbeiten 1988 bis 1990*. Exh. cat. by Julian Heynen. Krefeld: Krefelder Kunstmuseen.

1992
Valencia, Instituto Valenciano de Arte Moderno (IVAM), Centre del Carme. *Juan Muñoz: Conversaciones*. Exh. cat. by Vicente Todolí.

1994
Nîmes, Carré d'Art-Musée d'Art Contemporain. *Juan Muñoz*. Exh. cat. by Guy Tossatto.

1995
Boston, Isabella Stewart Gardner Museum. *Juan Muñoz: Portrait of a Turkish Man Drawing*. Exh. cat. by Jill Medvedow.

Santiago de Compostela, Spain, Centro Galego de Arte Contemporánea. *Juan Muñoz*. Exh. brochure by Gloria Moure.

1996
Madrid, Museo Nacional Centro de Arte Reina Sofía. *Juan Muñoz: Monólogos y diálogos/Monologues and Dialogues*. Exh. cat. by James Lingwood. Translated and revised as Zurich, Museum für Gegenwartskunst Zürich, *Juan Muñoz: Monologe und Dialoge/Monologues and Dialogues*, exh. cat. by James Lingwood (1997).

Muñoz, Juan, et al. *Silence please!: Stories after the Works of Juan Muñoz*. Dublin and Zurich: Irish Museum of Modern Art and Scalo. (Published in lieu of an exh. cat. in conjunction with Dublin, Irish Museum of Modern Art, *Juan Muñoz: Sculpture, Drawings and Installation*, 6 July–4 August 1994.)

New York, Dia Center for the Arts. *Juan Muñoz: A Place Called Abroad*. Exh. brochure by Lynne Cooke.

Turin, Marco Noire Contemporary Art. *Juan Muñoz: Mobiliario, grabados 1996*. Exh. cat. by Jorge Marsá. Lanzarote: Línea.

1997
Washington, D.C., Hirshhorn Museum and Sculpture Garden, Smithsonian Institution. *Directions: Juan Muñoz*. Exh. brochure by Neal Benezra.

1998
Santa Fe, N. Mex., SITE Santa Fe. *Streetwise*. Exh. brochure by Lynne Cooke.

1999
Miengo, Spain, Sala Robayera. *Juan Muñoz: Certain Drawings in Oil and Ink/Algunos dibujos en óleo y tinta 1996–1998*. Exh. cat.

New York, Dia Center for the Arts. *Juan Muñoz*. Exh. cat. by Lynne Cooke.

2000
Humlebæk, Denmark, Louisiana Museum for Moderne Kunst. *Juan Muñoz: The Nature of Visual Illusion*. Exh. cat. by Adrian Searle and Åsa Nacking.

2001
London, Tate Modern. *The Unilever Series: Juan Muñoz*. Exh. cat. by Susan May. London: Tate Gallery Publishing Limited.

GROUP EXHIBITION CATALOGUES AND OTHER BOOKS

1981
Fribourg, Switzerland. *Fri-art 81*. Exh. cat.

1982
Berlin. *Büro Berlin*. Exh. cat.

1983
Madrid, Galería Fernando Vijande. *Seis españoles en Madrid*. Exh. cat.

Madrid, Palacio de las Alhajas, Caja de Ahorros y Monte de Piedad. *La imagen del animal: Arte prehistórico, arte contemporáneo*. Exh. cat. by Juan Muñoz. Madrid: Ministerio de Cultura with the collaboration of The British Council.

1985
Eindhoven, The Netherlands, Stedelijk van Abbemuseum. *Christa Dichgans, Lili Dujourie, Marlene Dumas, Lesley Foxcroft, Kees de Goede, Frank van Hemert, Cristina Iglesias, Harald Klingelhöller, Mark Luyten, Juan Muñoz, Katherine Porter, Julião Sarmento, Barbara Schmidt Heins, Gabriele Schmidt-Heins, Didier Vermeiren*. Exh. cat. by Jan Debbaut and Rudy Fuchs.

1986
Fontevraud, France, Abbaye Royale de Fontevraud, Fonds Régional d'Art Contemporain (FRAC) des Pays de la Loire. *Ateliers internationaux des pays de la Loire*. Exh. cat.

Ghent, Museum Van Hedendaagse Kunst. *Chambres d'amis*. Exh. cat. by Jan Hoet.

Madrid, Consejería de Cultura de la Junta de Andalucía. *Bienal de Venecia: Aperto 86— Cuatro artistas españoles: XLII Biennale de Venezia*. Exh. cat. by Kevin Power et al.

Madrid, Palacio de la Moncloa. *Arte joven en el Palacio de la Moncloa*. Exh. cat. by Carmen Giménez Martín.

Madrid, Sala de Exposiciones de la Fundación Caja de Pensiones. *Pintores y escultores españoles 1981–1986*. Exh. cat. by Maria Corral and Kevin Power. Barcelona: Fundación Caja de Pensiones.

Seville, Pabellón Mudéjar. *Diecisiete artistas, diecisiete autonomías*. Exh. cat. by Marga Paz. Seville: Consejería de Cultura, Junta de Andalucía.

Venice, 42nd Venice Biennale. *XLII esposizione internationale d'arte, la Biennale di Venezia: Arte e scienza*. Exh. cat. by Lynne Cooke et al. Venice and Milan: Edizioni La Biennale and Electa.

Zamora, Spain, VII Bienal de Escultura de la Ciudad de Zamora. *Escultura ibérica contemporánea*. Exh. cat. by Javier González de Durana and Kosmé María de Barañano.

1987
Amsterdam, De Appel. *Nightfire*. Exh. cat.

Fontevraud, France, Fonds Régional d'Art Contemporain (FRAC) des Pays de la Loire. *Juan Muñoz*. Exh. cat. by José-Luis Brea. (Published in conjunction with Fontevraud, France, Abbaye Royale de Fontevraud, Fonds Régional d'Art Contemporain [FRAC] des Pays de la Loire, *Lili Dujourie/Juan Muñoz*, summer.)

Paris, ARC-Musée d'Art Moderne de la Ville de Paris. *Espagne 87: Dynamiques et interrogations*. Exh. cat.

San Sebastian, Spain, Fondos del Museo de Bellas Artes de Álava Vitoria-Gasteiz. *Generación de los 80: Escultura—Fondos del Museo de Bellas Artes de Álava*. Exh. cat. Vitoria: Museo de Bellas Artes.

1988
Amsterdam, Maatschappij Arti et Amicitiae. *Juan Muñoz: Un objeto metálico/A Metallic Object*. (Published in lieu of an exh. cat. in conjunction with Amsterdam, Maatschappij Arti et Amicitiae, *Jan van de Pavert and Juan Muñoz*, 26 April–21 May.)

Annemasse, France, Villa du Parc, Fonds Régional d'Art Contemporain (FRAC) Rhônes-Alpes. *Presentation & propositions*. Exh. cat.

Celant, Germano. *Inespressionismo: L'arte oltre il contemporaneo*. Genova: Costa & Nolan. Translated as *Unexpressionism: Art Beyond the Contemporary* (New York: Rizzoli, 1989).

Graz, Austria, Stadtmuseum Graz. *Steirischer Herbst '88*. Exh. cat. by Peter Pakesch. Graz: Grazer Kunstverein.

Sicilia, José Mariá, Aurora García, and Axel Bolvig. *Spansk kunst i 1980'erne: De nyeste tendenser: José María Sicilia, Juan Muñoz, Pepe Espaliú, Susana Solano, Curro González, Ricardo Cotando, Xavier Grau, Txomin Badiola*. Holte: Gl. Holtegaard.

1989
Amsterdam, KunstRai 89. *Before and after the Enthusiasm 1972–1992/Antes y despues del entusiasmo*. Exh. cat. by José-Luis Brea. The Hague and Amsterdam: SDU Publishers and Contemporary Art Foundation.

Athens, DESTE Foundation for Contemporary Art. *Psychological Abstraction*. Exh. cat. by Jeffrey Deitch.

Brussels, Centre Albert Borschette. *Jeunes sculpteurs espagnols: Au ras du sol, le dos au mur*. Exh. cat. by Fernando Huici. Brussels: Ministero de Cultura and Centre Albert Borschette.

Karuizawa, Takanawa, Japan, The Museum of Modern Art. *Supein aato toudi/Spain Art Today*. Exh. cat. by Jaime Brihuega and Miguel Fernández-Cid.

Long Island City, N.Y., P.S.1 Contemporary Art Center. *Theatergarden Bestiarium: The Garden as Theater as Museum*. Exh. cat. by Chris Dercon et al. Cambridge, Mass.: The MIT Press. Translated as Poitiers, Entrepôt-Galerie du Confort Moderne, *Bestiarium, jardin-théâtre*.

Paris, Musée National d'Art Moderne, Centre Georges Pompidou and La Grande Halle-La Villette. *Magiciens de la terre*. Exh. cat. by Jean-Hubert Martin et al. Paris: Editions du Centre Pompidou.

Santiago de Compostela, Spain, Casa da Parra. *Presencias e procesos: Sobre as ultimas tendencias da arte*. Exh. brochure by Maria Luisa Sobrino Manzanares.

1990
Cortes, José Miguel G., ed. *La creacion artística como cuestionamiento/Artistic Creation at Stake, Discussions Held at the IVAM, 18–19 May 1990*. Valencia: Instituto Valenciano de la Juventud.

Epernay, France, Office Régional Culturel de Champagne-Ardenne. *Sculpture contemporaine espagnole*. Exh. cat. by X. Anton Castro et al.

Krefeld, Germany, Museen Haus Lange and Haus Esters. *Weitersehen (1980→1990→)*. Exh. cat. Krefeld: Krefelder Kunstmuseen.

London, Institute of Contemporary Arts and Serpentine Gallery. *Possible Worlds: Sculpture from Europe*. Exh. cat. by Iwona Blazwick, James Lingwood, and Andrea Schlieker.

Madrid, Sala Julio González, Museo Español de Arte Contemporáneo. *X salon de los 16*. Exh. cat. by Francisco Calvo Serraller et al. Madrid: Grupo 16.

Munich, Galerie Tanit. *Jardins de bagatelle*. Exh. cat.

Newport Beach, Calif., Newport Harbor Art Museum. *OBJECTives: The New Sculpture*. Exh. cat. by Paul Schimmel. Newport Beach and New York: Newport Harbor Art Museum and Rizzoli.

North York, Ontario, Art Gallery of York University. *Meeting Place: Robert Gober, Liz Magor, Juan Muñoz*. 4 vols. Exh. cat. by Gregory Salzman.

Rennes, Centre d'Histoire de l'Art Contemporain. *Le spectaculaire: Rebecca Horn, IFP, Niek Kemps, Claude Lévêque, Raoul Marek, Juan Muñoz, Emmanuel Saulnier, Haim Steinbach, Jan Vercruysse*. Exh. cat. by Karine Alexandre et al.

Sydney, Art Gallery of New South Wales. *The Readymade Boomerang: Certain Relations in Twentieth Century Art: The 8th Biennale of Sydney*. Exh. cat.

1991

Berlin, Martin-Gropius-Bau. *Metropolis: Internationale Kunstausstellung Berlin 1991*. Exh. cat. edited by Christos M. Joachimides and Norman Rosenthal. Stuttgart: Edition Cantz.

Krefeld, Germany, Krefelder Kulturstiftung, Kaiser Wilhelm Museum. *Skulpturen für Krefeld 2*. 2 vols. Exh. cat. Krefeld: Krefelder Kunstmuseen.

Krefeld, Germany, Museum Haus Lange and Haus Esters. *In anderen Räumen*. Exh. brochure by Julian Heynen. Krefeld: Krefelder Kunstmuseen.

Malmö, Sweden, Rooseum Center for Contemporary Art. *Trans/Mission: Konst i interkulturell limbo/Art in Intercultural Limbo*. Exh. cat. by Lars Nittve and Dick Hebdige.

Pittsburgh, The Carnegie Museum of Art. *Carnegie International 1991*. 2 vols. Exh. cat. by Lynne Cooke et al. Pittsburgh and New York: The Carnegie Museum of Art and Rizzoli.

Santa Monica, Calif., Meyer/Bloom Gallery. *History as Fiction*. Exh. cat.

1992

Barcelona, Fundació "la Caixa." *Tropismes: Collecció d'art contemporani Fundació "la Caixa."* Exh. cat. by Nimfa Bisbé, Dan Cameron, and Rosa Queralt.

Dusseldorf, Kunstverein für die Rheinlande und Westfalen. *Jahresgaben '92: Editionen*. Exh. cat.

Le Havre, France, Musée des Beaux-Arts André Malraux. *Ceci n'est pas une image: Les iconodules, l'image aujourd'hui*. Exh. cat. by Jérôme Alexandre. Paris: La Différence; Association des conservateurs de Haute-Normandie.

Kassel, Germany, Museum Fridericianum. *Documenta IX*. 3 vols. Exh. cat. by Baart de Baere et al. Stuttgart and New York: Edition Cantz and Harry N. Abrams.

Ljubljana, Slovenia, Moderna Galerija. *Tišina: Protislovne oblike resnice/Silence: Contradictory Shapes of Truth*. Exh. cat. by Zdenka Badovinac.

London, Hayward Gallery. *Doubletake: Collective Memory and Current Art*. Exh. cat. by Lynne Cooke et al. London and New York: South Bank Centre and *Parkett*. Translated as Vienna, Kunsthalle Wien, *Doubletake: Kollektives Gedächtnis & heutige Kunst* (1990), exh. cat. edited by Toni Stooss and Eleonora Louis.

Madrid, Sala de Plaza de España. *Artistas en Madrid: Años 80*. Exh. cat. by Miguel Fernández-Cid. Madrid: Dirección General de Patrimonio Cultural de la Consejería de Educación.

Munich, Galerie Bernd Klüser. *Portfolio lettre international.*

Seville, Expo 92. *Fundação de Serralves, um museu português.* Exh. cat. Porto: Fundação de Serralves.

Seville, Pabellón de España, Expo 92. *Pasajes: Actualidad del arte español.* Exh. cat. by José-Luis Brea and Teresa Blanch.

Seville, Pabellón de España, Expo 92, Salas del Arenal. *Los últimos días.* Exh. cat. by José-Luis Brea et al.

Sydney, 9th Biennale of Sydney. *The Boundary Rider: 9th Biennale of Sydney.* Exh. cat. by Anthony D. Bond.

Valencia, Instituto Valenciano de Arte Moderno (IVAM), Centre Julio González. *La colección del IVAM: Adquisiciónes 1985–1992.* Exh. cat. by Tomàs Llorens, Vicente Todolí, and J. F. Yvars.

1993
Albuquerque, N. Mex., The Albuquerque Museum. *The Human Factor: Figurative Sculpture Reconsidered.* Exh. cat. by Christopher C. French and Kathleen Shields.

Antwerp, Koninklijk Museum voor Schone Kunsten, Antwerp 93, *Het sublieme gemis/The Sublime Void: On the Memory of the Imagination.* Exh. cat. by Bart Cassiman.

Antwerp, Antwerpen 93, and Middelheim, Openluchtmuseum voor Beeldhouwkunst Middelheim. *Nieuwe beelden/New Sculptures.* Exh. cat. by Bart Cassiman, Menno Meewis, and Barbara Vanderlinden.

Arnhem, The Netherlands. *Sonsbeek 93.* Exh. cat. edited by Jan Brand, Catelijne de Muynck, and Valerie Smith. Ghent: Snoeck-Ducaju & Zoon.

Beja, Portugal, Galeria dos Escudeiros. *Juan Muñoz–Julião Sarmento: Metalúrgica alentejana.* Exh. cat. by Jorge Castanho, Maria Filomena Molder, and Herberto Helder. Beja: Câmara Municipal de Beja.

Bignan, France, Centre d'Art Contemporaine du Domaine de Kerguéhennec. *Domaine: L'ordre du temps.* Exh. cat.

Copenhagen, Charlottenborg. *JuxtaPosition.* Exh. cat. by Mikkel Borgh and John Peter Nielson.

Eindhoven, The Netherlands, Stedelijk Van Abbemuseum. *Aanwinsten/Acquisitions 1989–1993.* Exh. cat. by Jan Debbaut et al.

Rome, Palazzo delle Esposizioni. *Tutte le strade portano a Roma.* Exh. cat.

Venice, Peggy Guggenheim Collection, 45th Venice Biennale. *Drawing the Line Against AIDS.* Exh. cat. by John Cheim et al. [United States] and New York: American Foundation for AIDS Research and Rizzoli.

1994
Basel, Kunsthalle Basel. *Welt-Moral: Moralvorstellungen in der Kunst heute.* Exh. cat. by Thomas Kellein.

Bordeaux, Capc Musée d'Art Contemporain. *<<Même si c'est la nuit>>.* Exh. cat.

Cirlot, Lourdes. *Historia universal de arte: Últimas tendencias.* Barcelona: Editorial Planeta.

Madrid, Galería Soledad Lorenzo. *Malpaís: Grabados y monotipos 1994.* Exh. cat. Lanzarote: Línea.

Moure, Gloria. *Configuraciones urbanas.* Barcelona: Ediciones Polígrafa. Translated as *Urban Configurations* (Barcelona: Ediciones Polígrafa).

Las Palmas de Gran Canaria, Canary Islands, Centro Atlántico de Arte Moderno. *Entre la presencia y la representación.* Exh. cat. by Nimfa Bisbe.

Porto, Fundação Serralves. *Fragmentos para um museo imaginario.* Exh. cat.

San Sebastian, Spain, Arteleku. *1m = c.299792458⁴s.* Exh. cat. by Philippe Bouthier.

Storrs, Conn., Atrium Gallery, University of Connecticut. *Selections from the Le Witt Collection.* Exh. cat. by Walter McConnell.

1995
Athens, Panhellenios Syndesmos Aithouson Technis. *Art Athina 3 '95: Synantisi sygchronis technis.*

Barcelona, Museu d'Art Contemporani. *L'escultura. Creacions paral·leles. Metáfores del real.* Exh. cat. by Teresa Blanch.

Helsinki, Nykytaiteen Museo-Valtion Taidemuseo. *Yksityinen/Julkinen/Private/Public: Ars 95.* Exh. cat.

Luxembourg, Musée National d'Histoire et d'Art. *<<Collection>>: Art moderne et contemporain au Van Abbemuseum Eindhoven.* Exh. cat.

Maastricht, The Netherlands, Bonnefantenmuseum. *Sculpture from the Collection of Marlies and Jo Eyck/Sculpturen uit de colectie var Marlies en Jo Eyck.* Exh. brochure by Aloys van den Berk.

Manchester, England, Rochdale Canal. *Duck not on a Pond, Ganders never Laid a Golden Egg.* Exh. brochure.

Palma de Mallorca, Mallorca, Centre de Cultura. *Arquitectures plurals.* Exh. cat.

Rotterdam, Caldic Collection. *A Collection [of] Sculptures.*

Santiago de Compostela, Spain, Casa de la Para. *Incidentes.* Exh. cat.

Tokyo, The Watari Museum of Contemporary Art. *Ripple across the Water.* Exh. cat.

1996
Athens, DESTE Foundation for Contemporary Art. *Everything That's Interesting is New: The Dakis Joannou Collection.* Exh. cat. by Jeffrey Deitch et al. Athens and Ostfildern: DESTE Foundaiton for Contemporary Art and Cantz Verlag.

Berwick-Upon-Tweed, England. *Berwick Ramparts Project.* Exh. cat. by Pippa Coles. Berwick-Upon-Tweed: Berwick-Upon-Tweed Borough Council, English Heritage, Northern Arts and Northumberland County Council.

Copenhagen. *CitySpace 1996: Sculptures and Installations Made for Copenhagen 96*. Exh. cat.

Jerusalem, Israel Museum. *Marks: Artists Work throughout Jerusalem*. Exh. cat. by Suzanne Landau.

Savy, Robert, et al. *Fonds Régional d'Art Contemporain-Limousin: 1989–1995: "Deuxième époque."* Limoges: Fonds Régional d'Art Contemporain (FRAC)-Limousin.

Turin, Museo d'Arte Contemporanea, Castello di Rivoli. *Collezioni di Francia: Le opere dei Fondi Regionali d'Arte Contemporanea*. Exh. cat. by Giorgio Verzotti. Milano and Turin: Edizioni Charta and Castello di Rivoli.

Zurich, Museum für Gegenwartskunst Zürich. *Museum für Gegenwartskunst Zürich*. Exh. cat. by Arina Kowner and Rein Wolfs.

1997

Los Angeles, Margo Leavin Gallery. *Maxwell's Demon*. Exh. cat.

Lyon, Musée d'Art Contemporain. *4ᵉ Biennale d'art contemporain de Lyon: L'autre*. Exh. cat. by Harald Szeemann. [France]: Réunion des Musées Nationaux.

Madrid, Museo Nacional Centro de Arte Reina Sofía. *En la piel de toro*. Exh. cat. by Aurora García and Joaquím Magalhaes.

North Miami, Fla., Museum of Contemporary Art. *Tableaux*. Exh. cat. edited by Bonnie Clearwater.

Paris, Fondation Cartier pour l'art contemporain. *1: La collection de la Fondation Cartier pour l'art contemporain*. Exh. cat.

Venice. *La Biennale di Venezia: XLVII esposizione internationale d'arte*. Exh. cat. edited by Germano Celant.

Zurich, Museum für Gegenwartskunst Zürich. *Hip*. Exh. cat. by Marleen Wolfs et al.

1998

Antwerp, Museum van Hedendaagse Kunst. *Subjective Presences: A Choice from the Collection of Fundació "la Caixa."* Exh. cat.

Bernier, Jean, and Marina Eliades. *Jean Bernier Gallery: 1977–1998*. Athens: AGRA Publications.

Gainesville, Fla., Samuel P. Harn Museum of Art. *Inner Eye: Contemporary Art from the Marc and Livia Straus Collection*. Exh. cat.

Ghent, Stedelijk Museum voor Actuele Kunst. *Watou: 'Voor het verdwijnt en daarna.'* Exh. cat.

Gijón, Spain, Centro Cultural Caja de Asturias, Palacio Revillagigedo. *II trienal de arte gráfico: La estampa contemporánea*. Exh. cat.

Humlebæk, Denmark, Louisiana Museum of Modern Art. *Louisiana at 40—The Collection Today*. Exh. cat. Special issue of *Louisiana Revy* 38, no. 3 (June).

London, Hayward Gallery. *Voice Over: Sound and Vision in Current Art*. Exh. cat. by Michael Archer. London: South Bank Centre.

Madrid, Museo Nacional Centro de Arte Reina Sofía. *Dibujos germinales: 50 artistas españoles*. Exh. cat.

Oostende, Belgium, Museum voor Moderne Kunst. *René Magritte en de hedendaagse kunst/René Magritte and the Contemporary Art*. Exh. cat.

Pontevedra, Spain, Museo de Pontevedra. *Fisuras na percepción: 25 Bienal de arte de Pontevedra*. Exh. cat. by Alberto González-Alegre et al.

Ribalta, Jorge, ed. *Servicio público: Conversaciones sobre financiación pública y arte contemporáneo*. Salamanca and Barcelona: Ediciones Universidad de Salamanca and Unión de Asociaciones de Artistas Visuales.

Stockholm, Moderna Museet. *Wounds: Between Democracy and Redemption in Contemporary Art/Mellan demokrati och forlosning i samtida konst*. Exh. cat. by David Elliott and Pier Luigi Tazzi.

1999

Bonn, Kunstmuseum Bonn. *Zeitwenden: Ausblick*. Exh. cat. by Dieter Ronte and Walter Smerling. Cologne: DuMont.

Boston, The Institute of Contemporary Art. *Collectors Collect Contemporary: 1990–99*. Exh. cat. by Jessica Morgan.

Istanbul. *The Passion and the Wave: 6th International Istanbul Biennial*. Exh. cat. by Paolo Colombo et al.

Krefeld, Germany, Krefelder Kunstmuseum. *C/O Haus Lange-Haus Esters, 1984/1999*. Exh. cat.

Künzelsau, Germany, Museum Wurth. *Spanische Kunst am Ende des Jahrhunderts*. Exh. cat. by Kosme María de Barañano Letamendía and C. Sylvia Weber. Sigmaringen: Thorbecke.

Leipzig, Germany, Galerie für Zeitgenossische Kunst. *Life Cycles*. Exh. cat.

Liverpool, Tate Gallery Liverpool. *Trace: 1st Liverpool Biennial of International Contemporary Art*. Exh. cat. by Anthony Bond et al. Liverpool: Liverpool Biennial of Contemporary Art in association with Tate Gallery Liverpool.

Middelburg, The Netherlands, Zeeuws Museum. *Het betoverde plein*. Exh. cat. by Florent Bex. Middelburg: Stichting Wim Riemens.

Nuremberg, Kunsthalle Nürnberg. *Vergiß den Ball und spiel' weiter*. Exh. cat.

Warsaw, Mediterrean Foundation and the National Museum. *North-South: Transcultural Visions*. Exh. cat.

2000
Ghent, Stedelijk Museum voor Actuele Kunst. *Over the Edges*. 2 vols. Exh. cat. by Jan Hoet and Giacinto Di Pietrantino.

London, Tate Modern. *Between Cinema and a Hard Place*. Exh. brochure by Frances Morris et al.

Long Island City, N.Y., P.S.1 Contemporary Art Center. *Around 1984: A Look at Art in the 80's*. Exh. cat. by Carolyn Christov-Bakargiev.

Las Palmas de Gran Canaria, Canary Islands, Centro Atlántico de Arte Moderno. *Máquinas*. Exh. cat. by Marga Paz.

Sydney, Art Gallery of New South Wales. *Biennale of Sydney 2000: 12th Biennale of Sydney*. Exh. cat. by Fumio Nanjo et al.

2001
New York, Museum of Modern Art. *Parkett: Collaborations and Editions since 1984*. Exh. cat. by Deborah Wye and Susan Tallman. Zurich and New York: Parkett Publishers.

New York, Museum of Modern Art. *Collaborations with Parkett: 1984 to Now*. Exh. brochure by Deborah Wye.

Oakland, Calif., California College of Arts and Crafts Institute. *A Contemporary Cabinet of Curiosities: Selections from the Vicki and Kent Logan Collection*. Exh. cat. by Ralph Rugoff.

Warner, Marina. "Here Comes the Bogeyman: Goya, the Late Grotesque, and Juan Muñoz." In *Robert Lehman Lectures on Contemporary Art*, vol. 2, edited by Karen Kelly and Lynne Cooke. New York: Dia Center for the Arts.

ARTICLES AND REVIEWS

1984
Serraller, Francisco Calvo. "La tercera mirada del misterio." *El País* (Madrid), 17 November, Art section.

1985
Collado, Gloria. "70, 80, 90 . . . La historia interminable: Rumbo a lo desconocido." *Lápiz* 3, no. 23 (February): 35–38.

Pinharda, Joao. "Retrato de una epoca." *Mais* (Lisbon), 15 March.

Porfírio, José Luís. "Quatro caminhos: Simetrias e contrastes." *Expresso* (Lisbon), 16 March.

1986
Cameron, Dan. "Spain is Different." *Arts Magazine* 61, no. 1 (September): 14–17.

Koether, Jutta, and Diedrich Diederischsen. "Jutta and Diedrich Go to Spain: Spanish Art and Culture Viewed from Madrid." *Artscribe*, no. 59 (September–October): 56–61.

S. C. "El arte joven español en la Fundación Cartier." *ABC* (Madrid), 24 December.

Serraller, Francisco Calvo. "Las imágenes rotas de un agonista." *El País* (Madrid), 19 December, section C.

Tazzi, Pier Luigi. "Albrecht Dürer Would Have Come Too." *Artforum International* 25 (September): 124–28.

1987
Albertazzi, Liliana. "Espagne aujourd'hui." *Galeries Magazine*, no. 17 (February–March): 50, 57, and 116–17.

Brea, José-Luis. "Juan Muñoz: Nada es tan opaco como un espejo." *Sur Exprés*, no. 1 (15 April–15 May): 32–33.

Collado, Gloria. "Tierra desierta." *Guía del ocio*, no. 576 (29 December 1986–4 January 1987): 42.

Danvila, Jose Ramon. "Contra todo tipo de circunstancias." *El Punto de las Artes* (Madrid), 19 December 1986–8 January 1987.

———. "Un encuentro con el arte en Marga Paz." *El Punto de las Artes* (Madrid), 9–15 October.

"El estado del arte." *Sur Exprés* (November–December): 49–55.

Power, Kevin. "Juan Muñoz." *Artscribe*, no. 64 (summer): 93.

Serraller, Francisco Calvo. "Cuatro artistas españoles jóvenes exponen en Burdeos." *El País* (Madrid), 30 September.

———. "La nouvelle sculpture espagnole." *Art Press*, no. 117 (September): 17–20.

1988
Aliaga, Juan Vicente. "Spanish Art: A History of Disruption." *Artscribe International*, no. 68 (March–April): 64–67.

Brea, José-Luis. "Juan Muñoz." *Flash Art* (Spanish edition), no. 1 (February): 70. Also published as "Juan Muñoz: The System of Objects," *Flash Art*, no. 138 (January–February): 88–89.

Christov-Bakargiev, Carolyn. "Something Nowhere." *Flash Art*, no. 140 (May–June): 80–85.

203

Phillipson, Michael. "Juan Muñoz." *Artscribe*, no. 68 (March–April): 88–81.

Power, Kevin. "Das Wesen des Tanzes." *Kunstforum International* 94 (April–May): 233–36.

———. "Spanien—Künstlerportraits: Juan Muñoz." *Kunstforum International* 94 (April–May): 148–49.

Steenbergen, Renée. "Juan Muñoz." *NRC Handelsblad* (Rotterdam), 29 April.

1989
Brea, José-Luis. "Juan Muñoz: The Other Speaks." *New Art International* 4, no. 2 (March): 62–64.

Cembalest, Robin. "Spain: Learning to Absorb the Shock of the New." *Artnews* 88 (September): 127–31.

Costa, José Manuel. "Juan Muñoz." *ABC* (Madrid), 5 May.

———. "Juan Muñoz, la metáfora entre los pucheros." *Guía de Madrid*, no. 80 (April).

———. "Juan Muñoz: La temperancia del objeto." *El Punto de las Artes* (Madrid), 21–27 April: 164–65.

Danvila, Jose Ramon. "Juan Muñoz, la reflexión sobre lo cotidiano." *El Punto de las Artes* (Madrid), 20–26 October.

Deitch, Jeffrey. "Psychological Abstraction." *Flash Art*, no. 149 (November–December): 164–65.

Fernández-Cid, Miguel. "Una consulta en la galería." *Diario 16* (Madrid), 14 April, Art section.

Grout, Catherine. "Cristina Iglesias, Juan Muñoz: Sculptures." *Artstudio*, no. 14 (autumn): 110–17.

Jimenez, P. "Juan Muñoz, metáfora de lo cotidiano." *ABC* (Madrid), 28 November.

Lambrecht, Luk. "Juan Muñoz." *Flash Art*, no. 148 (October): 143–44.

Melo, Alexandre. "Some Things That Cannot Be Said Any Other Way." *Artforum International* 27 (May): 119–21.

Nazaré, Leonor. "Crise de l'object— Cómicos." *Expresso* (Lisbon), 4 November.

Serraller, Francisco Calvo. "La danza inmóvil." *El País* (Madrid), 21 October, Art section.

1990
Aliaga, Juan Vicente. "Discursos alienados." *El País* (Madrid), 1 December, Art section.

Arnaudet, Didier. "Des pratiques de l'objet dans l'art des années 80: Apparences, metaphores et empreintes." *Colóquio artes* 32, no. 85 (June): 54–61.

Bradley, Kim. "Juan Muñoz at Galería Marga Paz." *Art in America* 78 (February): 179.

Cantor, Judy. "Juan Muñoz." *Artnews* 89 (April): 181.

F. B. "Muñoz: Un œil noir vous regarde." *Beaux-Arts Magazine*, no. 85 (December): 127.

García, Aurora. "Juan Muñoz, Galería Marga Paz." *Artforum International* 28 (February): 149.

Hall, James. "Near-Mystical Meltings." *Art International*, no. 10 (spring): 65–68.

Jimenez, Carlos. "España, el cierre de una década/The Close of a Decade." *Arte en Colombia*, no. 43 (February): 76–79, 147–49.

Llorca, Pablo. "La tercera via." *Guía de Madrid* (June).

Marlow, Tim. "London, Lisson Gallery, Juan Muñoz." *The Burlington Magazine* 132, no. 1043 (February): 144.

Melo, Alexandre. "A propósito de objectos complexos." *Ler*, no. 11 (summer): 57–9.

———. "Cartografía de la supervivencia." *Diario 16* (Madrid), 2 May.

Olivares, Rosa. "Beyond Form: An Update on Spanish Sculpture." *Arts Magazine* 65, no. 4 (December): 52–57.

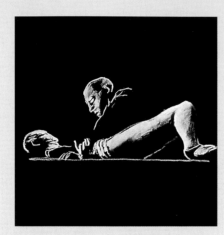

Exhibition invitation, *Juan Muñoz: Drawings and Prints*, Frith Street Gallery, London, 1992

Packer, William. "Some Transubstantiation Needed." *Financial Times* (London), 20 November, Arts section.

Roberts, James. "Juan Muñoz." *Artefactum* 7, no. 32 (February–March): 44.

1991
Blase, Christoph. "Wohnen in Krefeld." *Das Kunst-Bulletin*, no. 3 (March): 10.

Brenson, Michael. "Juan Muñoz." *New York Times*, 26 April.

CDG. "Genf: Juan Muñoz im Centre d'Art Contemporain." *Das Kunst-Bulletin*, no. 1 (January): 42.

Chauvy, Laurence. "Des ballerines aux jambes coupées." *Journal de Genève*, 8 January.

Dohnalek, Claudio. "Inaugurada en Berlín la exposición 'Metropolis,' símbolo de la unificación." *El País* (Madrid), 27 April.

Hixson, Kathryn. "Chicago in Review." *Arts Magazine* 65 (February): 106–8.

Lambrecht, Luk. "Juan Muñoz, Centre d'Art Contemporain, Geneva, and Museum Haus Lange, Krefeld." *Forum International* 8 (May–August): 67.

Levels, Marlies. "Pose (pauze) posa: Momenten van stilstand in het werk van Juan Muñoz." *Archis*, no. 12 (December): 27–30.

Poiatti, Myriam. "Juan Muñoz: Quatorze 'ballerines.'" *Tribune de Genève*, 5–6 January.

Praplan, Geneviève. "La paix de l'esprit." *La Suisse* (Geneva), 22 January.

Savioz, Cathy. "Muñoz: Ni Lucio, ni Carlos, Juan!" *Voir*, no. 76 (February): 23.

Searle, Adrian. "Waiting for Nothing." *Frieze*, no. 2 (December): 24–29.

Serraller, Francisco Calvo. "Juan Muñoz." *Beaux-Arts Magazine*, no. 96 (December): 104–6.

Tager, Alisa. "The Essence of Absence: The Sculpture of Juan Muñoz." *Arts Magazine* 65 (summer): 36–39.

Van den Boogerd, Dominic. "Bevroren barok." *Metropolis M*, no. 6 (December): 28–35.

1992
Bourriaud, Nicholas. "Figuration in an Age of Violence." *Flash Art* 25, no. 162 (January–February): 87–91.

Charbonnier, Jean-Michel. "Les jeunes talents." *Beaux-Arts Magazine*, no. 106 (November): 22–29.

Cork, Richard. "Do You See What They See?" *Times* (London), 28 February, Features section.

Deitcher, David. "Art on the Installation Plan." *Artforum International* 30 (January): 79–84.

Fernández-Cid, Miguel. "La apariencia y el sentido." *Cambio* 16 (Madrid), 25 May.

Jinkner-Lloyd, Amy. "Musing on Museology." *Art in America* 80 (June): 43–51.

Maldonado, José. "Cascando: Aun por terminar, aun por ver." *Papers d'art* (December): 10–11.

Peters, Philip. "En Route: Jan Hoet's Documenta." *Kunst & Museumjournaal* 4, no. 2: 25–32.

Pol, Marta. "Jose Maldanado/Juan Muñoz." *Papers d'art* (September).

Searle, Adrian. "Juan Muñoz: Un recuerdo de Londres." *Revista de Occidente*, no. 129 (February): 47–56.

Smolik, Noemi. "Aspekte der Skulptur: Zwischen fester Form und Grenzlosigkeit." *Kunstforum International* 199: 201–4.

Tarantino, Michael. "Juan Muñoz." *Artforum International* 30 (April): 111–12.

Villén, Ángel L. Pérez. "La vanitas neobarroca." *Lápiz* 10, no. 87 (May–June): 64–67.

Zaya, Octavio. "Juan Muñoz: A Theater of Appearances (Between Transit and Inertia)." *Balcon*, no. 10: 15–25.

1993
Barriga, Paulo. "Très airosas saídas." *Diário do Alentejo* (Beja), 3 December.

Krumpel, Doris. "'Doubletake' in der Wiener Kunsthalle." *Der Standard* (Vienna), January.

Melo, Alexandre. "A importância de ser actual." *Expresso* (Lisbon), 10 December.

Oliveira, Luísa Soares de. "Arte radical." *Público* (Lisbon), 29 November.

Pinharanda, João. "Julião Sarmento e Juan Muñoz." *Público* (Lisbon), 17 December.

Schwabsky, Barry. "Reviews: New York." *Sculpture* 12, no. 4 (July–August): 54–55.

Shone, Richard. "London: Recent Exhibitions." *The Burlington Magazine* 135, no. 1078 (January): 45–47.

Stegeman, Elly. "The Sublime Void." *Kunst & Museumjournaal* 5, no. 2: 53–57.

Titz, Walter. "Die Gedachtnisse der Welt." *Kleine Zeitung* (Graz), January.

1994
Jocks, Heinz-Norbert. "Juan Muñoz." *Kunstforum International*, no. 125 (January–February): 344–45.

Piguet, Philippe. "Nîmes: Juan Muñoz." *L'oeil*, no. 461 (May): 15.

1995
"Beide kehren zur menschlichen Figur zurück." *Hamburger Abendblatt*, 7 July.

Bensley, Lis. "Viewers are Actors in Muñoz's Sculpture Dramas." *New Mexican* (Santa Fe), 13 October.

Bryars, Gavin. "A Man in a Room, Gambling." *Parkett*, no. 43 (March): 52–55. Translated as "Ein Mann in einem Zimmer beim Kartenspiel": 56–61.

Cooke, Lynne. "Juan Muñoz and the Specularity of the Divided Self." *Parkett*, no. 43 (March): 20–23. Translated as "Juan Muñoz und die Spiegelungen des Geteilten Selbst": 24–27.

205

Danek, Sabine. "Feuer zum Mitnehmen." *Szene Hamburg*, August.

Durden, Mark. "Duck not on a Pond, Ganders never Laid a Golden Egg." *Art Monthly*, no. 191 (November): 33–35.

Giuliano, Charles. "Juan Muñoz: Portrait of a Turkish Man Drawing." *Art New England* 17, no. 1 (December 1995–January 1996): 64.

Hermida, Xosé. "Juan Muñoz expone su última obra, basada en la 'absorción y teatralidad.'" *El País* (Madrid), 21 December.

J. S. M. "Klapperschlange mit Tränenkette." *Stuttgarter Zeitung*, 14 August. Also published as "Wie bestellt und nicht abgeholt," *Landeszeitung für die Lüneburger Heide*, 8–9 July.

Melo, Alexandre. "The Art of Conversation." *Parkett*, no. 43 (March): 36–41. Translated as "Die Kunst der Konversation": 28–35.

Melrod, George. "Post-Pop Pizzazz." *Art and Antiques* 18, no. 10 (November): 39–40.

Schupp, Ulrike. "Theatralische Reminiszenen: Skulpturen von Juan Muñoz und Henk Visch im Kunstverein." *Hamburger Rundschau*, 20 July.

Sherman, Mary. "Xu Bing and a Prayer." *Artnews* 94 (December): 55–56.

Sierra, Rafael. "El regreso del escultor pródigo." *El Mundo* (Madrid), 21 December, Culture section.

Temin, Christine. "Juan Muñoz Practices the Gentle Art of Dislocation." *Boston Globe*, 24 September, Art section.

Unger, Miles. "Juan Muñoz." *New Art Examiner* 23 (December): 37–38.

1996

Borràs, Maria Lluïsa. "Una muestra de naderías." *La Vanguardia* (Barcelona), 8 November.

Dannatt, Adrian. "Juan Muñoz." *Flash Art*, no. 191 (November–December): 105–6.

Danvila, Jose Ramon. "Juan Muñoz: Intensidad interior, espacio y escenografía." *El Punto de las Artes* (Madrid), 7 November.

———. "La mirada dinámica." *El Mundo* (Madrid), 8 November.

Erausquin, Victoria. "Misterio en el Retiro." *Expansión* (Madrid), 9 November.

"Esculturas de Juan Muñoz en el Palacio de Velázquez." *Egin* (San Sebastian), 23 October.

Fernández-Cid, Miguel. "Presencias y ecos de Juan Muñoz." *ABC* (Madrid), 25 October.

Flórez, Fernando Castro. "El espacio inquietante del hombre: En lugar del ventrílocuo." *Cimal Arte Internacional*, no. 47: 25–32.

———. "La figuración desviada." *Diario 16* (Madrid), 2 November.

Foix, Vicente Molina. "Nueva York–Valencia." *El País* (Madrid), 5 November.

Gonzalez García-Pando, Carmen. "Juan Muñoz: Eculturas públicas con pensamientos privados." *Reseña*, no. 278 (December): 44.

Hunt, Ian. "Making It All Up." *Art Monthly*, no. 200 (October): 70–71.

Jarque, Fietta. "La primera antológia del escultor Juan Muñoz transforma radicalmente el Palacio de Velázquez." *El País* (Madrid), 25 October.

"Juan Muñoz at the Palacio de Velázquez." *Guidepost* (29 November): 10–11.

"Juan Muñoz, bellezza y originalidad." *Noticias Médicas*, no. 3.635 (November): 46.

Lloyd, Ann Wilson. "Empty Hands, Silent Mouths." *Art in America* 84, no. 3 (March): 50–51.

———. "Juan Muñoz." *Sculpture* 15 (January): 78.

Princenthal, Nancy. "Artist's Book Beat." *On Paper* 1, no. 2 (November–December): 40–1.

Reyes, J. A. Álvarez. "La derecha ha dado un golpe de Estado en el IVAM." *Diario 16* (Madrid), 25 October.

Serraller, Francisco Calvo. "Un montaje magistral." *El País* (Madrid), 25 October.

Sierra, Rafael. "El Reina Sofía resume la trayectoria del escultor Juan Muñoz." *El Mundo* (Madrid), 25 October.

Smith, Roberta. "Wandering through a Place That Never Was." *New York Times*, 27 September, section C.

Van Hove, Jan. "Voorzichtig optimisme op Lineart." *De Standaard* (Brussels), 29 November.

1997

Billeter, Fritz. "Kunst: Warum lachen diese Chinesen?" *Brückenbauer* (Zurich), 12 February.

Cañas, Susana. "Las misteriosas figuras de Juan Muñoz." *El tiempo latino* (San Francisco), 14 March.

Canning, Susan M. "Juan Muñoz." *Sculpture* 16, no. 3 (March): 58–59.

Cassiman, Bart. "Juan Muñoz." *Dietsche Warande & Belfort* 6 (December): 681–82.

Cochran, Rebecca Dimling. "Juan Muñoz." *Art Papers* 21 (March–April): 81.

Cohn, David. "Juan Muñoz." *Artnews* 96 (February): 126.

Cruz, Juan. "Gavin Bryars and Juan Muñoz." *Art Monthly*, no. 211 (November): 30–31.

Dixon, Glenn. "Stage Fright." *Washington City Paper*, 14 March.

Eccles, Tom. "Juan Muñoz at Dia." *Art in America* 85 (May): 121.

F. J. "Gavin Bryars clausura con un concierto la exposición de Juan Muñoz en el Retiro." *El País* (Madrid), 11 January.

Gerster, Ulrich. "China grinst—Juan Muñoz im Museum für Gegenwartskunst." *Neue Zürcher Zeitung*, 6 February.

Grabher, Ariane. "Vom Leben in einem Schuhkarton." *Vorarlberger Nachrichten* (Wichnergasse), 6 February.

Hanks, Robert. "Music—Contemporary: A Sound Strategy." *Independent* (London), 22 September, Features section.

Harris, Jane. "Juan Muñoz." *Art Papers* 21 (March–April): 64.

Howell, George. "Cheryl Donegan; Juan Muñoz." *Art Papers* 21 (July–August): 35.

———. "Juan Muñoz: Figurative Metaphors on the Washington Mall." *Sculpture* 16, no. 1 (January): 8–9.

Kuoni, Gisela. "Von der Faszination der lähmenden Abwesenheit." *Bündes Zeitung*, 19 March.

Llorca, Pablo. "Juan Muñoz." *Artforum International* 35 (February): 95–96.

McEvilley, Thomas. "The Millennial Body: The Art of the Figure at the End of Humanity." *Sculpture* 16, no. 8 (October): 24–29.

McFadden, Sarah. "The 'Other' Biennial." *Art in America* 85 (November): 84–91.

Muñoz, Jorge. "El impacto de Juan Muñoz." *Inversión* (Madrid), 10 January.

Oberholzer, Niklaus. "Lauter lächelnde Unbekannte um uns." *Neue Luzerner Zeitung*, 10 February.

Richard, Paul. "Laughing in the Faces of Danger." *Washington Post*, 10 March, Style section.

Rosa, Tessa. "L'infinita solitudine di Juan Muñoz." *Azione* (Naples), 1 May.

SFD. "Irritierend: Juan Muñoz im Museum für Gegenwartskunst." *Tagblatt der Stadt Zürich*, 11 February.

Searle, Adrian. "Hush! Listen to the Sound of Sculpture." *Guardian* (London), 18 September, section 2.

Vachtov, Ludmila. "Die Falle der Mutanten." *Neue Nidwaldner Zeitung* (Luzern), 6 February.

Vignjevic, Tomislav. "Prireditev v znamenju neizogibnih sprememb." *M'ars* 9, no. 2: 54–57.

Vogel, Wolfram. "Schrecken des Kriegs als Disco." *Südkurier* (Konstanz), 6 February.

Wüst, Karl. "Sisyphos in der Schuhschachtel." *Bischofszeller Nachrichten*, 8 February.

Zwez, Annelise. "Geschichten ohne Worte, Lachen ohne Laute." *Anzeiger von Ulster*, 4 February.

———. "Kunst-Geschichten ohne Worte." *Schaffhauser Nachrichten*, 11 February.

1998

Berger, John. "El cæ fuego." In *La ciutat de les paraules*. Barcelona: Edicions de l'Eixample.

———. "Hotel Declercq." *Eaeyoepotynia* (Athens), 6 April. Also published in *Triquarterly* (fall): 91–96.

Brea, José-Luis. "'En la piel de toro,' Palacio de Velázquez." *Artforum* 36 (January): 107–8.

Cruz, Juan. "Hearing Voices." *Art Monthly*, no. 214 (March): 12–15.

Rinne, Hannu. "Museossakin kamppailevat ja muoto." *Taide*, no. 3: 19.

Romano, Gianni. "Juan Muñoz: Galeria Continua, San Gimignano." *Untitled: A Review of Contemporary Art*, no. 15 (spring): 25.

Tosatto, Guy. "Juan Muñoz." *L'oeil*, no. 492 (January): 56–59.

1999

Antmen, Ahu, and Vasif Kortun. "The Istanbul Fall." *Flash Art* (Italy) 32, no. 209 (November–December): 84–85.

Barragán, Paco. "Ya no tiene sentido la representación nacional." *El Periodico del Arte*, no. 25 (August–September).

Bröder, F. J. "Ab in die Ecke und schäm dich." *Nordbayerischer Kurier* (Bayreuth), 23–24 October.

Buck, Louisa. "It's not So Cold up North." *Art Newspaper*, no. 95 (September).

207

Chambert, Christian. "The International Curators Had Moved On." *Nu*, pt. 2: 88.

Massey, Diane. "A Sharp Satire on City's Greats." *Daily Post* (New York), 6 October.

Muñoz, Juan, with Attilio Maranzano. "The Burning of Madrid as Seen from the Terrace of My House" (photo essay). *Janus* 3 (March): 22–27.

Schmidt, Kristin. "Vergiß den Ball und spiel' weiter—Das Bild des Kindes in der zeitgenössischen Kunst." *Monatsanzieger* (Nuremberg), no. 223 (October).

Searle, Adrian, and Jonathan Jones. "Venice on the Mersey." *Guardian* (London), 28 September, section 2.

2000

Alberge, Dalya. "Company of Men to Replace Giant Spider." *Times* (London), 3 October.

Bergendahl, Berit. "104 leende kineser." *Götesborgs-Posten*, 18 March.

Berger, John. "A Mouth Speaks Out Alone." In *LAB. Academy of Media Arts Yearbook*. Cologne: Verlag Walter König.

Bergström, Lotta. "Vad skrattar de åt, kinesrna?" *Hallands Nyheter* (Falkenberg), 22 March.

Bonde, Lisbeth. "Det aktive værk." *Information* (Copenhagen), 18 March.

Carlsson, Larsolof. "Kineser på bred front." *Helsingborgs Dagblad*, 17 March.

Castro, Fernando. "El narrador de historias." *ABC* (Madrid), 1 December.

Charpentier, C-J. "Hundra spanska kineser." *Nya Läns-Tidningen/Nya Lidköpings Tidning*, 29 March.

Costa, José Manuel. "Juan Muñoz realizará una escultura de seseuta metros para la Tate Gallery." *ABC* (Madrid), 4 October.

Dakinah. "Louisiana: Muñoz' optiske illusion." *Lokal-Avisen Ugebladet* (Vestfyn), 22 March.

"El escultor Juan Muñoz obtiene el premio Nacional de Artes Plásticas." *ABC* (Madrid), 1 December.

Ersgård, Stefan. "Leende kineser gästar Louisiana." *Arbetet Nyheterna* (Malmö), 18 March.

Feinstein, Roni. "Report from Sydney: The Biennale of Reconciliation." *Art in America* 88 (December): 38–45.

Fernández-Cid, Miguel. "Artista polémico, obra inquietante." *La Razón*, 1 December.

H. D. "Spektakulær udstilling på Louisiana." *Frederiksborg Amts Avis* (Hillerød), 18 March.

Hansen, Jørgen. "De fremmede." *Jyllandsposten, Morgenavis*, 22 March.

———. "100 kinesere og en spanier." *Jyllandsposten, Morgenavis*, 17 March.

Hemming, Sarah. "Sarah Hemming Wonders How You Replace a Seven-Tonne Spider." *Daily Express* (London), 30 December, Weekend section.

Holmqvist, Åke. "Kinesiska leenden som provocerar." *Norra Skåne* (Hässleholm), 25 March.

Hörle, Suzanne. "Leende kineser på Louisiana." *Nya Wermlands-Tidningen* (Karlstad), 23 March.

Hornung, Peter. "Muñoz' verdensteater." *Politiken* (Copenhagen), 17 March.

J. P. "The Dis-Orient Express." *Copenhagen Post*, 24–30 March.

Jones, Jonathan. "Big and Beautiful?" *Guardian* (London), 4 October.

Jørgensen, Tom. "Magien mangler." *Ekstra Bladet* (Copenhagen), 20 March.

Malmqvist, Conny C-A. "Kineser, kineser— överallt kineser." *Kvällspoten* (Malmö), 22 March.

Misfeldt, Mai. "100 kinesere på museums-besøg." *Berlingske Tidende* (Copenhagen), 17 March.

Moe, Helene. "Under smilets syntetiske maske." *Kristeligt Dagblad* (Copenhagen), 16 March.

Montigny, Britte. "Skenet bedrar." *Skånska Dagbladet* (Malmö), 24 March.

Nielsen, Elisa. "Beskuer eller aktør." *Aktuelt* (Copenhagen), 20 March.

Prassad, Raeckha. "Muñoz Moves into Spider's Space." *Guardian* (London), 4 October.

Rifbjerg, Synne. "En Kinamands chance." *Week-end Avisen* (Copenhagen), 18 February.

Rodriguez, Juan Carlos. "La fama interna-cional de Juan Muñoz le da el Premio Nacional de Artes Plásticas." *La Razón*, 1 December.

Scavenius, Bente. "100 små kinesere." *Børsen* (Copenhagen), 20 March.

Serraller, Francisco Calvo. "El escultor Juan Muñoz obtiene el Premio Nacional de Artes Plásticas." *El País* (Madrid), 1 December.

Sierra, Rafael. "España intenta reconciliarse de nuevo con Juan Muñoz." *El Mundo* (Madrid), 1 December.

Waak, Malin. "Kineser som konstverk." *Sydsvenska Dagbladet* (Malmö), 24 March.

Win. "Juan Muñoz er naeste satsning." *Helsingør Dagblad*, 25 February.

2001
Adams, Tim. "Breaking the Mould." *Life: The Observer Magazine* (3 June): 11–14.

Campbell-Johnston, Rachel. "The Urbane Spaceman." *Times* (London), 11 June, Arts section.

Cumming, Laura. "Don't Mention the War . . ." *Observer Review*, 17 June, Arts section.

Jarque, Vicente. "La Figura táctil, o las imágenes de Juan Muñoz." *Arte y parte*, no. 32 (April–May): 22–31.

Muñoz, Juan, and Julian López. "Escena de desaparición" (photo essay). *Arte y Parte*, no. 32 (April–May): n. pag.

Searle, Adrian. "We Are Not Alone." *Guardian* (London), 12–13 June, Visual Arts section.

Exhibition brochure, *Steetwise*, SITE Santa Fe, 1998

List of Illustrations

Works listed here are by Juan Munoz unless otherwise noted. For a list of plates, see "Catalogue of the Exhibition," pp. 140–43.

FIGURE ILLUSTRATIONS

Neal Benezra, "Sculpture and Paradox"

Fig. 1
Two Figures for Middelheim, 1993
Bronze
Figures: $66^{15}/_{16}$ x $27^9/_{16}$ x $27^9/_{16}$ and $51^3/_{16}$ x $31^1/_2$ x $27^9/_{16}$ in. (170 x 70 x 70 and 130 x 80 x 70 cm)
Openluchtmuseum voor beeldhouwkunst Middelheim, Antwerp

Fig. 2
Untitled, 1979–80
Reel-to-reel tape players, audio tape, plaster, and wood
Dimensions variable
Courtesy of the artist

Fig. 3
Croydon Drawing, 1980
Chalk on wall
Dimensions variable
Courtesy of the artist

Fig. 4
Juan Muñoz, Malaga, 1980
Courtesy of the artist

Figs. 5a–c
Juan Muñoz, P.S.1 Contemporary Art Center, Long Island City, New York, 1982
Courtesy of the artist

Figs. 6a–c
Juan Muñoz, New York, 1982
Courtesy of the artist

Fig. 7
Installation view of "Juan Muñoz: Últimos trabajos," Galería Fernando Vijande, Madrid, 1984, with *General Miaja Looking for the Guadiana River* installed on four columns

Fig. 8
Bunker overlooking Juan Muñoz's house in Torrelodones, Spain
Courtesy of the artist

Fig. 9
Édouard Manet (French; 1832–1883)
The Balcony, 1868
Oil on canvas
$66^1/_2$ x $49^1/_4$ in. (168.9 x 125.1 cm)
Musée d'Orsay, Paris

Fig. 10
North of the Storm, 1986
Welded iron
H. $47^1/_4$ in. (120 cm); diam. $78^3/_4$ in. (200 cm)
© IVAM (Institut Valencià d'Art Modern), Generalitat Valenciana, España

Fig. 11
Edgar Degas
Henri Michel-Lévy, 1878
$16^1/_8$ x $10^5/_8$ in. (41 x 27 cm)
Calouste Gulbenkian Foundation

Fig. 12
Jeff Wall (Canadian; b. 1946)
A Ventriloquist at a Birthday Party in October 1947, 1990
Transparency in light box
$90^3/_{16}$ x $138^9/_{16}$ in. (229 x 352 cm)
J. P. Berghmanns/Collection Lhoist, Brussels

Fig. 13
Robert Gober (American; b. 1954)
Untitled, 1990
Wax, cotton, wood, leather, shoe, and human hair
$10^3/_4$ x $20^1/_2$ x $5^5/_8$ in. (27.3 x 52.1 x 14.3 cm)
Hirshhorn Museum and Sculpture Garden, Smithsonian Institution, Joseph H. Hirshhorn Purchase Fund, 1990

Fig. 14
Honoré Daumier (French; 1808–1879)
Le Souffleur, 1870
Lithograph
From *Le Charivari*, 7 February 1870

Fig. 15
Ballerinas in Apartment (detail), 1990
Bronze and wood
$35^7/_{16}$ x $78^3/_4$ x $78^3/_4$ in. (90 x 200 x 200 cm); ballerinas: $23^5/_8$ x $22^7/_{16}$ x $22^7/_{16}$ in. (60 x 57 x 57 cm) each
Private collection

Fig. 16
Opposite Balconies, 1991
Steel and terracotta
39³/₈ x 19⁵/₈ x 8⁵/₈ in. (100 x 50 x 220 cm)
Private collection, Switzerland

Fig. 17
Georges-Pierre Seurat (French; 1859–1891)
Bathers at Asnières, 1884
Oil on canvas
79¹/₈ x 118¹/₈ in. (201 x 300 cm)
The National Gallery, London

Figs. 18a–b
Square (Madrid) (detail), 1996
Resin and pigment
Dimensions variable
Collection of Simone and Heinz Ackermans,
London

Figs. 19a–b
Installation views of "A Place Called Abroad,"
Dia Center for the Arts, New York, 1996–97,
including *Shadow and Mouth* (fig. 19b)
Courtesy of Dia Center for the Arts, New York

Figs. 20a–c
Table with Hold-Out, 1994
Wood, felt, metal, playing cards, and raising
mechanism
35⁷/₁₆ x 35⁷/₁₆ x 31¹/₂ in. (90 x 90 x 80 cm)
Collection of the artist

Fig. 21
Waiting for Jerry, 1991
Wall, light, and audio soundtrack
Dimensions variable
Collection of the artist

Michael Brenson, "Sound, Sight, Statuary"

Fig. 1
Conversation Piece (Dublin) (detail), 1994
Resin, sand, and cloth
Figures: 55¹/₈ x 7⁷/₈ x 7⁷/₈ in. (140 x 20 x
20 cm) each
Collection Irish Museum of Modern
Art, Dublin; on long-term loan from the
artist, 2000

Fig. 2
Blotter Figure, 1999
Resin
63 x 36 x 21 in. (160 x 91.4 x 53.3 cm)
Courtesy of Marian Goodman Gallery,
New York

Fig. 3
Wax Drum, 1988
Metal and wax
15³/₄ x 15³/₄ x 11¹³/₁₆ in. (40 x 40 x 30 cm)
Private collection, Madrid

Fig. 4
Jack Palance at the Madeleine, 1986
Wood and knife
31¹/₂ x 31¹/₂ x 17⁵/₁₆ in. (80 x 80 x 44 cm)
Fonds Régional d'Art Contemporain (FRAC)
des Pays de la Loire, La Fleuriaye

Fig. 5
First Banister, 1987
Wood and knife
78³/₄ x 3¹/₈ x 2³/₄ in. (200 x 8 x 7 cm)
Private collection, Madrid

Fig. 6
Sara in front of a Mirror, 1996
Resin and mirror
86⁵/₈ x 55¹/₈ x 22¹³/₁₆ in. (220 x 140 x 58 cm)
Private collectors Mr. and Mrs. Van Daele,
Belgium

Fig. 7
Crossroads Cabinet October, 1999
Cabinet; steel, glass, lead, and mixed media
98 x 31¹/₂ x 9⁷/₈ in. (248.9 x 80 x 25.1 cm)
Courtesy of Marian Goodman Gallery,
New York

Fig. 8
Last Conversation Piece, 1994–95
Bronze
Overall dimensions: 66¹/₂ x 244³/₄ x 321¹/₈ in.
(168.9 x 621.7 x 815.7 cm)
Hirshhorn Museum and Sculpture Garden,
Smithsonian Institution, Museum
Purchase, 1995

Olga M. Viso, "Suspicions of the Gaze"

Fig. 1
Two Figures Looking Sideways, 1996–97
Resin and lamp
Dimensions variable
Collection Migros Museum, Zurich

Fig. 2
School of Piero della Francesca (Italian;
1415–1492)
The Ideal City, ca. 1470
Panel
23⁵/₈ x 78³/₄ in. (60 x 200 cm)
Palazzo Ducale, Mantua

Fig. 3
Diego Velázquez (Spanish; 1599–1660)
Las Meninas, 1656
Oil on canvas
125 x 108 in. (317.5 x 274.3 cm)
Museo Nacional del Prado, Madrid

Fig. 4
Baroque Exercise, 1984
Metal, cement, and pigment
41⁵/₁₆ x 21⁵/₈ x 7⁷/₈ in. (105 x 55 x 20 cm)

Fig. 5
Portraits B (detail), 1985
Wood, iron, stone, and charcoal
61 x 23¹/₄ x 12 in. (154.9 x 59 x 30.5 cm)
Blake Byrne Collection, Los Angeles

Fig. 6
Parmigianino (Girolamo Francesco Maria
Mazzola) (Italian; 1503–1540)
Self-Portrait in a Convex Mirror, 1524
Oil on wood
Diam. 9²/₃ in. (24.4 cm)
Kunsthistorisches Museum, Vienna

Fig. 7
Alberto Giacometti (Swiss; 1901–1966)
Four Figurines on a Base, 1950–65
Bronze
H. 61¹/₂ in. (156.2 cm)
Collection Tate Gallery, London; purchased
with assistance from the friends of the
Tate Gallery, 1965

Fig. 8
Balcony on the Ceiling of a Basement, 1986
Iron
27¹⁵/₁₆ x 36¹/₄ x 7¹/₂ in. (71 x 92 x 19 cm)
Susan and Michael Hort

Fig. 9
Neal's Last Words, 1997
Resin, silicone, motor, and mirror
Dimensions variable
Louisiana Museum for moderne kunst,
Humlebæk, Denmark

Fig. 10
No. 9, 1994
Rubber and iron
Dimensions variable
Collection of the artist

OTHER ILLUSTRATIONS

Cover and back cover:
Five Seated Figures, 1996 (cat. no. 54)

Pages 1–12
The Burning of Madrid as Seen from the Terrace of My House, 1999
Photo essay

Page 54
Juan Muñoz's studio, Madrid, 1999

Page 63
Jacob Epstein (American; 1880–1959)
Rock Drill
Reconstruction by K. Cook and
A. Christopher of the 1913–15 original,
1973–74
Resin, metal, and wood
Birmingham Museum and Art Gallery,
Great Britain

Page 64
Parmigianino (Girolamo Francesco Maria
Mazzola) (Italian; 1503–1540)
Lady with Three Children, 1533–35
Oil on panel
$50^{3}/_{8}$ x $38^{3}/_{16}$ in. (128 x 97 cm)
Madrid, Museo Nacional del Prado

Agusti Centelles
Riots in St. James Square, February 17, 1936
Black-and-white photograph

Page 66
Installation view of *The Prompter* (cat. no. 24),
P.S.1 Contemporary Art Center, Long Island
City, New York, 1989

Page 68
Aztec statue of the goddess Coatlique,
15th century
Andesite
H. 8 ft. (2.4 m)
Museo Nacional de Antropología,
Mexico City

Page 70
Illustration from *Segment* (Chicago
and Geneva: The Renaissance Society at
The University of Chicago and Centre
d'Art Contemporain, 1990).

Page 82
Juan Muñoz's studio, Madrid, 2001

Page 144
Juan Muñoz in a performance of
A Man in a Room, Gambling, BBC Studio
One, London, 1997
Performance commissioned by Artangel,
London

Page 148
Three-Card Trick, 1995
Black-and-white photographs
Courtesy of the artist

Page 151
A Winter's Journey (detail), 1994
Silicone, resin, wood, and electric motor
Dimensions variable
Fonds National d'Art Contemporain,
Ministère de la Culture et de la
Communication, Paris
Carré d'Art-Musée d'Art Contemporain,
Nîmes

Page 182
Juan Muñoz's studio, Madrid, 1999

Page 184
Juan Muñoz and John Berger in a performance of *Will It Be a Likeness?*, Frankfurt, 1996

Page 185
Alberto Iglesias and Juan Muñoz, Madrid, 2000

Gavin Bryars and Juan Muñoz, London, 2001

Page 186
Exhibition invitation, "Juan Muñoz," Galerie
Ghislaine Hussenot, Paris, 1988

Page 188
Sara with Mirror, 1996
Resin and mirror
120 x 45 x 78 in. (304.8 x 114.3 198.1 cm)
Collection of Camille O. Hoffman

Page 190
Juan Muñoz in his studio, Madrid, 1987
(cat. no. 1)

Page 193
Installation view of "Juan Muñoz: The
Nature of Visual Illusion," Louisiana
Museum for Moderne Kunst, Humlebæk,
Denmark, 2000

Page 195
Program cover, *A Man in a Room, Gambling*,
BBC Studio One, London, 1997

Page 197
Exhibition invitation, "Juan Muñoz:
A Brief Description of My Death,"
Bernier/Eliades Gallery, Athens, 1999–2000

Page 204
Exhibition invitation, "Juan Muñoz:
Drawings and Prints," Frith Street Gallery,
London, 1992, with detail of *Untitled*, 1992

Page 209
Exhibition brochure, "Streetwise," SITE
Santa Fe, 6 June–2 August 1998

Page 214
Disappearance Piece 1–4, 1995
Black-and-white photographs with ink
Courtesy of the artist

Pages 216–28
Artist's sketch and installation views
of *Double Bind*, Tate Modern, London
From "The Unilever Series: Juan Muñoz,"
12 June 2001–10 February 2002

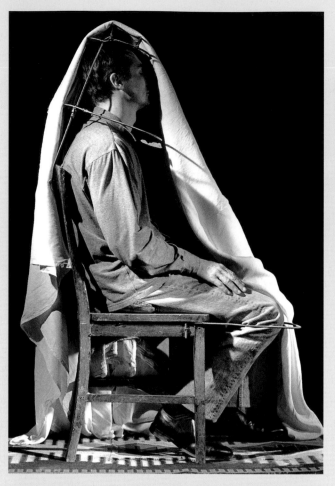

Disappearance Piece 1–4, 1995

Double Bind

Tate Modern, London, 12 June 2001–10 February 2002

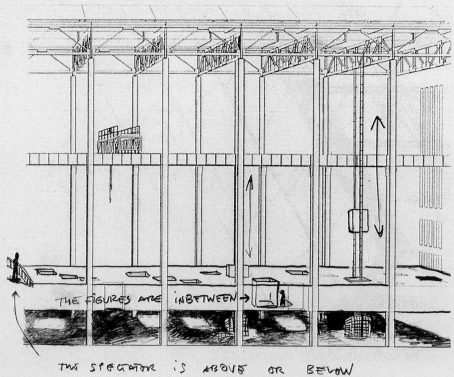